BRAINMATICS

IVAN MOSCOVICH

BrainMatics
LOGIC
PUZZLES

h.f.ullmann

PUZZLE NUMBERS

The puzzles in this book are accompanied by two numbers in a small box: a white number which indicates the puzzle number and a red number which indicates the puzzles difficulty. If you are searching for the solution of a special puzzle in the solutions part, you can easily identify the solution by the white number.

All puzzles in this book have been designed and carefully checked by the author.

© 2009 Tandem Verlag GmbH
h.f.ullmann is an imprint of Tandem Verlag GmbH

Idea & Concept: Ivan Moscovich
Text: Ivan Moscovich
Project Coordination: Daniel Fischer
Layout: scripta, Cologne
Cover Design: Jeff Beebe

Printed in China

ISBN 978-3-8331-5365-5

10 9 8 7 6 5 4 3 2 1

www.ullmann-publishing.com

> "Imagination is more important than knowledge. Knowledge is limited."
>
> *Albert Einstein*

EINSTEIN ON MATH

"Never before in my life have I troubled myself over anything so much and I have gained enormous respect for mathematics, whose more subtle parts I considered until now, in my ignorance, as pure luxury!"

Einstein, in a letter to a friend, 1916

"Our experience hitherto justifies us in believing that nature is the realization of the simplest conceivable mathematical ideas. I am convinced that we can discover by means of purely mathematical constructions the concepts and the laws connecting them with each other."

(Einstein in the Herbert Spencer lecture at Oxford, 1933)

This book is a labor of love. I dedicate it to my wife Anitta, with love and gratitude for her infinite patience, valuable judgment, and assistance; to my daughter Hila, who is my harshest but fairest critic, inspiring me with new insights; to my lovely granddaughter Emilia, who is well on her way with her own wonderful life journey; and to all those who like beauty, surprises, challenges, puzzles, and mathematics.

I.M.

Brain

"Someone not particularly interested in mathematics, or someone fearful of the subject, must be presented with illustrations that are extremely easy to comprehend. He or she needs to be presented with examples that do not require much explanation, ones that sort of 'bounce off the page' in their attractiveness. It is also helpful if the examples are largely visual. They can be – but don't have to be – recreational in nature. Above all, they should elicit the 'wow' response, that feeling that there really is something special about the nature of mathematics."

Alfred S. Posamentier
Professor of Mathematics
City University of New York

(from an article that first appeared in the New York Times January 2, 2002)

Humans derive great satisfaction from finding patterns, but we gain an even greater pleasure from understanding what lies behind the *patterns*.

The discovery of an unexpected connection, of some hidden magical regularity, provokes a delightful combination of surprise and intellectual satisfaction. We may feel a sense of awe at the beauty of what we have uncovered. This combination is what this book is about...

Matics

BrainMatics is a tribute to American mathematician Martin Gardner. It is a collection of mathematical ideas and theorems, incorporating major milestones in the history of mathematics, and including classic puzzles, games, paradoxes, and illusions, some simple and lesser known, but all revealing the profound beauty and power of mathematics. Yet the book is not a random collection of single topics, for I have taken great care to create a logical continuity, presenting the topics in line with the historical development of mathematics and in a way that clarifies the main ideas.

My work was inspired and driven forward by the encouraging reviews and valuable comments I received in response to my **1000 PlayThinks** (published by Workman in 2001) and the several other books that followed (published by Sterling). **BrainMatics** is much more than a puzzle book, but it includes puzzles wherever they can contribute to an easier understanding of mathematical ideas. The puzzles make great conversation pieces and interactive problem-solving activities for friends and family and in the classroom. Many new topics are tackled, ones that are often avoided in most puzzle books for the general public. The selection of ideas has inevitably been subjective, but I hope it will prove to have been well judged.

This book is for lovers of mathematics and for people who do not see themselves as mathematically oriented. It is my sincere hope that the book will help people who are not immediately warm to mathematics to understand some of the great ideas of the subject.

Mathematical understanding leads to insights about our everyday life, but it also opens up to us exciting worlds far beyond our own. I trust you will enjoy reading and using this book as much as I enjoyed creating it. And if you are unable to resist exclaiming "It's beautiful!" at least once, then my work on this book will have proved a worthwhile effort.

I.M.

"Nothing has been done if something remains to be done"
Carl Friedrich Gauss

"Why is the world written in mathematics?"
Italian mathematician and physicist Galileo Galilei (1564–1642)

"Martin Gardner has turned dozens of innocent youngsters into math professors and thousands of math professors into innocent youngsters."
Persi Diaconis, Professor of Math, Stanford University.

ACKNOWLEDGMENTS

First and foremost, I would like to thank Martin Gardner for everything. His work, personality and friendship have been a profound inspiration to me since the mid-1950s when I read his first "Mathematical Games" column in the journal *Scientific American*. Martin's immense contribution to the popularization of recreational mathematics – and of mathematics in general – has fostered a community of creativity.

Without Martin, there would have been fewer "puzzle parties" and mathematical exhibitions – and certainly no "Gatherings for Gardner," those events like no others. Over the last 50 years or so at these conventions of like-minded souls, I have met "Martin's People," a wonderfully diverse group of mathematicians, scientists, puzzle collectors, magicians, inventors, publishers, and others, all united by a fascination with mental games, a love of recreational mathematics, and a deep affection for Martin himself. These events have provided me with hours of enjoyment and intellectual enrichment and, very often, with precious friendships. I send my appreciation and thanks to all my friends among "Martin's People," and in particular: Paul Erdos, my famous relative, who tried to provide the first sparks; David Singmaster with whom I dreamed of a very special puzzle museum; Ian Stewart for his early help; John Horton Conway, D. Coxeter, Solomon Golomb, Frank Harary, Raymond Smullyan, Edward de Bono, Richard Gregory, Tom Rodgers, Victor Serebriakoff, Edward Hordern, Nick Baxter, Jerry Slocum, Nob Yoshigahara, Lee Sallows, Greg Frederickson, James Dalgety, Mel Stover, Mark Setteducati, Bob Neale, Tim Rowett, Scott Morris, Will Shortz, Bill Ritchie, Richard Hess, Jeremiah Farrell – and many, many others. I also owe a debt of gratitude to the work of pioneers – Sam Loyd, Henry Dudeney, Lancelot Hogben and others – whose early books provided so much inspiration. Special thanks should also be offered to Oliver Caldecott, Peter Workman, Charles Nurnberg and my great friend Hal Robinson for their encouragement.

In a way *BrainMatics* is a visual synthesis of the whole of recreational mathematics.

Martin Gardner
on the beauty of mathematics:

"I enjoy mathematics so much because it has a strange kind of unearthly beauty. There is a strong feeling of pleasure, hard to describe, in thinking through an elegant proof, and even greater pleasure in discovering a proof not previously known. On a low level I have experienced such a pleasure four times:

1. I discovered the minimal number of acute triangles into which a square can be dissected;

2. I found the minimal network of Steiner trees that join all the corners of a chessboard;

3. I constructed a bicolor proof that every serial isogon of 90 degrees – a polygon, with all right angles, and sides in 1, 2, 3,.... sequence – must have a number of sides that is a multiple of 8;

4. I devised a novel way to diagram the prepositional calculus."

(from an interview with Martin Gardner by Don Albers, 2005)

BRAINMATICS

CONTENTS

The numbers following the puzzles' titles indicate the puzzles and their rankings. The puzzles' numbers are set bold, the ranking is set in italics. The numbers are corresponding to the red and white boxes on the puzzle pages.

INTRODUCTION

I am passionate about mathematics. Over the past 50 years I have collected, designed, and invented thousands of mathematical toys, games, and interactive exhibits. I believe so strongly in mathematics and mathematical games because I have seen that they can change the way people think. They can make us more inventive, more creative, more artistic, and more human. They may even make us healthier. They prompt us to see the world in new ways. They inspire us to tackle the unknown. And they remind us to have fun.

Like so many who lived through the 20th century, I witnessed repeated attempts to snuff out humanity's creative spark – and not only by political tyrants. I saw the creative impulse wither away in schools. I saw creativity devalued at work. And along the way I learned that our society must do more than repel dictators in order to make its citizens fully free. We must encourage what is best – and what is most human – within ourselves. One of the most effective ways to foster the special creative part that resides in each of us is through imaginative thinking and play.

Child psychologists have known for many years that children learn about the world through games. Now it is time to extend that model to adults. We can understand the most abstract and difficult concepts if we allow ourselves the luxury of approaching them not as work, but as fun – as a form of exploration.

The adventure of play

People have always felt the urge to explore new worlds. Today, most of the physical frontiers have been crossed, but mental ones still exist and they beckon to us. Yet often we act as if challenges to the mind are too difficult to contemplate. We judge the effort needed to push into new mental territories as simply too great. And so we turn back.

When self-doubt and fear threaten to derail our urge to explore, play becomes a truly essential activity. Seeing hard work as fun is what keeps the amateur athlete training for the marathon, and it is what keeps a child or an adult struggling to find the answer to a puzzle. At the end of a race, the winning runner feels immensely proud. At the end of a game, or after solving a puzzle, a player feels smart, successful – and, perhaps, at one with the beauty of mathematics. In the words of Irish playwright George Bernard Shaw (1856–1950), "We do not stop playing because we get old, we get old because we stop playing." In an era when so many are obsessed with staying and looking young, let's not forget the power of play.

"Hands-on" learning

Shortly after I emigrated to Israel in 1952, I began creating one of the first fully "hands-on" science museums, one in which the exhibits invited the visitor to think and participate in learning. This interactive, "hands-on" concept became the model for many later science museums, including the world-famous Exploratorium in San Francisco, California. At these museums, children and adults alike feel their minds awaken, and stir: they suddenly grasp concepts they have previously rejected as "too difficult" or "impossible to understand." They find that "doing the problem" is fun and so they understand it.

BrainMatics applies these principles. It is intended for the general reader, for those not yet converted to the glory and inherent beauty of mathematics. Humans derive great satisfaction from discovering patterns, but we gain an even greater pleasure from understanding what lies behind the patterns. The discovery of an unexpected connection, of some hidden magical regularity, provokes a delightful combination of surprise, intellectual satisfaction and awe.

Beauty, pleasure, and understanding

This book is packed full of puzzles, games, paradoxes, illusions, challenging mathematical concepts, theorems, and problem-solving challenges. The criteria of selection were based on the description offered by Charles W. Valentine in his 1962 book The Experimental Psychology of Beauty – namely, that the enjoyment of beauty is accompanied by pleasure, and this pleasure is related to the pattern and form, to the line and colors presented.

In addition to giving pleasure, moreover, BrainMatics aims to foster understanding, the capacity identified by English philosopher John Locke (1632–1704) as "the most elevated faculty of the soul." Well-placed quotations, historical anecdotes, biographical notes and clear explanations create the ideal framework for creative discovery. And they aim to develop understanding and knowledge through doing, for as 18th-century German physicist GC Lichtenberg (1742–99) noted, "What you have been obliged to discover by yourself leaves a path in your mind which you can use again when the need arises."

COMMUNICATION AND THE BOOK

The most important thing a person inherits is the ability to learn a language. Language – especially written language – makes connections possible between people living in vastly different circumstances, places, and times.

Language is carried visually either by signs, which are written marks that stand for units of language, or by symbols, which represent objects. In the 20,000 years since humans first scratched simple tallies on animal bones, the visual aspect of language has flourished. First objects, then words, were abstractly represented. By 300 BCE, the great library at Alexandria, in Egypt, contained around 750,000 papyrus scroll books, the greatest storehouse of knowledge that the world had ever seen.

Later technological developments such as block printing by the Chinese and movable type by Johannes Gutenberg (c.1400–68) have enabled written language to reach virtually every person on the planet. Symbolic language promotes a type of visual thinking that today's designers and communication engineers must take into account.

Thanks to globalization and the Internet, we are today at the beginning of a revolution in the communication of ideas. Older ways of presenting complex ideas and purely verbal forms of storing and transmitting information are, perhaps, being rendered obsolete. Change is occurring so quickly in this area that written language may not be prove the most trustworthy means of communicating with future generations.

As in the "butterfly effect" described by scientists in chaos theory (whereby a butterfly flapping its wings can effect weather systems thousands of miles away), new trends are born and new knowledge transferred through a chain reaction beginning from a small change but capable of causing far-reaching consequences. Someone somewhere has an idea and in no time it can become a worldwide craze.

TYPE MANUFACTURING

TYPESETTING

PRINTING

MOVABLE TYPE OF GUTENBERG

In 1440 German craftsman Johannes Gutenberg began using a wine press in conjunction with a series of blocks, each bearing a single letter on its face. Ink was rolled over the raised surfaces of the hand-set letter blocks, which were held together within a wooden frame. The set frame was then pressed against a sheet of paper.

Gutenberg's development of the printing press and of moveable type was probably the greatest invention of all time. With it, the modern revolution in mass communication began.

VISUAL COMMUNICATION

From the cave paintings of the Stone Age, through Gutenberg's typographic innovation to the binary system of electronic computers, we see a steady development towards the refinement of meaning and the streamlining of communication.

If visual persuasion can be used so effectively in advertising and even in forms of propaganda, why could it not be put to use in teaching, and in popularizing basic mathematical and scientific concepts? Communication designers are finding ways to make it easier for people to understand ideas and remember information.

MATHEMATICS IS BEAUTIFUL!

Our universe is mathematical. This idea goes all the way back to the philosophers of ancient Greece. Today, some mathematicians push the concept to the extreme by arguing that the universe is not just described by *mathematics* – *it is mathematics*.

The foundation of their argument is the assumption that an external mathematical reality exists independently of human observers. In other words, we don't invent mathematical structures – we discover them, and invent only the notations for describing them. We encounter mathematics everywhere. Even though we don't see brass plates on every building advertising professional mathematicians within, we could stick a label on practically every product around us advertising "Math inside."

Beautiful ideas

Ideas – intriguing, surprising, fascinating, and beautiful – are truly at the heart of mathematics. As a way of thinking, mathematics is diverse, creative, full of novelty and originality. And it is not only about solving equations. Donald Coxeter, a celebrated figure in geometry, declared that he was motivated exclusively by beauty. According to Coxeter, the goal of geometry is not so much to prove a theorem but to discover geometry's elegant rules. Many mathematicians describe mathematics as an art form and as a creative activity.

Mathematics is an artistic pursuit for everyone, not just for professional mathematicians. I am a non-mathematician. I discovered the beauty of mathematics in 1957, reading Martin Gardner's monthly mathematical column in the *Scientific American* magazine. Martin Gardner is also a non-mathematician. Ever since that time, when I particularly enjoy a mathematical idea, I have often said, "It's beautiful," or sometimes "It's amazing; elegant; surprising; astonishing; unbelievable; impossible; fun." Or I simply exclaimed, "Aha!" or "Wow!"

Enduring truth – and progress

One of the most beautiful characteristics of mathematics is the enduring truth of its laws. A theorem correctly proved within the severe constricts of mathematical logic is a theorem forever. The ancient Greek mathematician Euclid's proof of the Pythagorean theorem from nearly 2,500 years ago has lost none of its beauty or validity. In mathematics each generation builds on existing foundations and structures, while in most other sciences one generation often tears down what another has built.

The steady growth of mathematical knowledge and its many applications are essential to solving new problems in the modern world. Mathematics is an essential interdisciplinary language that we all need today – more than ever before – for survival in the modern world.

The fact that non-mathematicians can enjoy the beauty of mathematics should be central to the teaching of mathematics. We should enable non-mathematicians to discover a much broader picture of the subject at a much earlier stage in their mathematical development. Mathematics rules the world, and everybody should be a mathematician.

MODERN BLACK HOLE UNIVERSE

The universe may have been created by an explosion within a black hole, according to a new theory.

ANCIENT GREEK UNIVERSE

The ancient Greeks started with a fairly organic view of the creation of the universe – four separated properties later "hardened" to become four fundamental elements. The Greeks then added another dichotomy in a pair of (symmetrically) opposed forces – what we would call today attraction and repulsion.

CREATIVITY IN MATHEMATICS

What is a Man?

A beautiful mathematical machine – a computer?

"A self-balancing, 28-jointed adapter-base biped; an electrochemical reduction plant, integral with segregated stowages of special energy extracts in storage batteries for subsequent actuation of thousands of hydraulic and pneumatic pumps with motors attached; 62,000 miles of capillaries...

"Millions of warning signs, railroad and conveyor systems; crushers and cranes (of which the arms are magnificent 23-jointed affairs with self-surfacing and lubricating systems) and a universally distributed telephone system needing no service for 70 years, if well managed...

"The whole, extraordinarily complex mechanism guided with exquisite precision from a turret in which are located telescopic and microscopic self-registering and recoding range finders, a spectroscope etc; the turret control being closely allied with an air-conditioning intake-and-exhaust, and a main fuel intake...

"Within the few cubic inches housing the turret mechanism, there is room also for two sound-wave and sound direction-finder recording diaphragms, a filing and instant reference system, and an expertly devised analytical laboratory large enough not only to contain minute records of every last and continual event up to 70 years' experience, or more, but to extend, by computation and abstract fabrication, this experience with relative accuracy into all corners of the observed universe.

A man, indeed."

R Buckminster Fuller
Nine Chains to the Moon (J.B. Lippincott Co, 1938)

> "Creativity, it has been said, consists largely of rearranging what we know in order to find out what we do not know."
> *George Keller*

"EXECUTIVE OF THE FUTURE"
by Boris Artzybasheff,
Dodd, Mead & Company
New York, 1954, Used by permission of the publisher

NEANDERTHAL

Scientists are tantalizingly close to learning just what genetic changes distinguish modern humans from our closest evolutionary relatives, the Neanderthals, who became extinct around 30,000 years ago. In 2006 researchers assembled parts of a Neanderthal man's genetic code from a fossil bone: as it turns out, the genome of this particular Neanderthal – who lived around 38,000 years ago – was more than 99.5 per cent identical to the genome of modern humans.

CREATIVITY, PROBLEM SOLVING AND INTUITION

People once assumed that the Earth was flat, that the Sun revolved around the Earth, and that evil spirits caused diseases. Creative thinkers challenged these ideas. If we accept what we are told without ever questioning its truth, we may never discover better ways of doing and thinking.

Throughout human history, people have regarded creativity with wonder. Creative thinkers seem to be able to maintain a connection to a childlike state of wonder, and to use it for creative ends. How do they do it? How can we learn to be more creative?

Creativity is the most powerful mode of human thought, a resource we can all draw upon in order to understand our life and build a better world and future. From earliest history human beings needed creativity to solve practical problems. If our ancestors had not been creative, we would still be living in the Stone Age. And for this reason we all have a creative urge hard-wired within us.

Yet creativity is difficult to define. More than just the process by which new ideas are generated, it is really a different way of thinking, one less preoccupied with details than with fundamental relationships, less concerned with facts and numbers than with arrangements and connections. The ability to "think outside the box" is highly sought after today. A new age is upon us, in which creativity is increasingly important and more highly valued than ever.

Many researchers into creativity have noted the element of chance in the creative process. American scientist Linus Pauling (1901–94), two times winner of the Nobel Prize, was asked at one of his lectures how to create scientific theories: he replied that one must endeavor to come up with many ideas – then discard the useless ones.

Recent research suggests that the unconscious mind plays a key role in creativity. The research, published in 2006 by Ap Dijksterhuis and others at the University of Amsterdam, indicates that complex decisions are best left to your unconscious mind and that the conscious mind should be trusted with simple decisions only. Thinking hard about complex decisions based on multiple factors appears to confuse the conscious mind: people concentrate on only a subset of the available information, often resulting in unsatisfactory decisions. In contrast, the unconscious mind appears better able to consider the information as a whole, and produce a more satisfactory decision.

We use intuition constantly in our everyday life. Yet until recently the scientific study of intuition was largely ignored. New research has found that intuition springs from a set of important human skills that all act together to give a so-called "gut reaction." The more you use these skills, the better your intuition becomes.

Research evidence shows that mental stimulation through brain games and interactive puzzles encourages brain cells to develop more connections with each other, improving our general thinking. There is also good scientific evidence to show that exercising the brain can slow, delay, and protect against age-related decline.

**The Only Solution –
a Grook, by Piet Hein**
*We shall have to evolve
Problem solvers galore –
since each problem they solve
creates ten problems more*

THINKING AS A SKILL

Your brain works better than you might think. It is capable of making a virtually unlimited number of synaptic connections, each of which is a pattern of thought. The number of possible connections has been calculated, and the result is astonishingly huge – 1 followed by 60 million miles of zeros.

BrainMatics includes carefully designed visual problems that will sharpen your ability to recognize and perceive patterns, to stretch your imagination, to make the most of your thinking. And as you do these puzzles and problems, you will improve your creativity, insight, and intuition. Thinking is a learnable skill, like cooking or golf. If you make even a small effort to develop it, you will see improvement. As Japanese puzzle genius Nob Yoshigahara said: "What jogging is to the body, thinking is to the brain. The more we do it, the better we become."

KEEPING THE BRAIN FIT

The "brain-training" craze is flourishing. Among the many programs, the most popular product is a computer game called "Brain Training," developed by the neuroscientist Ryuta Kawashima. It gives an answer to the question "How old is your brain?" and is endorsed by actress Nicole Kidman. All the brain-training programs broadly claim either to enhance brain function – memory, concentration, processing speed – or to slow down the inevitable decline that comes with age. Many say "use it or lose it," but it is less clear how to define "use" and "it."

Is there reliable evidence that brain training can work? Yes, there is. In 2006, at the University of Alabama, a group led by Karlene Ball published the results of a study of the "use-it-or-lose-it" hypothesis. They put 1,884 healthy older adults through an intensive six-week program, which resulted in significant improvement in brain performance, such as memory and other tasks. Brain-training research by Mike Merzenich, at the University of California, San Francisco, on schizophrenia and depression produced miraculous improvements. Many older people seem to remain sharp as a tack well into their eighties and beyond. Although their pace may have slowed, they continue to work, play cards and board games, travel, use computers, write books, do puzzles, and perform other mentally challenging tasks that can befuddle people much younger. Further research has shown that when these sharp old folks die, autopsy studies often reveal extensive brain abnormalities, such as those found in patients with Alzheimer's. Up to two-thirds of people with autopsy findings of Alzheimer's disease were cognitively intact when they died. Nikolaos Scarmeas and Yaakov Stern at Columbia Medical Center deduced that something must account for the disjunction between the degree of brain damage and its outcome. And that something, they and others suggest, is cognitive reserve.

The theory of cognitive reserve refers to the brain's ability to change and maintain extra neurons and connections between them via axons and dendrites. Later in life, these connections may help compensate for the rise in dementia-related brain pathology that accompanies normal aging. Efforts are being invested to determine how people can develop cognitive reserve. There is no quick fix for the aging brain, but, nonetheless, well-designed recent studies suggest ways to improve the brain's viability. It is never too late to start building up cognitive reserve. The more intellectual challenges to the brain as early as possible in life, the more neurons and connections the brain is likely to develop and perhaps maintain into later years. But brain stimulation should not stop with the diploma. Constant new challenges are crucial to providing stimulation for the aging brain.

If you are doing the same thing over and over again without introducing new mental challenges, it won't be beneficial in this respect. This is an interesting point to ponder. Perhaps you devote most of your free time to solving Sudoku or crossword puzzles, or playing Scrabble, and conclude that you are doing your utmost to exercise your brain, but this may not be enough. You may become very good at these games but they stop offering you fresh challenges and proper stimulation. It may be that playing the same games becomes too automatic, using established brain connections, and so new ones are not developed.

Thus, as with muscles, it's "use it or lose it." The brain requires continued stresses or stimuli to maintain or enhance its strength. This means that it is necessary to play as many brain games and solve as many diverse puzzles, recreational problems as possible, each one providing you with a new challenge and new stimulation. This requirement may be the secret to why we like to play games and solve puzzles.

As living, intelligent organisms, we humans possess curiosity about our environment, about one another, and about ourselves. Putting that curiosity to use through an exploration of the unknown energizes us; no one knows why this is so, but we can feel that it is true. Likewise, playing games that engage our curiosity makes us feel more alive. Again, we don't clearly understand why, but it may have a lot to do with the risk of losing.

FRIENDS MEET

Your first serious challenge is one of the most beautiful puzzles of recreational math and comes from Russia. Its solution requires thinking, concentration, creativity, logic, insight, and attention to the smallest details.

Two Russian mathematicians meet on a plane:

"I believe you have three sons, what are their ages today?" asks Ivan.

"Yes, I do have three sons. The product of their ages is 36, and the sum of their ages is exactly today's date," answers Igor.

"I'm sorry, Igor, but that doesn't tell me the ages of your sons", says Ivan after a minute or two.

"Oh, I forgot to tell you. My youngest son has red hair."

"Ah, now it's clear. I now know exactly how old your sons are," concludes Ivan.

How did Ivan work out the ages of the sons?

THE BEAUTIFUL "EUREKA" MOMENT

Eureka (Greek: "I found it") – Archimedes uttered the word while bathing, when he suddenly understood how to calculate the volume of an irregular object, and continued to shout it repeatedly while running naked through the streets of Syracuse. Two thousand years later, researchers have found that this "AHA!" experience, when the answer to a problem pops out of thin air, involves a special kind of brain activity taking place in the unconscious mind. It has been recognized that thinking occurs not on stage, but off stage, out of sight. Thinking, memory, and attitudes all operate on two levels – conscious and deliberate, and unconscious and automatic – dual processing as researchers call it today.

We all have had sudden, smart insights. How do they arise? Is there a way we can conjure them up at will? Wiles (see above) describes beautifully the moment of his solution to a tough problem, and the extraordinary intellectual satisfaction accompanying it, the "AHA" experience, the "Eureka" moment. The light bulb goes on and the answer seems so obvious. But what happens in the mind to produce this miraculous revelation? Apparently, the unconscious processes that lead to insight tend to take place in the right hemisphere of the brain. The answer could help all of us to become more creative. Wiles's description related to a major mathematical discovery, but, interestingly enough, anybody can experience the same exhilarating feeling of intellectual satisfaction by merely solving a simple problem or a puzzle.

Intuition can often be deceiving as well. Intuition often errs. This frequently happens with optical illusions and probability problems, but they are not limited to perceptual tricks only. But in spite of these, "the really valuable thing is intuition," said Einstein. Inspiration and intuitive insights are part of creative thinking. In recent years, intuition is increasingly recognized as a natural mental faculty, a key element in discovery, problem-solving, and decision-making, a generator of creative ideas and a revealer of truth. We are all intuitive, and we can all be more intuitive. There is a growing conviction that perhaps we ought to trust the hunches, vague feelings, premonitions, and inarticulate signals we usually ignore. Creativity's intuitive dimension stems from unconscious processing. Insight popping into one's mind in times of relaxation illustrates the effortlessness of unconscious problem-solving.

> "Suddenly, unexpectedly, I had this incredible revelation. It was so incredibly beautiful; it was so simple and elegant. I couldn't understand how I'd missed it and I just stared at it in disbelief for 20 minutes. Then during the day I walked around the department, and I'd kept coming back to my desk looking to see if it was still there. It was. I couldn't contain myself. I was so excited. It was the most important moment of my working life."
>
> **Andrew Wiles, on discerning the proof of Fermat's Last Theorem, a momentous event in the history of mathematics.**

Design by Paddon & Miller; illustrations by R. Cartright (Cover of Invicta-Education Ltd. Catalog of 1970)

Question: "Where do you get your ideas?"

Answer: "I don't. They get me!"

Or, as German philosopher Friedrich Nietzsche (1844–1900) put it: "A thought comes when it wills, not when I will it."

Ideas and originality

Original thought is a straightforward process. It is easy enough when you know what to do. You simply combine in an appropriate dose the blatantly false and the patently true.

A Grook by Piet Hein

"The answer is 'Yes' or 'No,' depending on the interpretation."

Albert Einstein

THOUGHT EXPERIMENTS

In thought experiments we use the imagination to investigate the nature of what we don't know: the simple reasoning behind them is that by the power of thinking we discover new things about the world. Philosophers and mathematicians have used thought experiments since the time of ancient Greece and Rome and many have played an enormous part in advancing mathematics and science.

One of the most beautiful early thought experiments is the Infinite Space Experiment of ancient Greek philosopher Epicurus (341–270 BCE). Other celebrated thought experiments that are well worth looking up in books or on the Internet include: "Einstein's Elevator," "Schrodinger's Cat," "Maxwell's Demon," and "Newton's Satellite Principle."

Infinite space: Thought Experiment of Epicurus

Imagine an arrow flying endlessly through space without encountering any obstacle: this would prove that space is infinite. Then imagine the arrow flying through space and hitting an obstacle (such as a wall) before bouncing back: this would also prove that space is infinite, since there must be something behind the wall.

end of Space

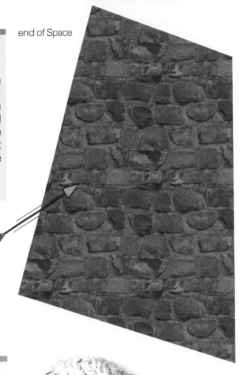

Epicurus (341–270 BCE)

According to Epicurus, philosophy should teach people how to be happy and attain *aponia* (a state of no pain and no fear). He proposed that the best way to achieve happiness and tranquillity was to reduce individual desires: the less a person wants, the happier she or he will be; therefore he advised people not to fall in love. He wrote more than 300 works, of which only a few fragments survive. The school of philosophy based on his works is called Epicureanism.

ROTATING TABLE PROBLEMS
A Modern Thought Experiment

Many of the best recreational mathematics problems are presented as thought experiments. One of these is the rotating table problem, published in 1979, by Martin Gardner. It is probably of Russian origin.

Imagine a square table freely rotating on a central column. At each corner there is a narrow pocket which can accommodate an empty glass that cannot be seen once inserted. When the four glasses are inserted in the four pockets and the table is spun, a bell will ring if all glasses are oriented in the same direction.

The game begins after the distribution of the four glasses in the four pockets, with their orientations chosen randomly. The table is then spun; when it stops and does not ring, a player chooses two pockets simultaneously, takes out the glasses and replaces them as he or she decides. The process is repeated indefinitely. After each spin the bell might or might not ring.

The problem is to find a procedure which will ensure with absolute certainty it will ring after a finite minimal number of spins.

To better understand the principle of the game and find ways for its solution, tackling simpler examples can be of help. In our case the simpler examples involve solving the problem for tables with two and three pockets.

Table with two pockets The problem is trivial. Since after the first spin the bell did not ring, all you have to do is invert one of the glasses, and both glasses will then have the same orientation and the bell will ring.

Table with three pockets The pockets are at the corners of a table in the shape of an equilateral triangle. How many spins will be necessary to ensure the bell ringing?

Table with four pockets How many spins will be necessary to ensure the bell ringing? The two chosen pockets can be along a side or along a diagonal.

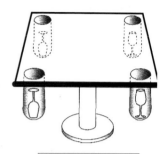

**ROTATING TABLE
WITH FOUR POCKETS**

**ROTATING TABLE
WITH THREE POCKETS**

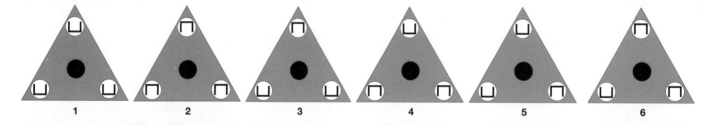

1 2 3 4 5 6

ROTATING TABLE WITH THREE POCKETS

Depending on the two chosen pockets, essentially there are six different possibilties before the initial first spin, as shown. In all cases the two chosen pockets are the two at the bottom. Can you work out the procedure to make the bell ring and also work out the minimal number of spins required to ensure that this will happen?

THE RIDDLE OF THE SPHINX

Can you solve the first I.Q. test ever devised, which is one of the oldest and most beautiful puzzles of antiquity? In Greek mythology the Sphinx was a creature with the head of a woman, the body of a lion, and the wings of an eagle, who guarded the gates of the ancient Greek city of Thebes. She challenged all who wished to enter with this simple riddle: "What creature goes on four legs in the morning, on two legs at noon, and on three legs at dusk?" Those who failed to solve the riddle were killed. Oedipus answered the riddle correctly, and the Sphinx killed herself.

Andrea Jemolo © 2009 Tandem Verlag GmbH 2009

OEDIPUS and the SPHINX

Oedipus in the garb of a traveler, sits before the legendary Sphinx, listening to the riddle.
Ceramics dated: c. 470 BC (Museo Gregoriano Etrusco)

The Great Sphinx at Giza, Egypt, is the world's largest stone sculpture – its body is more than 65 ft (20 metres) tall and 236 ft (72 metres) long. A similar Sphinx dated about 2500 BC guarded the ancient Greek city of Thebes and is associated, according to ancient Greek mythology, with the first recorded puzzle in history. While the Egyptian sphinxes were benevolent, the Theban Sphinx was a dangerous guardian that consumed people who could not answer the riddle.

PROBLEM-SOLVING AND PUZZLES

Marcel Danesi, in his challenging book *Ten Greatest Math Puzzles of all Time* mentions the Riddle of the Sphinx as an excellent example of insight thinking, so important in solving puzzles and problem-solving.

In general, there are three different types of strategy for solving puzzles:

Deduction: A strategy requiring previous knowledge related to the problem.

Induction: Observing the facts included in the problem, reaching a solution by reasoning and logic.

Insight thinking: A method that may start with trial-and-error approaches, then by guesses and hunches an intuitive grasp of the hidden answer to the problem is revealed. Insight thinking is responsible for some of the giant strides in the progress of mathematics. Many of the problems of mathematics were originally devised or disguised as challenging puzzles.

> "Not everything that can be counted counts; and not everything that counts can be counted."
> *A sign in Albert Einstein's office*

COUNT FUN – YOUR UNCONSCIOUS PROBLEM-SOLVING CREATIVITY TEST
Just counting from 1 to 90!
Two puzzle-tests reveal how your creative subconscious mind works, and how it can help you to solve problems.

Counting is the oldest mathematical activity and also one of the most powerful and fundamental ideas ever conceived. The simple notion that for each natural number, there is a following number offered great mathematical advances. We shall give counting a new twist of play

Counting is what allowed people to take the measure of their world, to understand it better and to put some of its innumerable secrets to good use.

and fun. The object in both games is simply to discover how long it will take you to find in succession, consecutive numbers from 1 to 90, without skipping any number. Playing these two games may offer you a few surprises.

To play these two games, you must start by finding 1, then 2, 3, 4, up to 90. Cheating is of course not allowed and it would spoil the fun, believe me. Repeat both games three times and mark your times in minutes for each game. Your first surprise will be that it takes more time than you expect. You can count from 1 to 90 in 90 seconds but with these games it takes much longer. You will also note that as you repeat the games your times will improve. But your second surprise will be that the repeated tests of game two will be incomparably better than those of game one. Can you explain why? Could it be that your unconscious discovered a secret of game two, which resulted in great improvements without your conscious being aware of it? Now that you know a secret is involved, can you discover it?

SYNCHRONICITY AND COINCIDENCES

Synchronicity is a word that Swiss psychologist Carl Jung used to describe the "temporally coincident occurrences of causal events". He also wrote that: *Meaningful coincidences, significantly related patterns of chance are unthinkable as pure chance – the more they multiply and the greater and more exact the correspondence is… they can be no longer be regarded as pure chance, but, for the lack of causal explanantion, have to be thought of as meaningful arrangements.*

It is with the I Ching (Book of Changes) that the Chinese view of synchronicity reached its most advanced philosophical form. The most improbable coincidences are likely to result from the play of random events. The very nature of randomness assures that combing random data will yield some pattern. Still too often we hear: "It couldn't be just a coincidence."

There are two features of coincidences not so well known. First, we tend to overlook the powerful reinforcement of coincidences, both waking and in dreams, in our memories. Non-coincidental events do not register in our memories with nearly the same intensity. Second, we fail to realize the extent to which highly improbable events occur everyday to everyone. It is not possible to estimate all the probabilities of many paired events that occur in our daily lives. We often tend to assign coincidences a lesser probability than they deserve. Our intuitions can go easily astray of which a good example is the famous Birthday Paradox. Being part of only a group of 25 people and discovering there are two persons having the same birthday may have seemed to you like a coincidence. However, it is possible to calculate the probabilities of some seemingly improbable events with precision, as with the Birthday Paradox.

Still, there are coincidences not so easily explained, and many have happened to me. I shall tell you of two of the many.

The ancient view that many coincidences are too improbable to be explained by known laws has recently been revived. Paul Kammerer, an Austrian biologist, described 100 coincidences he was convinced that could be accounted for only by the existence of an universal law, independent of physical causality, that brought "like and like together." The parapsychologist Vaughn admits that there is definitely a synchronicity to coincidental happenings, but warns of the dangers of trying to predict the outcome of synchronistic happenings with accuracy. To illustrate the point he tells the story of a man who was the seventh child of parents who were each the seventh child in their families. The man was born on the Sabbath (seventh day), on the seventh day of July (the seventh month) in 1907. Over the course of time a number of other happenings occurred in his life, all related to number seven, which he, of course, saw as his lucky number. On his 27th birthday he went to the racetrack, and there he saw that a horse called Seventh Heaven was number seven in the seventh race. The odds were seven to one. Impressed by all this, the man borrowed all the money he could and bet on the horse. The horse came in seventh.

In any case, in everyday life we develop subjective concepts of probabilities which often lead us to wrong conclusions. We must learn how to relate to chance intelligently, and to do so, we must learn to understand the laws of chance and probability, which are by no means self-evident like many other fields of mathematics and science.

SEVENTH HEAVEN

MY COINCIDENCES

Coincidence 1
– Kidnapped in a Concentration Camp

During the war I was taken to Auschwitz concentration camp and from there to a nearby forced labor camp. The work was unbearably hard and the Nazi system was to provide food rations to permit a prisoner to stay alive for three months, after which they were supposed to starve to death in order to make room for new arrivals. Accordingly, after four months I felt a sudden deterioration and also got an infection on the index finger of my left hand, which prevented me from carrying rails which was my job. The inflamation on my finger grew to the size of a big ball and the next morning I had to stand in the sick row. The SS was impressed by my finger and allowed me to stay in the camp for a day and my finger to be operated by the camp doctor. After the operation I stayed alone in the deserted camp. I was standing in the middle of a giant courtyard with a broom in my hands, thinking and worrying about the late hearsay that there is soon going to be a selection to send the emancipated and weak prisoners into the crematoria to make place for a big new contingent of prisoners. I saw in the distance the gates of the camp opening and a command car swept into the courtyard with great speed. The next moment with astonishment I realized the car was heading straight toward me. I just stood there frozen. The car screechingly stopped just inches from me. An SS Officer jumped from the car, grabbed me by the scruff of the neck and threw me onto the back of the car and then drove out of the camp. I had been kidnapped. After two hours drive I was taken to another labor camp of which the SS officer was the commandant.

Later in my new camp I heard that there had been an escape and the SS Commandant decided to steal a prisoner from a neighboring camp which obviously was a better solution to him than to report the escape. The mathematics of death had to add up and the prisoner was me. After the liberation I heard from a surviving prisoner of my previous camp that the same evening I was kidnapped 50 percent of the camp was selected and sent to the crematoria to be killed.

335544

Coincidence 2
– The Lottery Number

In late 1945, after being in Auschwitz, Bergen-Belsen, and others, I returned home to Yugoslavia where I was born to resume normal life again. Some time later I attended a meeting of Holocaust survivors and sat near two nice old ladies. I couldn't avoid overhearing their amusing conversation during an otherwise somber occasion. One of them was telling the other that she had a dream in which a strange voice strongly advised her to search for a lottery ticket bearing her Auschwitz concentration camp number. As I was leaving the event I found in the street a banknote exactly the price of a lottery ticket. I remembered the ladies' conversation and for several months I was trying to find the lottery ticket bearing my concentration camp number. Finally I gave up and using the found banknote I bought a ticket at a kiosk without looking at it, putting it in my vest pocket. Next week as I was reading the newspaper I saw the results of the last lottery draw. Taking out my ticket, with utmost astonishment, unbeliavably, I was looking at ticket number 335544 – my Auschwitz camp number. I was sure that the great prize would be mine. It wasn't. All tickets with 4 as the last number earned back the stake and could choose a new ticket to play the lottery for an additional month. For exactly 12 months I was playing the lottery with the initial investment of my number, each month getting back my stake and continuing to play the lottery. Each month I expected that finally I would win the great prize. It never happened. But were the probabilities of these coincidences happening as interesting than getting the big prize? It seems to me that they were.

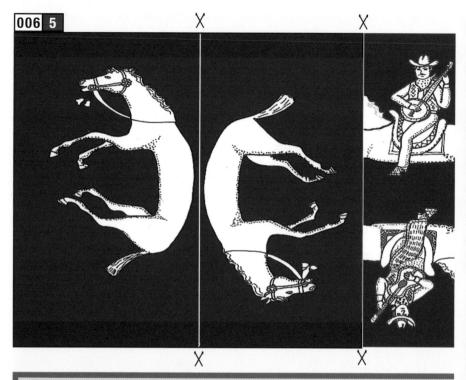

SAM LOYD (1841–1911)

The greatest American puzzle inventor and recreational mathematics popularizer. Loyd was also one of the best U.S. chess players of his time, ranked 15th in the world. He published a Tangram book containing 700 original designs. After his death, his puzzles were published in *Cyclopedia of 5000 Puzzles* – Tricks and Conundrums with Answers in 1914, which was one of the greatest puzzle books ever compiled.

TRICK HORSES PUZZLE

The Trick Horses puzzle is based on the original "Trick Mules" advertising puzzle by Sam Loyd, the greatest American puzzle inventor. He created it when he was still a teenager. It is one of the most beautiful puzzles ever devised, in a category of its own, and literally a visual masterpiece of lateral thinking.

Using only your imagination, can you mount the riders on their horses, when the strip with the two riders is cut out and placed on top of the two horses?

If you can't conceptualize the solution, copy the picture and cut it into three pieces along the white lines. Arrange the three resulting rectangles so that the two riders ride the horses

Hint: The problem looks deceptively simple until you try it. When the strip is correctly placed, the weary looking horses miraculously break into a frenzied gallop! No tricks, no bending, folding or cutting is allowed. Confronted with this puzzle many have a conceptual "block," and are simply unable to place the riders properly. But the solution is really easy. Loyd sold his Trick Mules puzzle to P.T. Barnum, who sold millions and earned $10,000 in royalties in just a few weeks – a fortune at the time. Ever since hundreds of variations of the puzzle appeared.

The Trick Mules puzzle by Sam Loyd may have been inspired by a Persian Horses ink drawing from the 17th century, shown at right (Courtesy, Museum of Fine Arts, Boston).

(The Trick Horses puzzle is from "Ivan Moscovich Supergames", first published by Hutchinson, 1984)

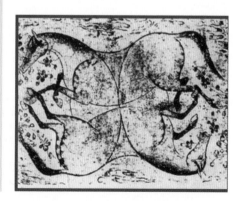

LEONARDO'S SELF-PORTRAIT

Can you read Leonardo's message? (From Leonardo's famous Notebooks, written in 1508.) Perhaps to disguise his work, which was too revolutionary, Leonardo made many of his famous Notes in mirror writing.

LEONARDO'S MATHEMATICS
Leonardo da Vinci – The greatest creative genius of all time

There is no person who better symbolizes the beauty of science, art and mathematics than Leonardo da Vinci (1452–1519), the quintessential Renaissance man: artist, mathematician, scientist, and engineer. He was a great lover of geometry and devoted much time to its study. His most outstanding geometrical accomplishments are the illustrations for Luca Pacioli's 1509 book *The Divine Proportion*. One of the 60 hand-colored illustrations from that book is shown here. These are the first illustrations of polyhedra ever in the form of "solid edges." The solidity of the edges lets one easily see which edges belong to the front and which to the back, unlike simple line drawings where the front and back surfaces may be visually confused. Yet the hollow faces allow one to see through to the structure of the rear surface. This is a brilliant new form of geometric illustration, and one worthy of Leonardo's genius for insightful graphic display of information.

Leonardo filled several notebooks with a wealth of his remarkable inventions. Each chapter emphasizes the complexity of Leonardo's mind, his unrestrained curiosity – the congruence of art and science. In all his work he made much practical use of mathematics and geometry. In any presentation of famous people associated with mathematics, science and art, his name cannot be omitted. Leonardo is simply amazing.

"Those who are inventors and interpreters between Nature and Man, as compared with the reciters and trumpeters of the works of others, are to be considered simply as an object in front of a mirror in comparison with its image when seen in the mirror; the one being something in itself, the other nothing: people whose debt to Nature is small, for it seems only by chance that they wear human form, and but for this one might class them with the herds of beasts.".

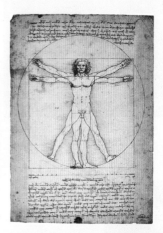

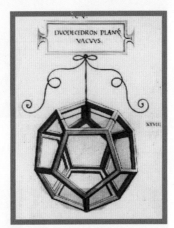

VITRUVIAN MAN OF LEONARDO

This pen and ink drawing by Leonardo, from 1492, depicting a man fitting his body into a circle and a square is probably the most famous drawing in the world. It is known as the Vitruvian Man and is named for the Roman architect Vitruvius. According to Pythagorian tradition, the circle represents the spiritual realm and the square, material existence, therefore the human body, as the model of perfection, represented the perfect marriage of matter and spirit, which is reflected in its proportions.

Leonardo was one of many artists who attempted to depict Vitruvius' perfect man, and possibly the only one who succeeded. His version is considered the most accurate depiction of the human body and the most beautiful of all attempts. It is the perfect blend of art and science.

Leonardo turned to science in the quest to improve his artwork. His study of nature and anatomy emerged in his stunningly realistic paintings, and his dissections of the human body paved the way for remarkably accurate figures. He was the first artist to study the physical proportions of men, women, and children and to use these studies to determine the "ideal" human figure.

Leonardo had for a long time displayed an ardent interest in the mathematics of art and nature.

...no human inquiry can be called science unless it pursues its path through mathematical exposition and demonstration.

Leonardo Da Vinci

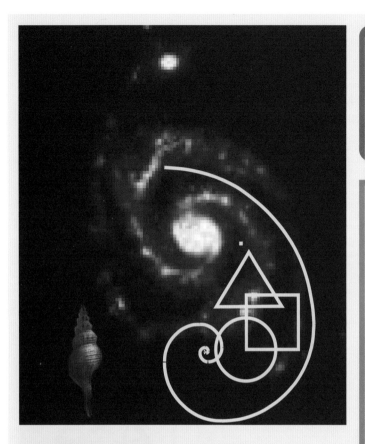

NATURE'S MASTER PLAN

Nature is a master builder playing endless variations on a number of basic shapes.

These basic shapes have existed since the beginning of time and remain unchanged – the circle, the square, the triangle, and the spiral may be compared to the letters of the alphabet, which can be used in combinations to form more elaborate shapes with new and unique properties. Much of the beauty we admire in the world around us is a result of nature's geometric skill: Every living thing – a shell, a plant, or a crystal – is a lesson in geometry. Nature seems to delight in the creation of varied geometric shapes, using circles, triangles, cubes, spirals, hexagons, and even stars, yet even the most simple forms may mask complexity.

Completely unrelated structures often show a surprising similarity, indicating the presence of basic principles in nature. A shell and a distant nebula are patterned alike – both are geometric spirals.

Crystals are the building blocks of most metals and many other solids, built on one another with mathematical precision, forming straight lines, edges, and layers. The atoms of different elements line up at different angles, resulting in attractive geometrical solids, such as cubes, prisms etc.

Design and order in nature – design is everywhere. All the shapes of nature, however disorderly they may appear at first glance – obey the laws of mathematical order.

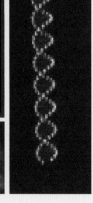

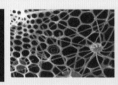

PREHISTORIC MATHEMATICS

Mathematical forms were present in nature before life appeared and long before humans walked the Earth. With the evolution of animal life came the possibility of the recognition of mathematical concepts such as form, number, and measurement. Spiders recognize regular polygons, logarithmic spirals, and similarity of figures in making a web. The laws of maxima and minima are followed by the bee in building up the hexagonal wax cells of the honeycomb. With the arrival of the humans there developed an opportunity for mathematics to show itself more consciously. Early art contributed to an appreciation of geometry, while religious mysticism and commerce contributed to the development of numbers, and each lent its influence to the creation of an interest in architecture and astronomy.

Dramatic natural events such as fire, solar eclipses, lightning, volcanoes erupting, the movement of the sun, moon, and stars all aroused man's inborn curiosity. Later this curiosity was disciplined by measurement and reinforced by mathematical reasoning and so humans became scientists. The cavemen who traded spears for an animal were using arithmetic. Probably they counted on their fingers and may be on their toes. Humans then began to own many things and had to keep count of them by making notches on a stick or trees (tally marks). Tally sticks were also used as calendars for marking the passage of days and seasons. Numbers were invented and at first they looked very much like tally marks. The ancient number systems, however, made it difficult to perform even the most simple arithmetical operations. A mechanical way of computation was necessary. The Romans did their arithmetic by counting pebbles, which was the most primitive form of the abacus, the forerunner of modern computers.

PREHISTORIC CAVE PAINTING

The number of hunters in the group doesn't match the number of animals killed, a fact that must have led to man's first mathematical ideas and problems – the concepts of MORE and LESS. Art was preparing the way for geometry.

THE WHEEL

Man's greatest invention is pure abstract geometry – the circle

The introduction of the wheel was an enormous advance in technology. It took thousands of years to conceive the idea of a new form unprecedented in nature, that of pure geometry. It required a capacity for abstract thinking and the ability to pass from the object to the idea of it, from the phenomenon to the theory. As with many other really great inventions, the wheel did not change essentially over the centuries. Our modern civilization runs on wheels and on the principle of rotary motion.

MAN –
THE MATHEMATICIAN

Mathematical forms existed before life appeared on our planet. One of the great cosmic forms is the spiral, which is the shape of many galaxies. While heavenly bodies move in elliptic or parabolic paths about some larger body. With the advent of humankind, there developed an opportunity for mathematics to show itself more consciously. Art contributed to an appreciation of geometry, religious mysticism and commerce contributed to the development of numbers, and each led to the stimulation of interest in architecture and in astronomy.

Beautiful dramatic natural events such as a solar eclipse, lightning, a volcano erupting, the path of the sun all aroused man's curiosity, but only when man's curisosity was disciplined by measurement and reinforced by mathematical reasoning could he become a scientist.

eclipse

lightning

volcano

sun's analemma

sun's path

concentric stars

finger-counting

sundial shadow

moon and its phases

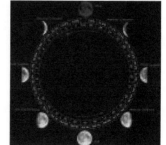

THE FIRST MATHEMATICAL CONCEPTS

The stars of the night sky offered a reliable clue to direction. Simple finger counting was useful for our forefathers when they wanted to exchange goods – it was the first arithmetic. By noticing the length of the shadow an early hunter could roughly tell what we call the time of day. To measure longer periods of time, our forefathers relied on the moon. Its gradual changes were recorded by cutting notches on a tree, stick or stone to match the passage of each day. Using the *trial-and-error method*, the ancient Egyptians developed the first crude form of geometry. They had only a basic understanding of the laws of mathematics and physics, yet they surveyed the land accurately, measured the passing of time by crude sundials, and constructed structures which have stood for thousands of years.

THALES – THE FIRST MATHEMATICIAN
Thales and his theorems

When we attempt to trace the beginnings of the history of mathematics, it is necessary to define what we mean by "history" and "mathematics." We may consider history as a narration of recorded events, or we may look upon it as a relation of incidents from the very beginning of the Universe. If mathematics means that "abstract science which investigates deductively the conclusions implicit in the elementary conceptions of spatial and numerical relations," then the history of mathematics cannot go back much earlier than the time of Thales (c. 624 B.C. – 546 B.C.). This would be a limitation, because a broader view tells the story of the genesis of mathematics, even before the period in which the science, as defined, began to exist. Early evidences of mathematics in the great cosmic plan assert that there are mathematical truths which have no beginning in time and which shall have no end.

Thales of Miletus was the first known Greek philosopher, scientist, and mathematician. He is credited with at least five classic theorems of elementary Euclidean geometry and with the first thoughts about world's microstructure. He believed that water was the original and absolute element and everything else came out of it, including motion and life as well. Before Thales, the ancient Greeks explained the origin and nature of the world through myths, gods, and heroes. Thales was an innovator. He attempted to explain the world without reference to the supernatural. But he is mostly known for his innovative use of geometry. He measured the height of the pyramids by their shadows at the moment when his own shadow was equal to his height. The length of the pyramid's shadow measured from the center of the pyramid at that moment must have been equal to its height.

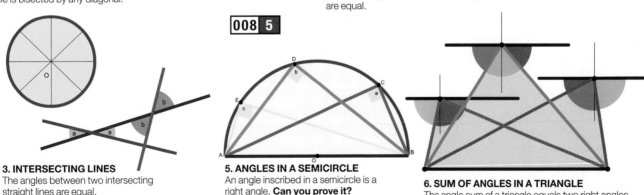

2. BASE ANGLES IN ISOSCELES TRIANGLES
The base angles of an isosceles triangle are equal.

4. CONGRUENT TRIANGLES
Two triangles are congruent if their two angles on the included side are equal.

1. CIRCLE DIAMETER
A circle is bisected by any diagonal.

008 5

3. INTERSECTING LINES
The angles between two intersecting straight lines are equal.

5. ANGLES IN A SEMICIRCLE
An angle inscribed in a semicircle is a right angle. **Can you prove it?**

6. SUM OF ANGLES IN A TRIANGLE
The angle sum of a triangle equals two right angles.

EUCLID AND EUCLIDEAN GEOMETRY

Euclidean geometry is a mathematical system attributed to the Greek mathematician Euclid of Alexandria. Euclid's book *Elements* is the first known systematic treatise of geometry. The method is based on a small set of intuitively appeealing axioms, upon which proofs of many other propositions (theorems) are based.

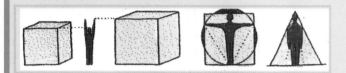

THE THREE CLASSICAL PROBLEMS OF GREEK ANTIQUITY

The ancient Greek mathematicians introduced problems that required figures to be constructed by the use of a compass and straightedge alone. These were the classical tools Euclid favored writing his Elements. At the time it was considered *"noble, elegant, and beautiful"* to solve problems without using anything else than just these tools. Three famous problems left by the ancient Greeks have resisted the efforts of many mathematicians over the centuries to be solved his way. The are:

1. duplicating the cube *(constructing a cube double the volume of a given cube);*

2. squaring the circle *(constructing a square equal in area to a given circle); and*

3. trisecting the angle *(dividing a given angle into three equal parts).*

They are based on the fact that when using only a compass and a straightedge there is a limit to the kind of mathematical operations that can be performed with these restrictions. None of the the three famous problems are solvable by using only a compass and unmarked straight edge although no one could prove this until the 19th century.

As the diagrams show, we can perform addition, subtraction, multiplication, division and square roots using only a compass and a straightedge.

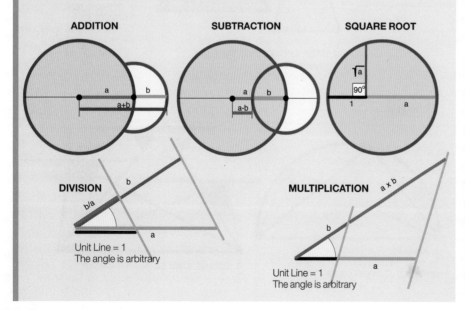

ADDITION

SUBTRACTION

SQUARE ROOT

DIVISION

Unit Line = 1
The angle is arbitrary

MULTIPLICATION

Unit Line = 1
The angle is arbitrary

EUCLID OF ALEXANDRIA

(c.365 BC--275 BC)

Euclid of Alexandria is the most famous mathematician of antiquity. His famous work on mathematics, *The Elements*, consists of 13 books, which constitute the greatest mathematical textbook of all time. Euclid was the leader of a team of mathematicians who contributed to this work, and so he can also be considered the greatest mathematics teacher ever. Little is known of Euclid's life. *The Elements* was a compilation of knowledge on mathematics that became the basis of mathematics teaching for 2000 years. Euclid's *Elements* is particularly remarkable for the clarity with which the theorems are stated and proved.

POINTS AND LINES
The Basic Tools of Geometry

The ancient Greeks developed the science of geometry from the practical study of measuring land, by inventing the science of abstract form and it was from this that mathematical proofs evolved. All of geometry begins with the point, which indicates a position on a two-dimensional plane or in three-dimensional space. The point, which is the intersection of two or more lines, is a pure *abstraction*. You must *imagine* that it is there, even though it does not exist as an entity in itself. It is a zero-dimensional mathematical object.

Because it is difficult to refer to something you cannot see, the point is usually represented by a dot, which is a small circle on a plane or a small sphere in three-dimensional space. So a point is "nothing", but it is also the fundamental particle upon which all of geometry is built. It is defined by Euclid's in his *Elements* as "that which has no part". His statement "Without Geometry, life is pointless" should be understood with reference to this, as well as in its broader meaning.

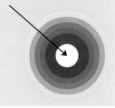

NON-EUCLIDEAN GEOMETRIES
ANGLES – TRIANGLES
Can you draw a triangle with the sum of its angles equal to 270°?

Geometry has roots in the measuring and division of land. Indeed, the literal translation of geometry is "measurement of the earth." But the complexity of the shapes of fields and the ingenuity ancient geometers employed to perform their jobs soon led geometry away from land surveys and toward the study of the relationships of abstract shapes.

For some 2,000 years, the geometry of Euclid was generally considered the only geometry that was possible, even though no one knew why his theorems were true. But since Euclid's theorems concerning straight lines and two-dimensional planes looked self-evident – in other words, they worked – no one thought to challenge them.

Early in the 19th century, however, mathematicians discovered that not only were many of Euclid's tenets not self-evident but they weren't true. For instance, when they substituted a sphere for Euclid's plane mathematicians found that, counter to Euclid's axiom, two parallel lines would meet. Why did it take so long to overturn Euclidean geometry? Because we occupy a tiny area of a huge sphere (the earth) and in such a limited area Euclidean geometry works quite well. For nearly all practical purposes architects can design and build structures as though the earth were flat. Indeed, in the ancient world there was little practical applications for any geometry that wasn't Euclidean. But non-Euclidean geometries have powerful and important applications in modern physics and cosmology. Astronomers use non-Euclidean geometry for describing the paths of light rays as they bend around very heavy bodies, such as stars, black holes, and galaxies. Combined with Einstein's theories of relativity, non-Euclidean geometry has solved many mysteries about space and time that could not be tackled in any other way.

Intersecting lines are great circles that intersect in Spherical geometry.

Parallel lines are great circles that intersect only at the equator in Spherical geometry. There are no parallels in Spherical geometry.

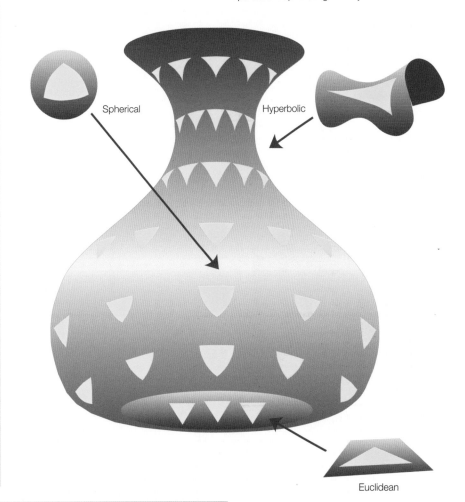

Spherical

Hyperbolic

Euclidean

ANGLES AND TRIANGLES IN GEOMETRIES

A typical vase possesses regions that have spherical, hyperbolic, and flat (Euclidean) geometries. These three triangles are determined by the sum of three interior angles of a triangle, formed by drawing the shortest distance between three points on the surface. This sum is greater than 180 degrees on a spherical space, lesser than 180 degrees for a hyperbolic space, and equal to 180 degrees on a flat Euclidean space.

THE SHADOW AND THE LAMPPOST

Jim liked to measure his shadow. Sometimes it was longer than his height, sometimes shorter. At this time of day it was exactly as long as his height. Jim also wanted to measure the height of the lamppost. Could he achieve this without actually being able to directly measure its height?

PROJECTIVE GEOMETRY

The origins of projective geometry are found in the works of Pappus, Desargues, and the Renaissance artists, who revived the ancient Greek doctrine that the essence of nature is mathematical law. Renaissance painters struggled for over 100 years to find a mathematical scheme to enable them to depict the three-dimensional world on a two-dimensional canvas. Finally they succeeded. The development of projective and analytical geometry led mathematicians to the possibility of studying the geometry of spaces with more than three dimensions. We see a distorted view of the world. The parallel tracks of a railroad should never meet, but rails in the distance do look as if they come to a point. Large things look small when they are far off, and distance can make two objects that are of equal size appear to be on radically different scales. The reverse is true as well – a thumb can obscure the largest galaxy.

Only during the Renaissance did painters solve the problem of representing the perspective of a three-dimensional space on a two-dimensional plane. That solution, called projection, created not only a breakthrough in art but also a new type of geometry – projective geometry, which is a form of mathematics that closely approaches the world of illusion. Projective geometry was one of the first non-Euclidean geometric theories.

We see the uses of projective geometry all around us. For example, maps are projections, photographs are images of projections, as are many mechanical and architectural drawings. Video games in realistic 3-D are possible because sophisticated computer programs can calculate the projection of imaginary three-dimensional objects.

DURER'S DRAWING MACHINE (1525)

Albrecht Durer's woodcut illustrates how a perspective drawing is produced by means of a projection. The glass plate held by the man shows a perspective drawing of the object on the table. Where the light rays from the object to the artist's eye intersect the plate they create an image of the object, known as its projection, onto the plate

SHADOW CUBE

Shadow seems to be a good example of a two-dimensional object. Projection unveils secret properties of shapes. A messy, seemingly random wire pattern in space produces a shadow of an ordered box, coming as a great surprise.

Implausible Container, a wire sculpture by Larry Kagan.

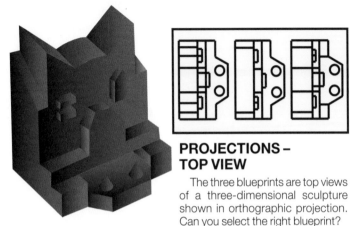

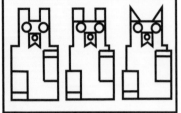

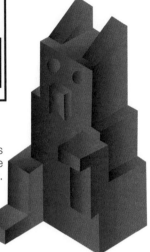

PROJECTIONS – TOP VIEW

The three blueprints are top views of a three-dimensional sculpture shown in orthographic projection. Can you select the right blueprint?

PROJECTIONS – FRONT VIEW

The three blueprints are front views of a three-dimensional sculpture shown in orthographic projection. Can you select the right blueprint?

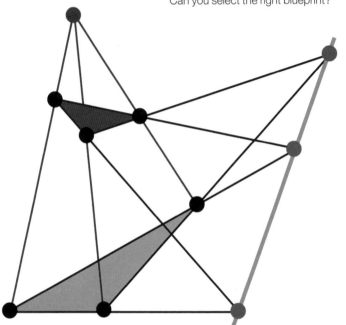

DESARGUES'S THEOREM

In 1641, Gerard Desargues, a French mathematician (1591–1661), published a book with a beautiful and mysterious title, *Shadow Lessons*. The subject of the book dealt with the relationship between perspective and shadow projections, which is known today as the simple and surprising Desargues's Theorem: *The points where the extensions of a triangle's sides meet the extensions of its shadow's sides lie along a straight line*. If the three straight lines joining the corresponding vertices of two triangles all meet in a point (the perspector), then the three intersections of pairs of corresponding sides lie on a straight line (the perspectrix). Equivalently, if two triangles are perspective from a point, they are perspective from a line. (When you try to check this, it always feels like a miracle when it works.)

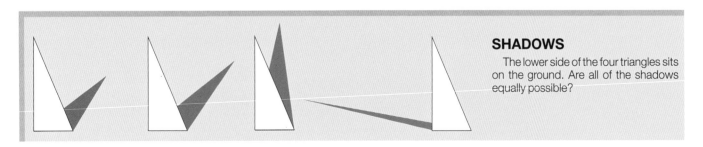

SHADOWS

The lower side of the four triangles sits on the ground. Are all of the shadows equally possible?

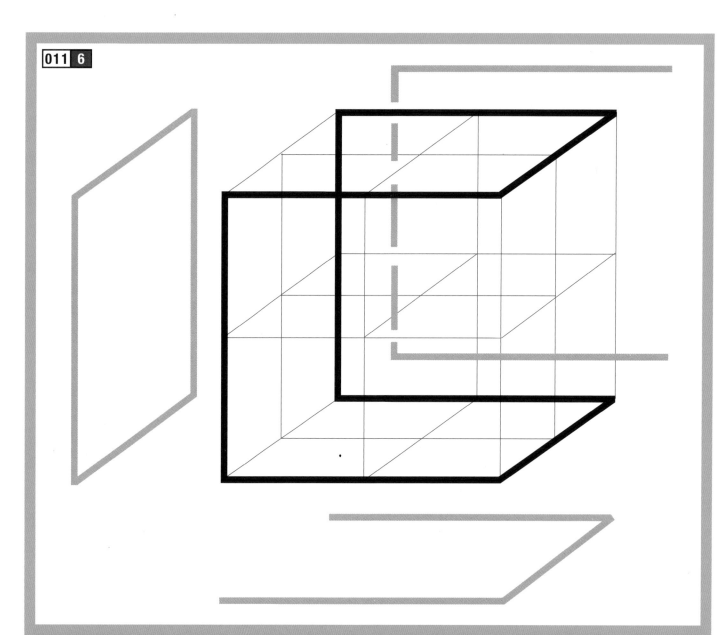

SHADOW TREES

A simple closed curve (black) is drawn along the grid lines (red) of a three-dimensional transparent 2 X 2 X 2 cube, forming its projections onto axis planes as shown. One of its shadows is a closed loop, while the other two are trees.

Can you draw another simple closed curve along the red grid lines of the cube, all three of whose projections onto axis planes are trees (not having any loops)?

(Mathematical Mind-Benders by Peter Winkler, published A.K. Peters)

TAXICAB GEOMETRY
The geometry of Gridlock City

One, easy to understand non-Euclidean geometry is the Taxicab geometry. It is a flat plane geometry along a square grid, like an orderly city map designed along straight lines with its streets at right angles, which can easily be explored as a paper-and-pencil game on squared paper. The first mathematician to research Taxicab geometry was Hermann Minkowski, a Russian mathematician who was a teacher of Albert Einstein in Zurich. In our Gridlock City of Taxicab geometry, the streets run either north–south or east–west. Many cities established in the 19th century possess just that sort of grid. Criss-crossing Gridlock City by taxicab, distances are measured along the lines of the square grid. For this reason taxicab distances from one point to another are in general longer than normal distances except when your taxi drives from one point to another in the same street.

The geometry of Gridlock City is quite different from Euclidean geometry. One of Euclid's axioms states that the shortest distance between two points is a straight line. This is not the case in Gridlock City. The shortest path is a series of short lines, since travel is restricted to the street grid. You must drive around the blocks, not through them. Therefore, there are several shortest distances between two points.

Since curves are not possible in taxicab geometry, do you think circles are impossible in Gridlock city? Not really. By definition a circle is a shape in which all points are equidistant from a fixed point. Suppose that there are six blocks to a mile in Gridlock City and you travel a mile by taxi from the center of the city. Where do you end up?

You could travel six blocks due east and stop. Or you could go five blocks east and one block north, or four blocks east and two blocks north. All those points lie on the "taxicab circle" of radius 1 mile. Can you plot the shape of such a "circle"?

Since the "straight lines" (the shortest paths) of taxicab geometry may be crooked from the Euclidean point of view, the concept of an "angle" becomes meaningless or different in this geometry. As with Taxicab circles, it is nonetheless possible to define equivalent analogues of Euclidean polygons, like triangles, squares, etc. The most interesting of these is the "biangle": a two-sided polygon is impossible in Euclid's geometry.

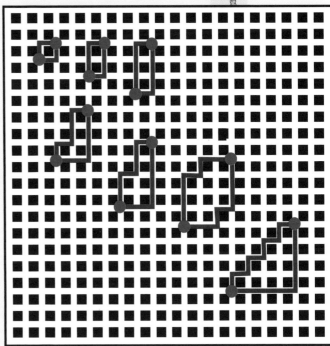

TAXICAB BIANGLES
Two-sided polygons

Interesting things can happen in non-Euclidean geometries. In our Euclidean geometry we know that the simplest polygon has three sides and that the shortest distance between two points is a straight line. But a two-sided polygon called a "biangle," non-existent in Euclidean geometry, can exist in taxicab geometry. Biangles of "side" lengths of 2 to 8 units between two points are shown. It should be obvious that different biangles can share the same pair of "corner" points, the two "sides" of any biangles must be equal because they join the same two points. How many different biangles of side lengths 4 and 5 units are possible?

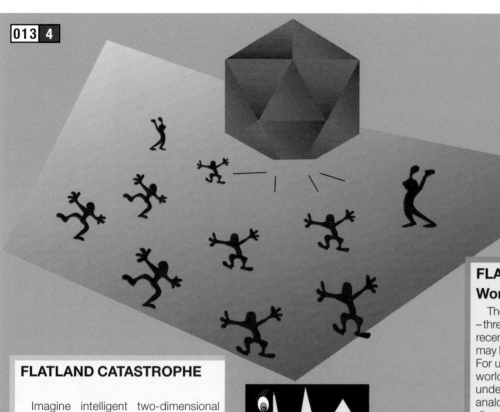

FLATLANDS
Worlds of two dimensions

The universe possesses four dimensions – three of space and one of time – and some recent theories have suggested that there may be even worlds of higher dimensions. For us, inhabitants of a three-dimensional world, a convenient way to try to understand higher dimensions is by analogy, imagining worlds of two dimensions. This was done in 1884, by Edwin A. Abbott, an English clergyman and popularizer of science. Abbott made a beautiful and now famous attempt to describe in charming detail a world made up of only two dimensions. In his satirical novel, called Flatland, the characters are basic geometrical figures gliding over the surface of an infinite two-dimensional plane – a vast tabletop. Apart from negligible thickness, Flatlanders have no perception of the third or any higher dimension (like we don't have of a fourth or any higher dimension). Abbott's book spawned many sequels tackling further details of an imaginary two-dimensional world, including its physical laws and workings of technological innovations, playing games, etc. One such book, *An Episode of Flatland*, written by Charles Howard Hinton in 1885, cleverly extends Abbott's ideas.

FLATLAND CATASTROPHE

Imagine intelligent two-dimensional aliens confined to a two-dimensional surface world called "Flatland." They are confined to Flatland not only physically but also sensuously – they have no faculties to sense anything out of their surface world. In an event that occurs every 100,000 years, a giant three-dimensional icosahedron meteorite collides and passes through Flatland. Can you describe how Flatlanders might observe this astronomical catastrophe?

FLATLAND HIERARCHY

In Edwin A. Abbott's Flatland ladies are just sharp straight lines; soldiers and workmen are isosceles triangles; the middle class are equilateral triangles; professionals are squares and pentagons; the upper class starts from hexagons and go up to circles, who are the high priests of Flatland. Ladies may be invisible from the back and dangerous to collide with. For these reasons, ladies are required by law to keep themselves visible at all times by executing a kind of perpetual twisting motion.

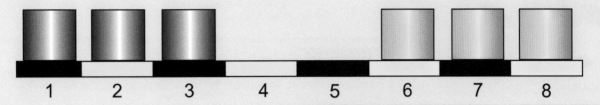

FLATLAND CHECKERS
Can flatlanders play games?

Flatland checkers are played on a two-dimensional "gameboard," with each player having three pieces, as shown in their initial positions. The moves are only in one direction, black to the right and yellow to the left. A piece can move one cell if empty, or jump over if occupied removing the piece jumped over. A move can cosist of a series of jumps, and jumps are compulsory if they are possible. Black starts first. Which player has an advantage in flatland checkers?

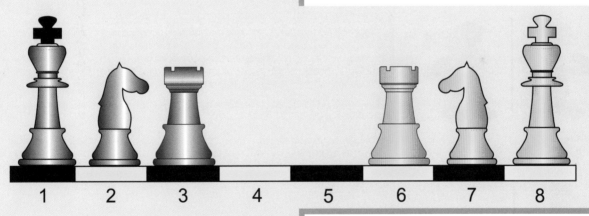

FLATLAND CHESS

Flatland chess is played on the same gameboard and each player has three pieces: king, knight, and rook, as shown in their initial positions. All pieces can move in either direction. A move ends on an empty cell, or at an occupied one by an enemy piece which is then removed. A rook moves any number of unoccupied cells. A king moves one cell at a time. A knight moves by jumping over an adjacent cell, either empty or occupied. A game can be a "draw" or a "checkmate" and won. Which player can force a win or force a draw?

1
TRANSLATION
(slide) – a parallel displacement

2
ROTATION
(turn) – rotation about a point

3
REFLECTION
(mirror image) – rotation about a straight line

4
GLIDE REFLECTION
(slide and reflection) – reflection and translation
combined

> "I see a certain order in the universe and symmetry is one
> way of making it visible"
> *May Sarton (1912–95)*

SYMMETRY

One of the most striking evidences of design and geometry in nature is the symmetry of many of its creations, symbolizing the unity of Science, Art, and Mathematics.

The most perfect natural examples of symmetry are in the arrangements of atoms and molecules in crystals. A common example is the snowflake, which possesses many axes of symmetry. Living creatures also display a remarkable amount of symmetry. Fivefold or pentagonal symmetry is found in many marine flowers and animals, such as the starfish, which has five, ten or even 23 symmetric arms. Human beings are roughly symmetrical about one axis, the spine, and display bilateral symmetry – the most common form of symmetry in nature. Objects that look the same as they are rotated about an axis have rotational symmetry. An equilateral triangle, for instance, will appear identical in three different positions as it rotates around a point at its center. Objects with lateral symmetry can be reflected on either side of a line or axis without appearing different.

We can easily make symmetrical patterns by folding and cutting paper or by using plane mirrors. What child hasn't made snowflakes or paper dolls that way? But symmetry is also an enormously important mathematical tool. Scientists could never have determined the structure of viruses and molecules without a full understanding of symmetry, and neither could they have built the standard model of particle physics.

Isometries are transformations that take any figure into a congruent one. Mirror symmetry is not the only type of symmetry in math. An object is symmetrical if it looks the same after being subjected to a transformation (a rotation, or reflection). This idea of symmmetry is studied in **group theory**. For example, a square has eight symmetries. A "group" in mathematical terms is the set of eight actions – the symmetry operations that preserve the square's appearance.

Evariste Galois invented a language, group theory, to descibe symmetry in mathematical structures. All of us have an idea of symmetry. Our ideas of beauty in art, music, and architecture are all heavily influenced by our notion of symmetry. To mathematicians, however, symmetry is known as a transformation that preserves an object's structure. Or, in simpler language, it is what you can do to a mathematical object that leaves it looking exactly the same.

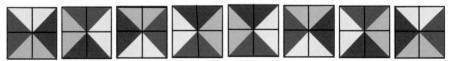

The eight symmetries of a square

TO THE LEFT: ISOMETRIES AND CATCHING SNOWFLAKES

There are four basic types of isometries of the plane, also called rigid motions.

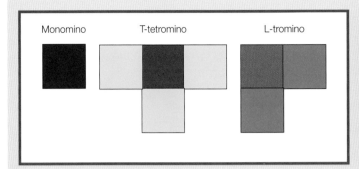

Monomino T-tetromino L-tromino

POLYOMINO SYMMETRY

Copy the monomino, T-tetromino, and L-tromino and cut them out and put them together to create symmetrical shapes, as shown in the example below. How many shapes can you create which have either reflected or rotational symmetry? There are 17 such symmetrical shapes, which is perhaps more than you would expect. We have shown where the monomino is placed in the other 16 shapes, can you complete them? Note that the colors are not relevant to the puzzle.

015 6

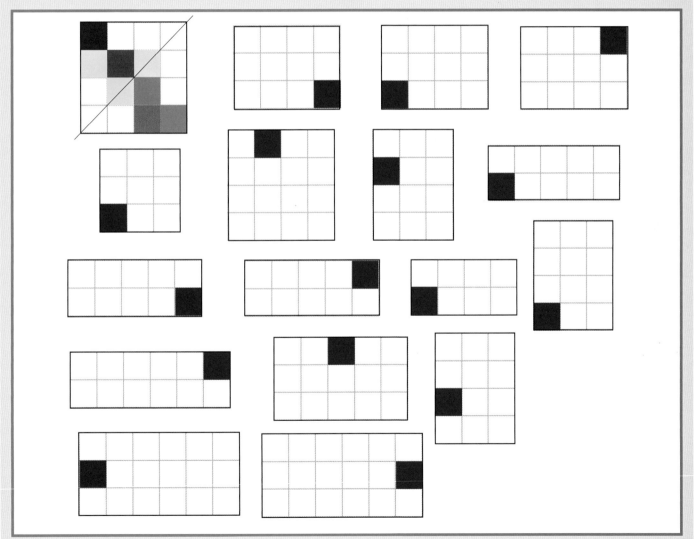

39

GOLDEN RATIO

Beauty can be achieved by the proportion, or comparative relationship, of one area

to another. Asymmetrical forms that seem beautiful to us have balance, or dynamic symmetry. The *Golden ratio*, **Golden section**, or the ***divine proportion*** as it was called by Leonardo da Vinci, is represented by the Greek letter phi (φ).

Where would you place a point on a line to divide the line in the most pleasing and meaningful way?

Among the multitude of points on the line, there is one very special point which divides the line into a mathematical ratio called the Golden Section or Golden Ratio, which since antiquity has played an important role not only in mathematics, but also in aesthetics, architecture, and art – not to mention nature as well.

Take a look at the diagram on the left. We've drawn a line and "snapped" it into two pieces. According to Euclid's definition, the larger segment/shorter segment is equal to whole line/larger segment. In other words:

Ratio of X to1 is the same as ratio X+1 to X or, AC/CB = AB/AC

Mathematically, we can write this as:

$$\varphi = \frac{X}{1} = \frac{X+1}{X}$$

Multiplying both sides by x, we get the simple quadratic equation

$$X^2 - X - 1 = 0$$

the two solutions of the equation for the golden ratio are:

$$\varphi = \frac{1+\sqrt{5}}{2} \approx \mathbf{1.618} \qquad \varphi = \frac{1-\sqrt{5}}{2} \approx \mathbf{0.618}$$

The positive solution = 1.61803398 ...... gives the value of the golden ratio, an irrational number.

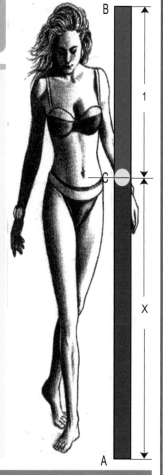

Dynamic Symmetry is an application of geometry with golden ratio in the main role. It is a pleasing type of symmetry dominating nature and man. Eudoxus (c. 408 B.C.–c. 347 B.C.), a Greek mathematician, was the first to try to find out why the golden section was so pleasing. He is said to have gone around with a stick, asking his friends to mark it at any point they found the most pleasing. He was astonished to find that the majority of people agreed almost exactly at the point which divided the stick into two parts in golden ratio. He also worked out the mathematics of golden ratio, expressing it by a formula, and calling it Phi, after Phidias, an artist, who used it extensively in his sculpture. They believed that art and architecture based on this ratio is unusually pleasing to the eye. They must have been surprised and reassured in their belief when they found this ratio in the Golden Rectangle and the pentagram, the sacred sign of the Pythagoreans, and in connection with the Fibonacci number sequence. An enormous literature has been accumulated around the golden ratio, with arguments that it is the key to the understanding of all morphology (including human anatomy), art, architecture and even music.

Who would have believed that this innocent looking line division, which Euclid defined for purely geometrical purposes, would have such enormous consequences in science, mathematics and art?

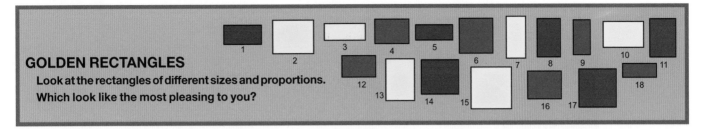

GOLDEN RECTANGLES

Look at the rectangles of different sizes and proportions.
Which look like the most pleasing to you?

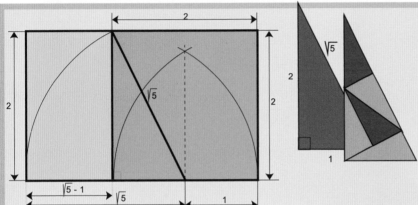

GOLDEN TRIANGLES

It is the only triangle that can be created from five smaller replicas of itself.

GOLDEN RECTANGLE
Whirling spiral

In probably what is a self-portrait of Leonardo da Vinci, he has overlaid the picture with a square subdivided into rectangles, some of which approximate golden rectangles. He was fascinated with golden proportions and the golden rectangle in, as he once described, "geometrical recreations." Leonardo illustrated Luca Pacioli's book on the golden sections, called *Divina Proportione* (Venice, 1509).

`016` `5`

BEAUTIFUL RECTANGLE

What are the proportions of the most pleasing rectangle?

Most scientists and artists over centuries have agreed that it is the rectangle having its sides in the proportion of the golden ratio – the Golden Rectangle. For its aesthetic appeal and elegance, it has played an important role in architecture, art, and even music.

The mathematical beauty of the Golden Rectangle will fully reveal itself if we construct it using the method of the ancient Greeks, that is, using a compass and a straightedge as visualized above.

1. We start with a perfect square and extend the line of its base.

2. From the midpoint of the base we draw an arc from the upper left corner of the square to the base.

3. We draw a perpendicular from this point and extend the top of the square to complete the **Golden Rectangle**.

We can use the Pythagorean theorem to check whether the proportions of the rectangle are those of the golden ratio. The right triangle used for this, is sometimes called the **Golden Triangle**. It is a triangle in which the height is twice the base. It also has an interesting property. While any triangle can be created from four smaller copies of themselves, only the golden triangle has the property that it can be created from five smaller copies of itself.

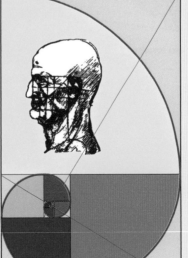

MODULAR MAN

Le Corbusier (1946) deconstructs the human form into the golden ratio and Fibonacci patterns.

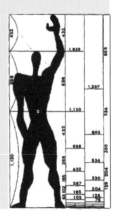

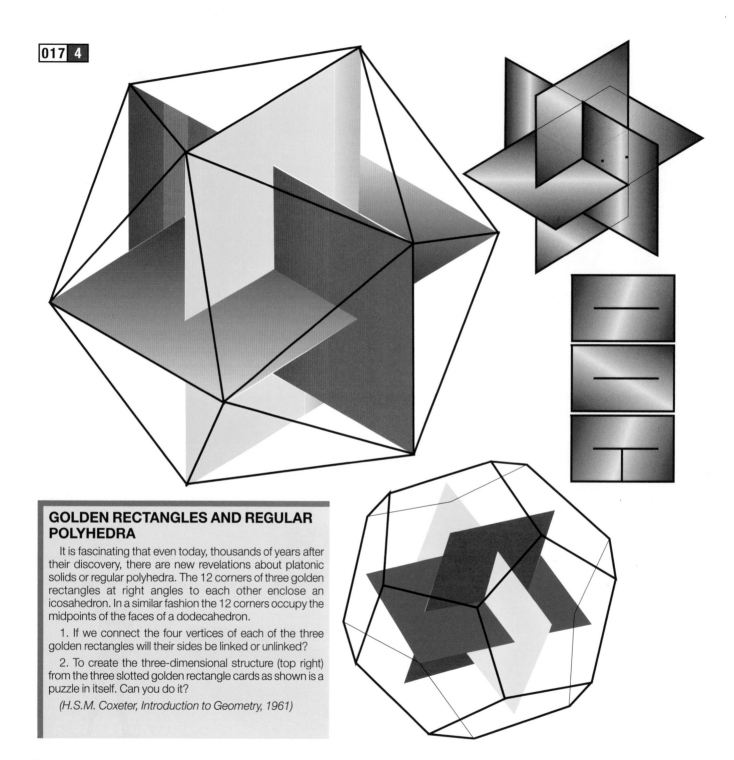

GOLDEN RECTANGLES AND REGULAR POLYHEDRA

It is fascinating that even today, thousands of years after their discovery, there are new revelations about platonic solids or regular polyhedra. The 12 corners of three golden rectangles at right angles to each other enclose an icosahedron. In a similar fashion the 12 corners occupy the midpoints of the faces of a dodecahedron.

1. If we connect the four vertices of each of the three golden rectangles will their sides be linked or unlinked?

2. To create the three-dimensional structure (top right) from the three slotted golden rectangle cards as shown is a puzzle in itself. Can you do it?

(H.S.M. Coxeter, Introduction to Geometry, 1961)

FIBONACCI RABBITS PUZZLE

The most famous recreational mathematics problem concerning number sequences is the classic dating from 1202.

This rabbit-breeding puzzle was found in a book called Liber Abaci (1202), written by Leonardo da Pisa, then a 27-year-old Italian mathematician, who is known by his nickname Fibonacci. In the puzzle, Fibonacci assumed that every pair of rabbits was made up of a male and a female rabbit and two months after their birth they produce another pair, when in reality they reach maturity only after four months.

This innocent mathematical puzzle revealed the most famous number sequence known today as the Fibonacci number sequence, which was later discovered to be everywhere in nature.

FIBONACCI RABBITS PUZZLE AND THE FIBONACCI NUMBER SEQUENCE

The Italian mathematician Leonardo Fibonacci invented a mathematical sequence (now called the Fibonacci sequence) as purely a recreational mathematics puzzle. But amazingly this invented sequence was later discovered to occur in many areas of science, math, and nature. Further than that, it bears a fascinating relationship to the golden ratio. What a coincidence! To stress its enormous importance, the Fibonacci Quarterly is a modern journal devoted entirely to mathematics related to the Fibonacci sequence.

JANUARY	1
FEBRUARY	1
MARCH	2
APRIL	3
MAY	5
JUNE	8
JULY	13

JULY	AUGUST	SEPTEMBER	OCTOBER	NOVEMBER	DECEMBER
?	?	?	?	?	?

Note: In the visualization of the problem above, each rabbit represents a pair of rabbits.

Fibonacci statue in Pisa

LEONARDO PISANO – FIBONACCI (1170–1250)

Leonardo Pisano, known by his nickname Fibonacci, was probably born in Pisa, Italy, and he certainly died there. Educated in North Africa, he traveled much with his father, who held a diplomatic post. Returning to Pisa around 1200, he wrote a number of important handwritten mathematical texts, the most important of which was *Liber Abaci* (1202). It was based on mathematical knowledge that Fibonacci had accumulated during his travels. Its most important contribution was introducing the Hindu-Arabic placed-valued decimal system and the use of Arabic numerals into Europe. A section contains a large collection of problems aimed at merchants. Another section is devoted to the introduction of the Fibonacci numbers and the Fibonacci number sequence.

FIBONACCI NUMBERS IN NATURE

Leonardo Fibonacci discovered the Fibonacci number sequence as a recreational mathematics exercise. However, it has been occurring in nature for millions of years.

Mathematical forms are present in plants. Certain leaves arrange themselves about a stalk in accordance to the law of number series first expressed by Leonardo Fibonacci. Was this the result of countless evolutionary experiments in the search of the most efficient configuration? Or is some other law involved which will be revealed in the future? The Fibonacci number series is produced by starting with 1 and adding the last two numbers to arrive at the next:

1 1 2 3 5 8 13 21 34 55 89 ....

Each term is the sum of the two terms which immediately precede it.

Each species of flower has a basic growth pattern and a corresponding number pattern, typical of the species but not always precisely followed in every single plant of the species. Although there are families of plants that follow other patterns (notably symmetrical development) the numbers of the Fibonacci sequence play an outstandingly siginificant role in the plant world.

SUNFLOWER

Two distinct sets of near-perfect spirals may be revealed in a sunflower, radiating clockwise and counterclockwise, with each set always made up of a predetermined number of spirals. How many spirals can you count in each direction?

Can you identify which of the two numbers are represented in the sunflower above?

You will discover that the two numbers will correspond to two consecutive numbers of the Fibonacci number sequence – the Fibonacci number ratio or Phi ratio.

019 3

LEAF PATTERNS

Many plants show Fibonacci numbers in the arrangement of leaves around the stem. If we look down at the plane from the top, the leaves are arranged so that the leaves above do not cover leaves below. The number of turns in each direction and the number of leaves are consecutive Fibonacci numbers. In the example above there are five complete turns and eight spaces from leaf 1 to leaf 9. The Fibonacci ratio for this plant is 5/8.

PINE CONE

Similar arrangements of opposing spirals are also found in the scales of a pine cone, as well as the leaves of many other plants with a spiral leaf-growth pattern. Can you count the two sets of spirals? How many spirals are there in each set?

FIBONACCI STAIRCASE AND THE GOLDEN RATIO

Can every natural number be expressed using only Fibonacci numbers?

The first 13 Fibonacci numbers are shown.

Can you, for example, try to form the natural number **232** using only Fibonacci numbers?

Is there any relationship between the Fibonacci number sequence and the Golden ratio?

The red numbers show how Fibonacci numbers grow relative to each other by looking at the quotients of two consecutive numbers, and look at how these fractions – one Fibonacci number divided by the previous one – change as the sequence grows. If you were to rewrite these fractions in decimal form, what amazing sequence would you find?

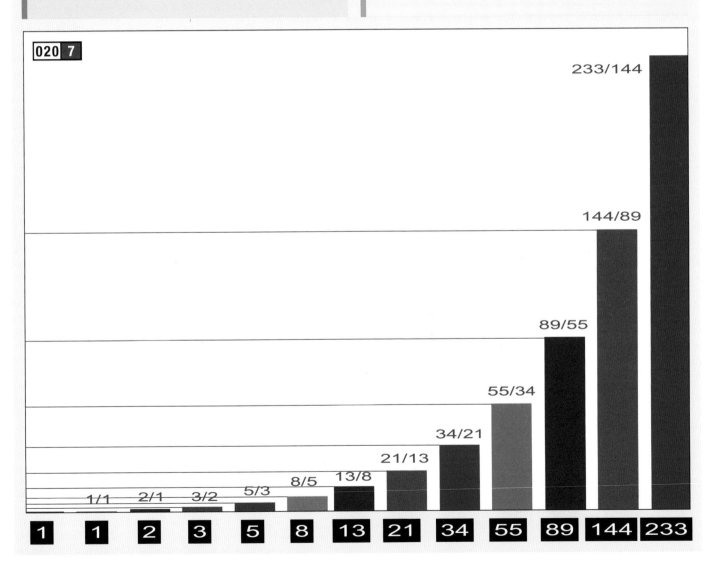

020 7

233/144
144/89
89/55
55/34
34/21
21/13
13/8
8/5
5/3
3/2
2/1
1/1

1 1 2 3 5 8 13 21 34 55 89 144 233

FRACTALS

The story of fractals began in the 17th century when Leibniz was considering recursive self-similarity, which he believed was a porperty that only the straight line had. In the late 19th century, mathematicians Gaston Julia, Pierre Fatou, and Georg Cantor experimented with a new family of curves made possible by computer programs.

In 1904, Helge von Koch introduced the beautiful *Koch Snowflake* and *Anti-Snowflake curves*, which were the earliest and most popular fractals. Although initially they were called *pathological curves*, because of their counterintuitive nature. Their lengths are infinite, while they enclose a finite area.

Benoit Mandelbrot showed in 1980 computer-created pictures of such objects created by Julia and the famous Mandelbrot set, which were strikingly beautiful and aroused great general interest worldwide. He also showed that these figures can be found in nature as well.

The main characteristics of fractals is self-similarity; patterns in the big fractal seen again and repeated in its parts in smaller and smaller dimensions.

SNOWFLAKE FRACTALS AND THE ANTI-SNOWFLAKE FRACTALS

Can you imagine a shape that has an infinite length yet encloses only a finite area? Sounds impossible, but surprisingly enough, such figures exist. One of them is the beautiful snowflake-curve and its opposite the anti-snowflake curve. These curves are growth patterns consisting of a sequence of polygons. The snowflake curve is created according to a very simple progression principle on the sides of an equilateral triangle. On the central third of each side another equilateral triangle is added, and so on to infinity.

The limit of this sequence of polygons is a remarkable curve (blue). Its length is infinite, yet the area it encloses is finite. The snowflake curve is an excellent visual way to demonstrate the concept of the limit and fractals, as it was later called. It is not possible to draw the limiting curve. We can only create the polygons for the next sequence, and the ultimate curve is left to the imagination.

As the curve grows, what will be the size of its area eventually?

On the next page the black outline shows the fifth generation of the Snowflake curve fractal.

In the inside of the initial equilateral triangle can you construct the first four generations of the Anti-Snowflake curve?

Are there three-dimensional analogs of the snowflake and similar curves?

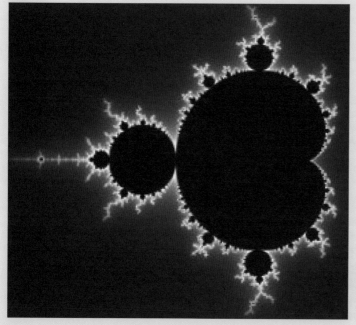

Two generations of the snowflake fractal

MANDELBROT SET

Unlike most other fractals, which are mainly geometrical constructions, the Mandelbrot set is a set of numbers and the image at left is just a plot of those numbers. Only a computer is capable of discovering whether a number is in the Mandelbrot set or not.

FRACTAL SNOWFLAKE AND ANTI-SNOWFLAKE CURVES

The outline of the black areas describes the fifth generation of the snowflake curve.

Can you draw along the triangular grid of the initial equilateral triangle the first four generations of the Anti-Snowflake curve?

FIBONACCI FRACTAL

The Fibonacci fractal was discovered by George W. Grossman in 1997, and is often called the Grossman Truss. It again demonstrates the mysterious and striking ways in which this sequence appears in nature and artificial objects. Like the snowflake curve it starts with a triangle, this time an isosceles right-angled triangle.

Its development is shown in six stages. Stage 1 illustrates the principle of its construction. In the next iteration the generative procedure will be applied only to the larger triangle. In the next generations we can see there will always be two groups of triangles, and the divisions will be applied only to the group of the larger triangles. It was convenient to color in each stage the larger triangle groups in red as shown.

The Fibonacci number sequence appears in each generation; as can be seen by counting the two groups of triangles as shown.

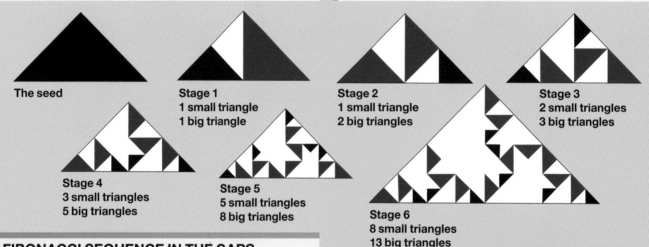

The seed

Stage 1
1 small triangle
1 big triangle

Stage 2
1 small triangle
2 big triangles

Stage 3
2 small triangles
3 big triangles

Stage 4
3 small triangles
5 big triangles

Stage 5
5 small triangles
8 big triangles

Stage 6
8 small triangles
13 big triangles

FIBONACCI SEQUENCE IN THE GAPS

But even more fascinating, the sequence appears also in each generation, in the triangles which were eliminated in each stage forming the gaps as shown below in green. Amazingly counting gaps in each stage will give us the whole sequence, even though it was not directly involved in the process that generated it.

(Ref.: The Fabulous Fibonacci Numbers, Alfred Posamentier, Ingmar Lehmann)

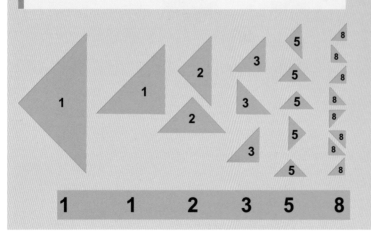

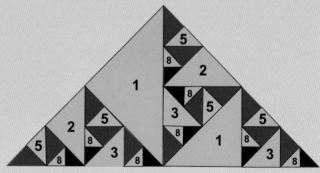

FIBONACCI FRACTAL GAPS

By counting the gaps in Stage 6, it is possible to express the whole Fibonacci sequence up to that stage.

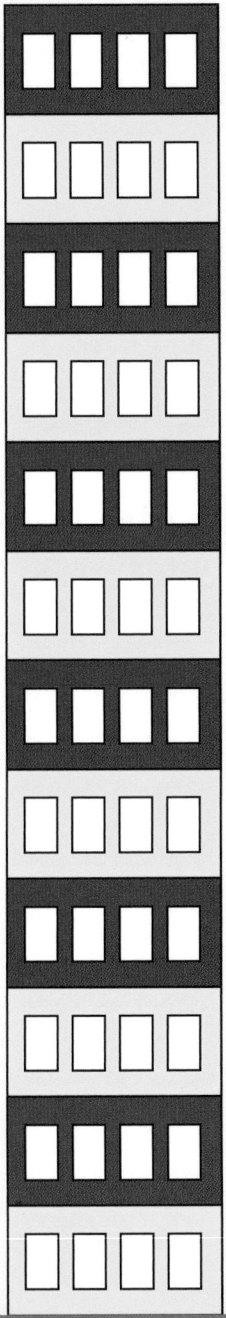

PACKING "2-BY-N" GAMEBOARDS WITH DOMINOS

In how many different ways can you cover with dominos (2-by-n rectangles) a 2-by-n gameboard. Find out for the first 6 boards shown.

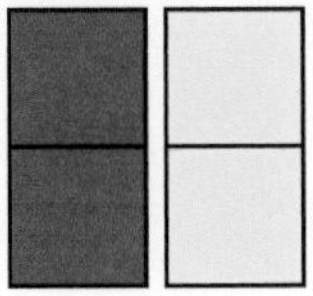

2 by 1

2 by 2

2 by 3

2 by 4

2 by 5

2 by 6

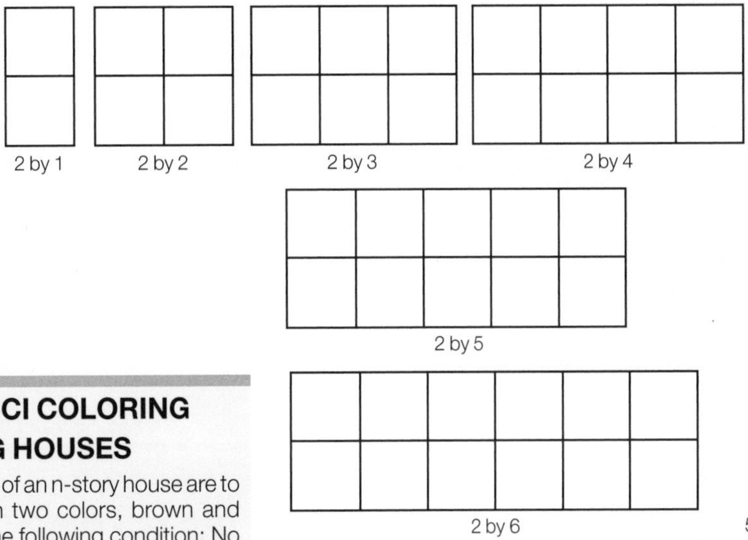

FIBONACCI COLORING
PAINTING HOUSES

The stories of an n-story house are to be painted in two colors, brown and yellow with the following condition: No two adjacent stories are brown. However, both of them can be yellow. In how many different possible ways can you paint a 12-floor house as shown following these rules? (A sample coloring is given.) Try first coloring houses from n=1 to n=5 floors.

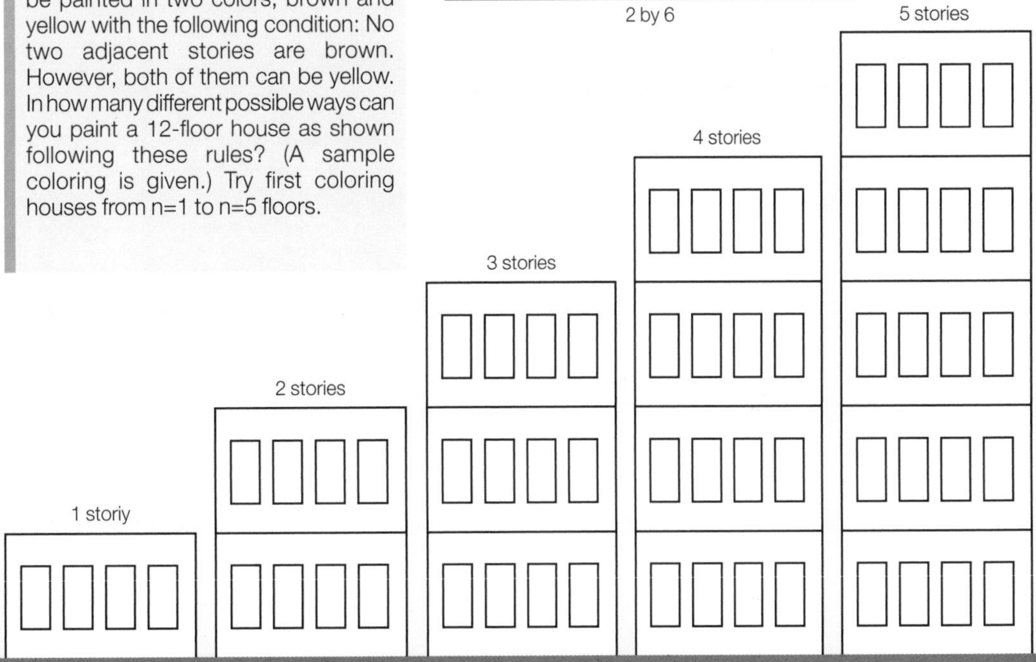

1 storiy

2 stories

3 stories

4 stories

5 stories

49

DIMENSIONS – PAPPUS'S THEOREM

The Power of the Moving Point – the dimensional progression from a point to a hypercube.

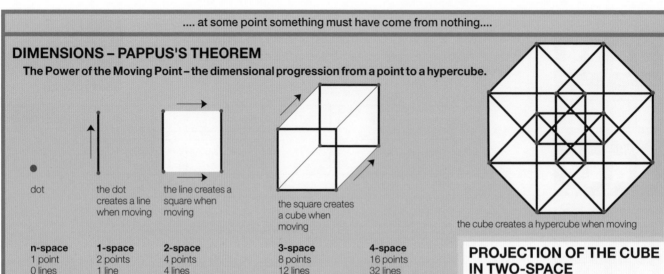

dot

the dot creates a line when moving

the line creates a square when moving

the square creates a cube when moving

the cube creates a hypercube when moving

n-space	1-space	2-space	3-space	4-space
1 point	2 points	4 points	8 points	16 points
0 lines	1 line	4 lines	12 lines	32 lines
0 squares	0 squares	1 square	6 squares	24 squares
0 cubes	0 cubes	0 cubes	1 cube	8 cubes
0 tesseracts	0 tesseracts	0 tesseracts	0 tesseracts	1 tesseract

DIMENSIONS – PAPPUS'S THEOREM

The Power of the Moving Point – the dimensional progression from a point to a hypercube.

A hypercube is an n-dimensional analogue of a square (n = 2) and a cube (n = 3). It is a closed, compact, convex figure consisting of groups of opposite parallel line segments aligned in each of the space's dimensions, at right angles to each other.

The great 4th-century mathematician Pappus of Alexandria first recognized that space could be filled with a moving point. A point moving in one dimension produces a straight line. That line moving in a direction perpendicular to the point defines a rectangle. And that rectangle moving in a direction at right angles to the point and the line creates a rectangular prism This same concept can be extended to include points that move along curves to define complex areas and volumes.

Thus the point is nothing, but paradoxically it is the fundamental "particle" on which the whole of geometry is built. So does all our geometry spring from nothing?

DIMENSIONS

The most fundamental concept in geometry is the idea of dimension. All of geometry begins with the point, which indicates a position on a two-dimensional plane or in three-dimensional space. The point, which is the intersection of two or more lines, is a pure abstraction. You must imagine that it is there. The position of a car on a road can be indicated by a single number; its distance from some location, such as a milestone. The location of a ship at sea can be determined by noting its latitude and longitude. Two dimensions, two numbers. The position of a point in a room can be pinned down with three numbers, or coordinates – say, the distance from two of the walls and its height off the floor. Three-dimensional coordinates are usually given an x, y, and z.

PROJECTION OF THE CUBE IN TWO-SPACE PROJECTION OF THE TESSERACT IN THREE-SPACE

The **tesseract**, is the four-dimensional analog of the (three-dimensional) cube, where motion along the fourth dimension is often a representation for transformations of the cube through time. The tesseract is to the cube as the cube is to the square; or, more formally, the tesseract can be described as a regular convex 4-polytope whose boundary consists of eight cubical cells.

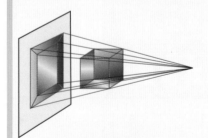

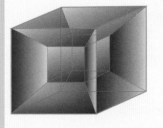

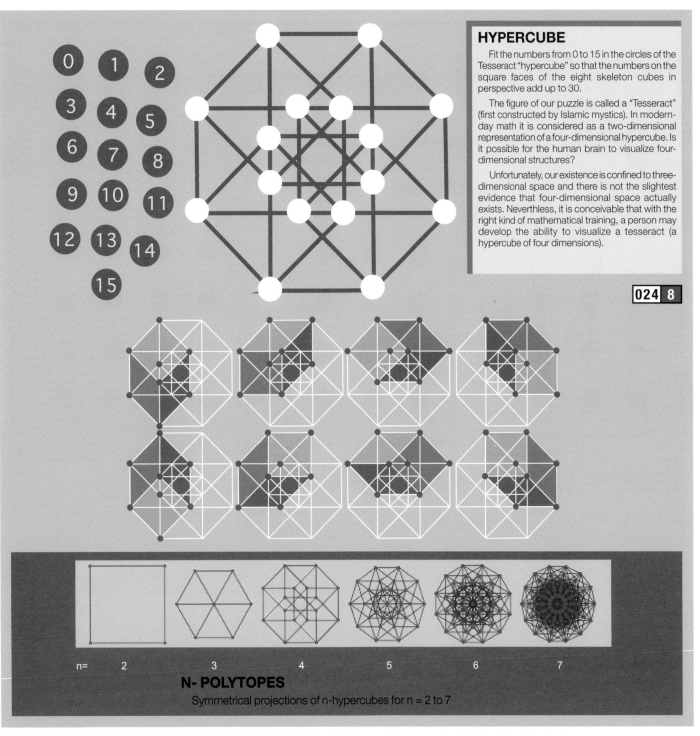

HYPERCUBE

Fit the numbers from 0 to 15 in the circles of the Tesseract "hypercube" so that the numbers on the square faces of the eight skeleton cubes in perspective add up to 30.

The figure of our puzzle is called a "Tesseract" (first constructed by Islamic mystics). In modern-day math it is considered as a two-dimensional representation of a four-dimensional hypercube. Is it possible for the human brain to visualize four-dimensional structures?

Unfortunately, our existence is confined to three-dimensional space and there is not the slightest evidence that four-dimensional space actually exists. Neverthless, it is conceivable that with the right kind of mathematical training, a person may develop the ability to visualize a tesseract (a hypercube of four dimensions).

024 8

n= 2   3   4   5   6   7

N- POLYTOPES

Symmetrical projections of n-hypercubes for n = 2 to 7

LINES THROUGH DOTS

The 9, 12, and 16-points problems.

The classical problem of connecting dots in different configurations with a minimum number of straight lines without lifting your pencil, is found in many books on recreational mathematics and IQ tests. Usually the number of lines to solve the problems is given.

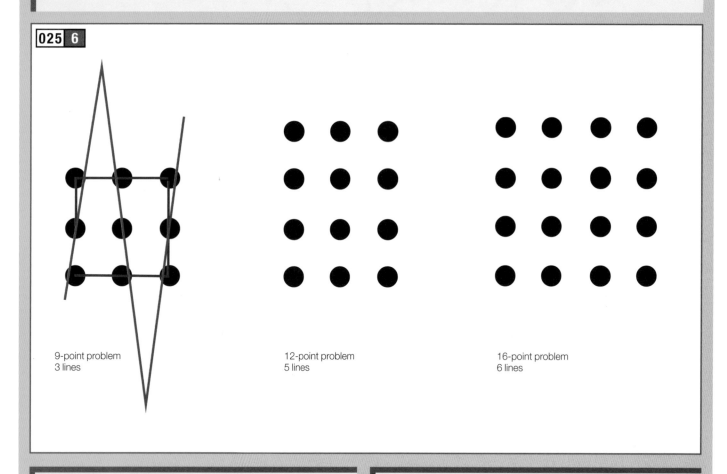

025 **6**

9-point problem
3 lines

12-point problem
5 lines

16-point problem
6 lines

At first attempts the problems appear to be impossible. For example, connecting eight points in the 9-point problem *(blue lines)* seems to be the minimum, but not three!

The reason may be a conceptual block, based on an initial assumption that the lines can only be horizontal and vertical, or that the lines should be confined to the "box" outlined by the points (blue). But no such restrictions were mentioned as part of the problems.

Slanted lines and lines that leave the boundaries of the points provide a way to the solutions *(red)*. Once such a general insights are gained, and the 9-point problem solved, the answer to problems involving a greater number of points should not be too difficult.

But can you extend further your imagination and solve the three problems by one single straight line?

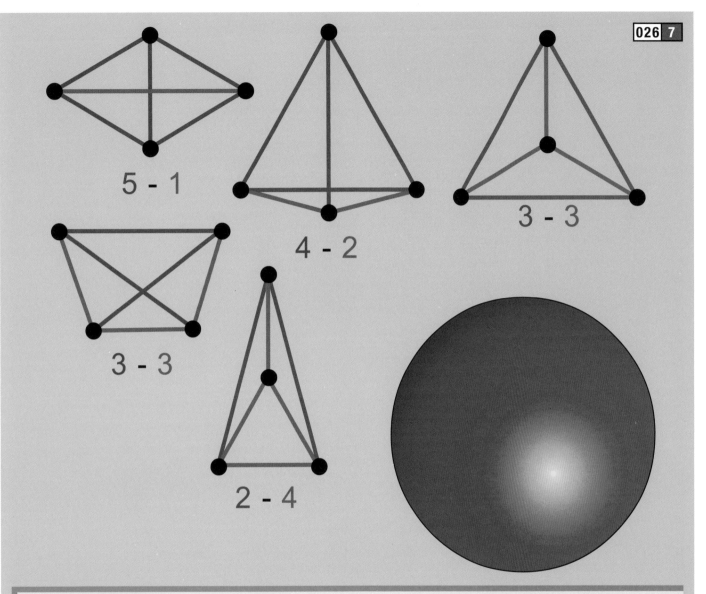

5 - 1

4 - 2

3 - 3

3 - 3

2 - 4

EQUIDISTANT POINTS

EQUIDISTANT TWO DISTANCES - FOUR POINTS

Puzzle 1. You have four points at your disposal (four small coins or something similar). Can you place them on the plane so that they determine only two different distances? There are only six possible different configurations – five of them are shown here. Can you find the sixth?

Puzzle 2. What is the largest number of points that can be placed on the surface of a sphere so that every point is exactly the same distance (equidistant) from every other point?

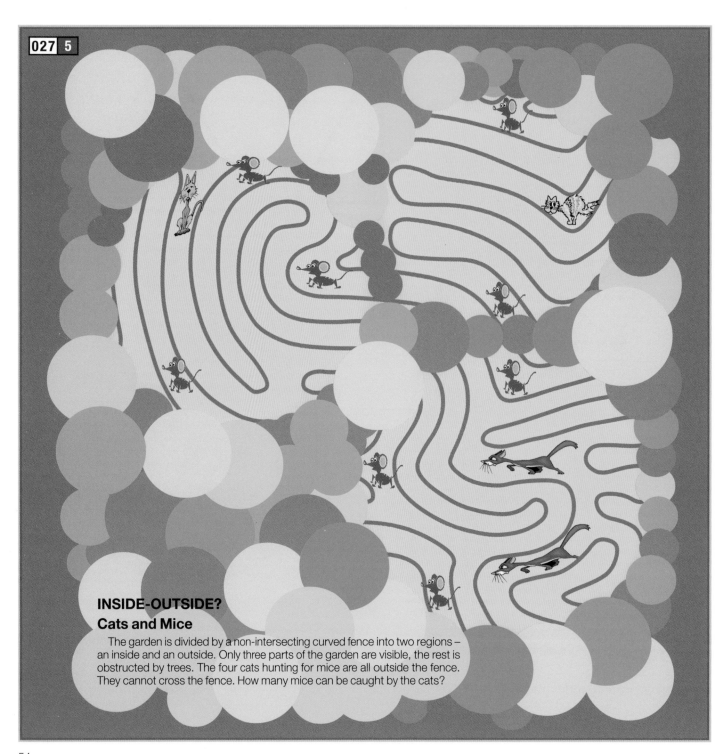

INSIDE-OUTSIDE?

Cats and Mice

The garden is divided by a non-intersecting curved fence into two regions – an inside and an outside. Only three parts of the garden are visible, the rest is obstructed by trees. The four cats hunting for mice are all outside the fence. They cannot cross the fence. How many mice can be caught by the cats?

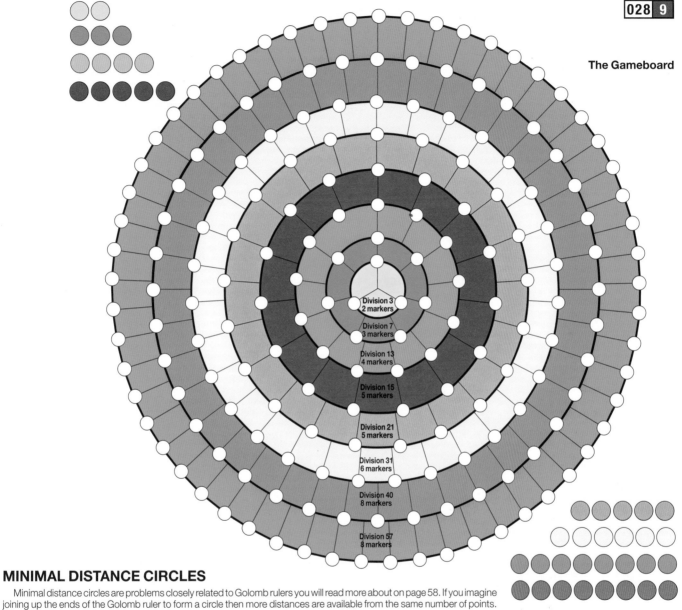

Division 3
2 markers

Division 7
3 markers

Division 13
4 markers

Division 15
5 markers

Division 21
5 markers

Division 31
6 markers

Division 40
8 markers

Division 57
8 markers

MINIMAL DISTANCE CIRCLES

Minimal distance circles are problems closely related to Golomb rulers you will read more about on page 58. If you imagine joining up the ends of the Golomb ruler to form a circle then more distances are available from the same number of points. Hence there are now many more perfect and optimal solutions than with the original linear ruler.

Circumferences of circles are divided into "n" equal parts, each part considered of unit length. The object is to distribute a certain number of markers on division points of each circle, so as to be able to measure every distance from 1 to n units, between any two marked points. There can be more than one way of measuring a distance, if you wish.

Can you place the given markers for circular Golomb rulers on the diagram for divisions of 3, 7, 13, 15, 21, and 31 units? Again, the object is to place the markers around each circle so that each distance from 1 to n units can be measured around the circle, not as straight lines between points.

EIGHTEEN-POINT CIRCLE GAME 1

Mathematicians sometimes invent seemingly simple, trivial-looking problems that prove to be much more difficult to solve than first thought. One such conundrum is the classic **18-point problem**. Our puzzle is an original design variation of the original problem in which the points were distributed along a straight line The object is to distribute 18 points in circular rings according to simple rules. Circles, of course, comprise a multitude of points – indeed, an infinite number of points form a circle. So you might imagine that with sufficient foresight, one could place a great number of points on a circle, certainly more than 18. That intuition, however, turns out to be wrong in this game.

The rules of the game are quite simple: Place a point anywhere on a circle (in the first white circle). Now place a second point on the next circle so that each of the two points lies on a different half of the line. One has to imagine that there is only one circle, the initial one, which grows into new generations into which the earlier placed points are placed along radial lines from the center of the growing generations of circles. Then place a third point on the next circle so that each of the three points is in a different third of the circle. At this stage it becomes clear that the first two points cannot be just anywhere; the points must be placed carefully so that when the third point is added, each will be in a different third of the circle. The game follows a predictable pattern – place the fourth point so that all are on different quarters, the fifth so that all are on separate fifths, and so on. You can proceed with this process as carefully as you wish, but it turns out, astonishingly, that you cannot go beyond placing 17 points. The 18th point will always violate the rules of the game. Even when you choose the locations of your points very carefully, placing 10 points is quite a good result. It should be noted that the 18 circles should really be imagined as one single circle, with each new "generation" subdivided into a continuously growing number of compartments as visualized in the sample game.

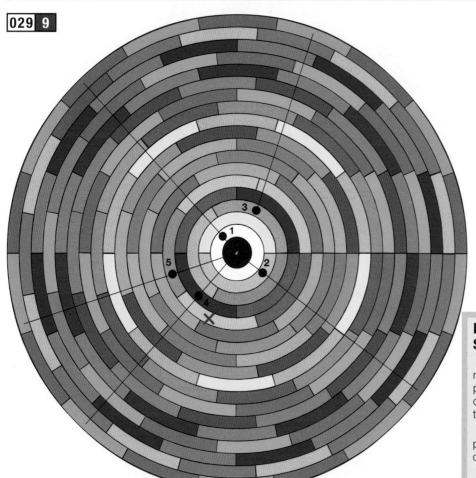

EIGHTEEN-POINT CIRCLE – SAMPLE GAME

The sample game ended at point five. No matter where point five is placed, the sixth point will fall into a compartment already occupied by a previously placed point and the game is ended.

Mieczyslaw Warmus in 1976 gave a 17-point solution and stated that there are 768 different patterns of 17-point solutions.

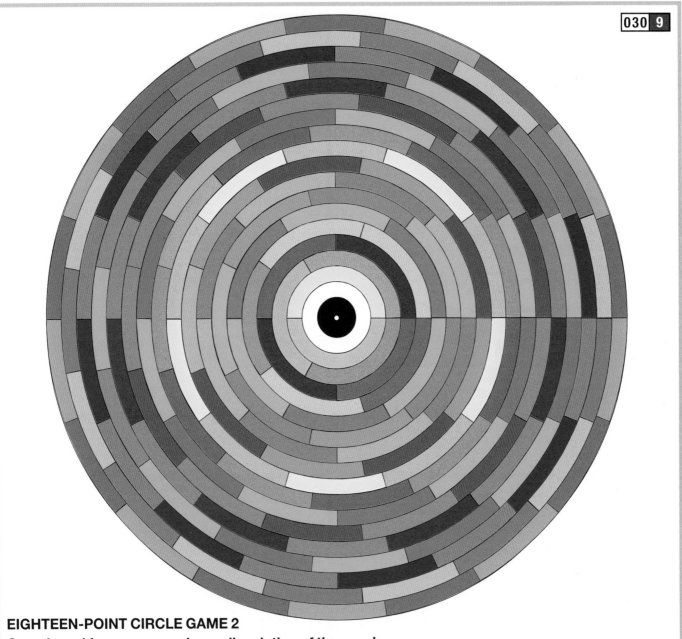

EIGHTEEN-POINT CIRCLE GAME 2

Gameboard for a paper-and-pencil variation of the puzzle game

The object is to draw 18 lines radiating from the center without two lines crossing the same color compartment.
How many lines can you draw before two lines will cross the same compartment?
(Use a very soft pencil and have an eraser ready.)

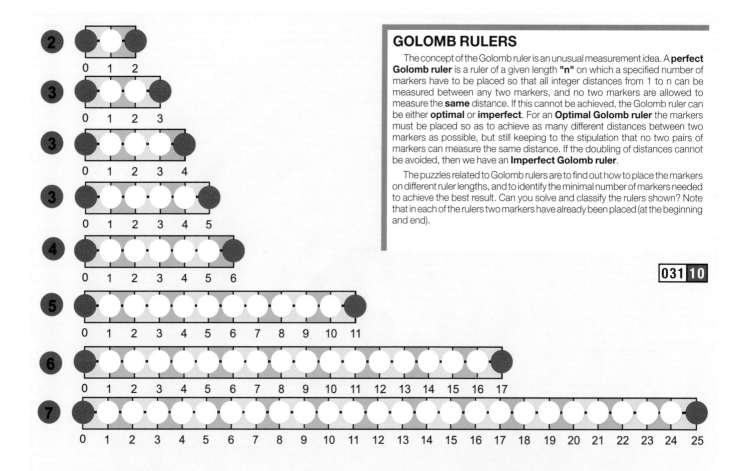

GOLOMB RULERS

The concept of the Golomb ruler is an unusual measurement idea. A **perfect Golomb ruler** is a ruler of a given length **"n"** on which a specified number of markers have to be placed so that all integer distances from 1 to n can be measured between any two markers, and no two markers are allowed to measure the **same** distance. If this cannot be achieved, the Golomb ruler can be either **optimal** or **imperfect**. For an **Optimal Golomb ruler** the markers must be placed so as to achieve as many different distances between two markers as possible, but still keeping to the stipulation that no two pairs of markers can measure the same distance. If the doubling of distances cannot be avoided, then we have an **Imperfect Golomb ruler**.

The puzzles related to Golomb rulers are to find out how to place the markers on different ruler lengths, and to identify the minimal number of markers needed to achieve the best result. Can you solve and classify the rulers shown? Note that in each of the rulers two markers have already been placed (at the beginning and end).

031 10

GOLOMB RULERS
Perfect and Optimal Golomb Rulers

The original concept of Golomb rulers was introduced in 1952 by W.C. Babcock. Today, they are called Golomb rulers for Solomon W. Golomb, a professor of mathematics and electrical engineering at the University of Southern California who extensively analysed and extended the concept into new and unexpected directions.

A Golomb ruler is a ruler constructed so that no two pairs of marks can measure the same distance. The markers on a Golomb ruler must be placed at integer multiples of fixed spacings. The object is to place the markers so to achieve as many distinct measures of distances between two markers as possible, with a given number of markers. In order to achieve this, the markers must be placed very efficiently, avoiding redundant distances between markers.

In a Perfect Golomb ruler of length n, *all* the distances from 1 – 2 – 3 – .... n can be measured exactly *once*. Perfect Golomb rulers exist only for ruler lengths up to four marks as shown.

For an Optimal Golomb ruler, or the shortest Golomb ruler possible for a given number of marks, the condition remains that no two pairs of marks can measure the same distance, however, it may *not* have all consecutive distances from zero to the ruler's length (they correspond to what Golomb calls the "best" numbering of complete graphs for more than four points).

Finding and proving optimal Golomb rulers becomes more and more difficult as the number of marks increases. Today, optimal Golomb rulers up to 24 marks are known, and presently the search is on for the 25 and 26 versions.

The Golomb rulers problem is one of the most beautiful problems in recreational mathematics, but such rulers are also needed in a variety of scientific and technical disciplines as well and are at the forefront of mathematical researches, proving the relevance of recreational problems to pure math. Golomb rulers provide a general spacing principle applied in astronomy (placement of antennas), x-ray sensing devices (placement of sensors), and in many other fields.

DOTS-AND-BOXES
A paper-and-pencil game for 2 players

The rules were very simple – draw a rectangular outline along the grid. Players take turns to join two neighboring intersections (horizontally or vertically, not diagonally). When a player closes a square box, it is marked in his or her color, and the player goes on playing as long as he or she can close boxes. The player with most boxes is the winner.

We may have not been aware that the game is possibly one of the most fiendishly complicated games ever devised in spite of its simplicity. Elwyn Berlekamp's book *The Dots and Boxes Game* reveals the subtleties and multilevel strategies of the game. A game is described in which players avoid giving away boxes as long as they can, by making moves that do not create the third side of a potential box. As a result the grid becomes divided into a series of "chains" – a state Berlekamp calls gridlock, which happens in our game at the 12th move. At this stage there are three chains which contain 2, 3, and 4 potential boxes respectively. So the red player gives away 2 boxes to the blue player, blue player gives away the next 3 boxes to the red player, who inevitably has to gives away the last 4 boxes to the blue player who wins the game. If the number of chains at a gridlock is even, then the player who opens the first chain wins; if odd, then the first player who opens the first chain loses.

Could player 1 have avoided losing the game?

Let's say, in move 15 player 1 declines to accept all three boxes opened to him in that chain and takes only one box, and then draws a line that leaves a domino rectangle, as shown below. The "sacrifice" thus changed the outcome of the game and player 1 wins. Even such a simple game shows the hidden sophistication of dots-and-boxes. No complete winning strategy is yet known.

032 **5**

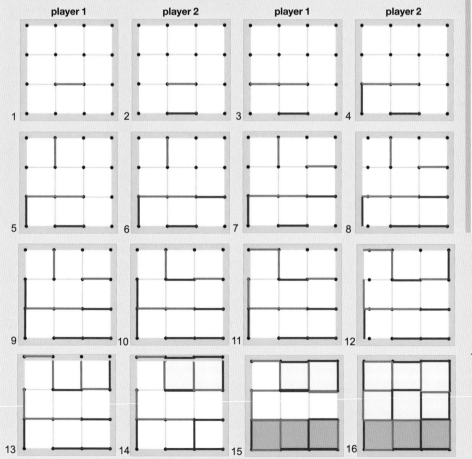

player 1 · player 2 · player 1 · player 2

1 · 2 · 3 · 4
5 · 6 · 7 · 8
9 · 10 · 11 · 12
13 · 14 · 15 · 16

15

16

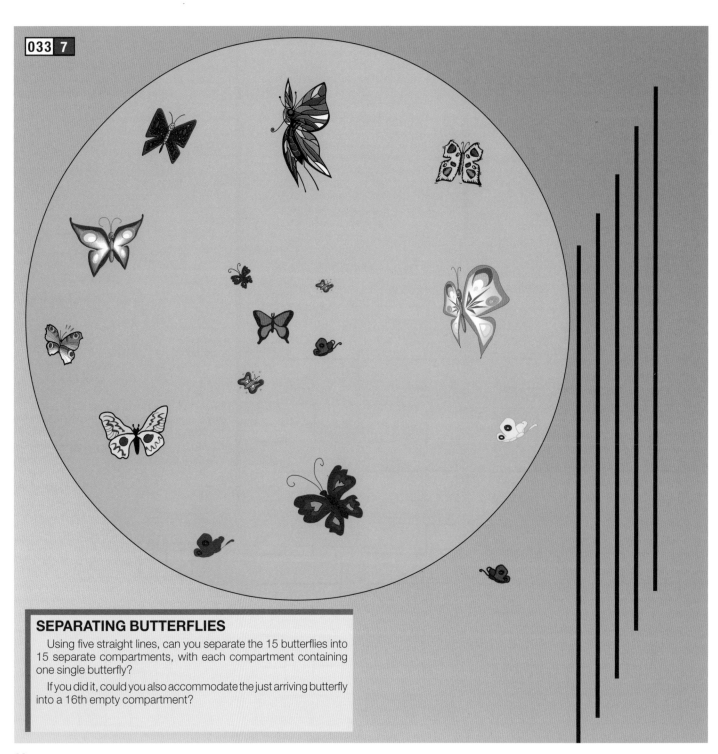

SEPARATING BUTTERFLIES

Using five straight lines, can you separate the 15 butterflies into 15 separate compartments, with each compartment containing one single butterfly?

If you did it, could you also accommodate the just arriving butterfly into a 16th empty compartment?

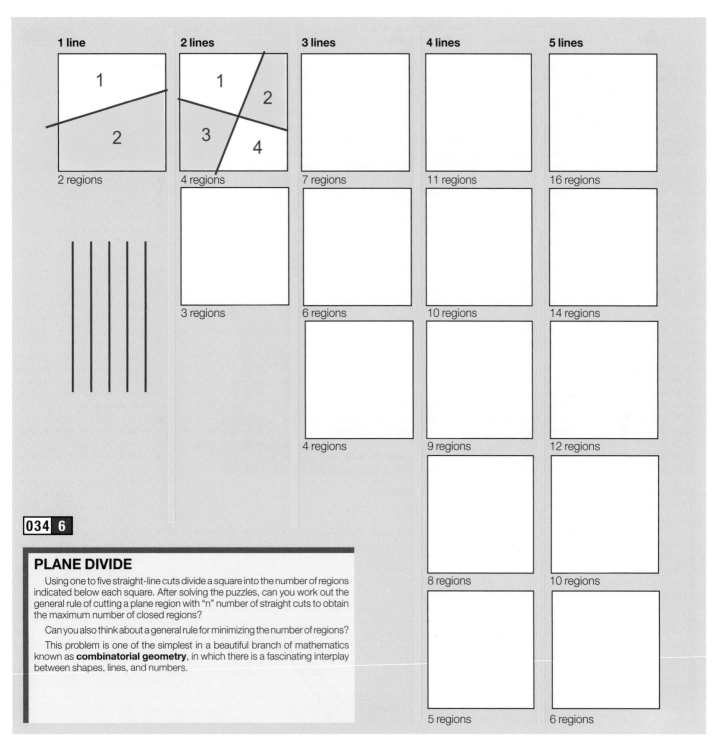

1 line

1

2

2 regions

2 lines

1

2

3

4

4 regions

3 regions

3 lines

7 regions

6 regions

4 regions

4 lines

11 regions

10 regions

9 regions

8 regions

5 regions

5 lines

16 regions

14 regions

12 regions

10 regions

6 regions

034 6

PLANE DIVIDE

Using one to five straight-line cuts divide a square into the number of regions indicated below each square. After solving the puzzles, can you work out the general rule of cutting a plane region with "n" number of straight cuts to obtain the maximum number of closed regions?

Can you also think about a general rule for minimizing the number of regions?

This problem is one of the simplest in a beautiful branch of mathematics known as **combinatorial geometry**, in which there is a fascinating interplay between shapes, lines, and numbers.

61

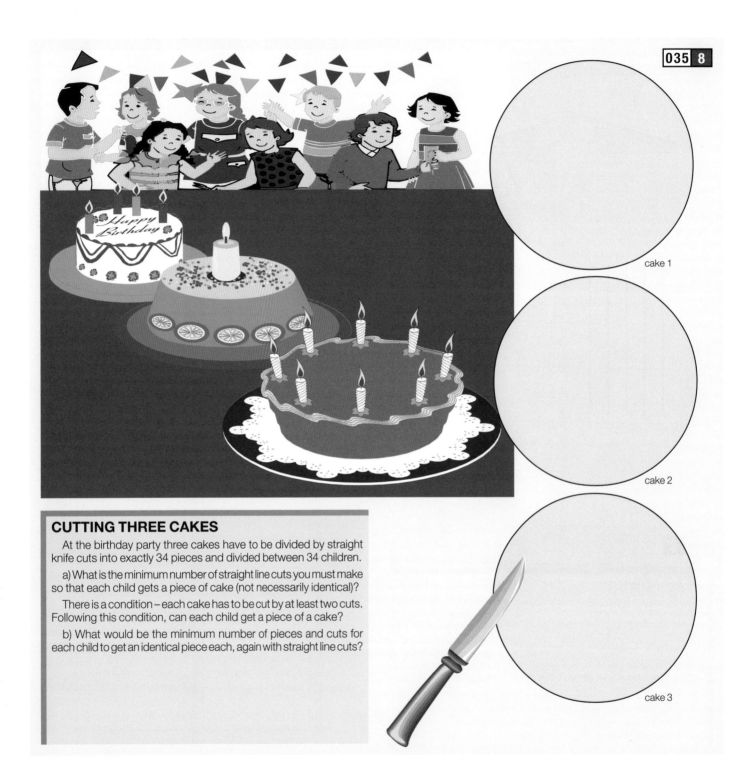

cake 1

cake 2

cake 3

CUTTING THREE CAKES

At the birthday party three cakes have to be divided by straight knife cuts into exactly 34 pieces and divided between 34 children.

a) What is the minimum number of straight line cuts you must make so that each child gets a piece of cake (not necessarily identical)?

There is a condition – each cake has to be cut by at least two cuts. Following this condition, can each child get a piece of a cake?

b) What would be the minimum number of pieces and cuts for each child to get an identical piece each, again with straight line cuts?

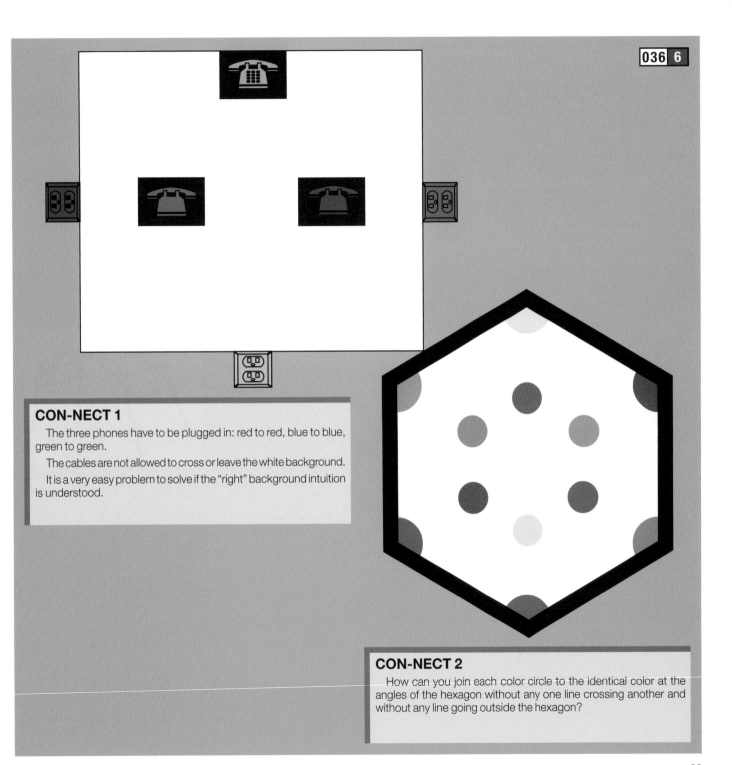

CON-NECT 1

The three phones have to be plugged in: red to red, blue to blue, green to green.

The cables are not allowed to cross or leave the white background.

It is a very easy problem to solve if the "right" background intuition is understood.

CON-NECT 2

How can you join each color circle to the identical color at the angles of the hexagon without any one line crossing another and without any line going outside the hexagon?

MATCHSTICK SQUARES PROBLEMS

The first known description of a matchstick puzzle was published in 1858 and ever since, volumes have been devoted to matchstick problems. Some of these became classics, such as:

1. Match Cube

Can you create a solid cube from matchsticks, without using glue or any other means for their joining?

2. Fifteen Matchsticks

Can you lift 15 matchsticks with one single match?

3. Match Bridge

Can you create a rigid, free-standing bridge from 18 matchsticks, again, without using any glue or any other means for joining?

The images to the right might give you an idea.

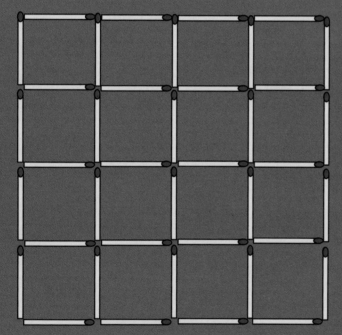

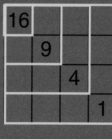

MATCHSTICK SQUARES ELIMINATION

What is the smallest number of matchsticks that you must remove so that it is impossible to find a square of any size (4 x 4, 3 x 3, 2 x 2, or 1 x 1) anywhere in this diagram?

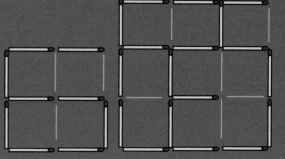

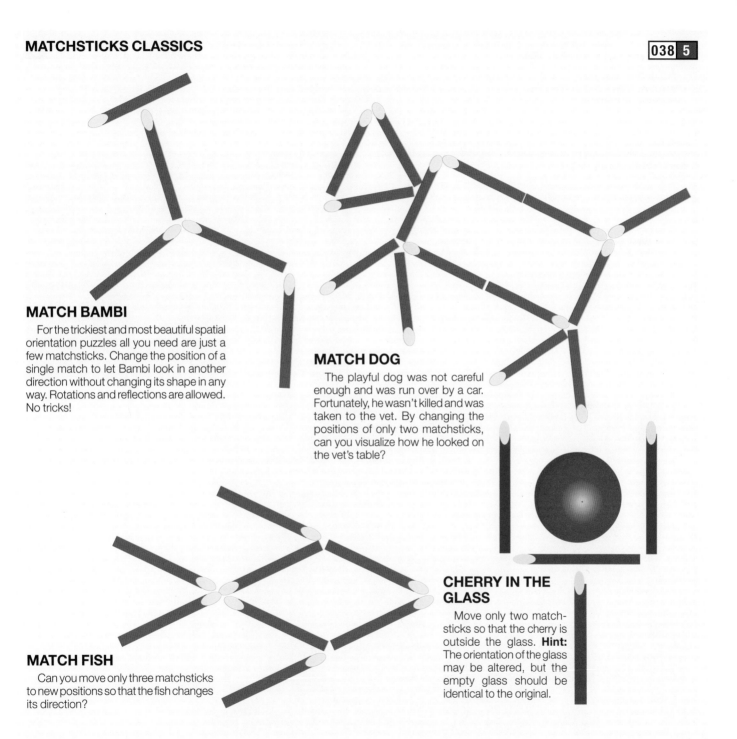

MATCH BAMBI

For the trickiest and most beautiful spatial orientation puzzles all you need are just a few matchsticks. Change the position of a single match to let Bambi look in another direction without changing its shape in any way. Rotations and reflections are allowed. No tricks!

MATCH DOG

The playful dog was not careful enough and was run over by a car. Fortunately, he wasn't killed and was taken to the vet. By changing the positions of only two matchsticks, can you visualize how he looked on the vet's table?

CHERRY IN THE GLASS

Move only two matchsticks so that the cherry is outside the glass. **Hint:** The orientation of the glass may be altered, but the empty glass should be identical to the original.

MATCH FISH

Can you move only three matchsticks to new positions so that the fish changes its direction?

MATCHSTICK PUZZLES

Matchsticks were used for centuries in recreational math problems. They can also be ideal tools to visualize problems and games in graph theory.

MATCH – MATCH 4

With four matches there are five possible topologically different configurations, as shown, taking the following conditions into account:

1. Matchsticks can only touch at their ends.

2. Matchsticks are flat on the plane.

Note: Once a configuration is formed, it can be transformed in an infinite number of ways into topologically equivalent structures, by deforming it without separating its connections at the joints. Each configuration is shown in two topologically equivalent configurations.

Can you match the 5 pairs?

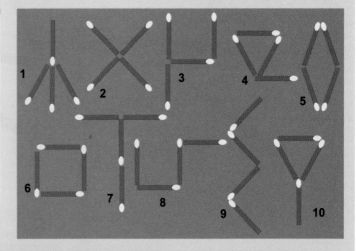

MATCH – MATCH 5

With five matches there are 12 possible topologically different configurations, as shown, taking the following conditions into account:

1. Matchsticks can only touch at their ends.

2. Matchsticks are flat on the plane.

Note: Once a configuration is formed, it can be transformed in an infinite number of ways into topologically equivalent structures, by deforming it without separating its connections at the joints. Each configuration is shown in two topologically equivalent configurations.

Can you match the 12 pairs?

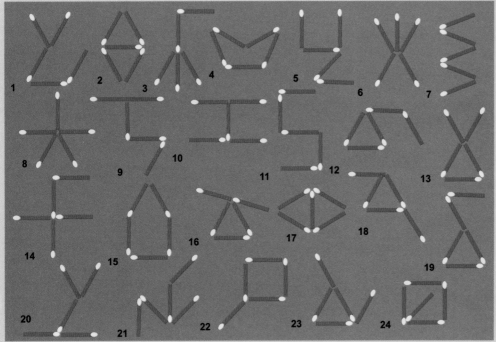

SHIPS MEET

This beautiful problem was invented by Edouard Lucas, the famous French 19th-century mathematician. Every day at noon, a ship leaves Le Havre for New York and another ship leaves New York for Le Havre exactly at the same time. The trip last seven days and seven nights. How many New York–Le Havre ships will the Le Havre–New York ship that departs today meet during its voyage to New York?

GRASSHOPPER PUZZLE GAME

This is an original puzzle game that is easy to learn, and can be played as a paper-and-pencil game on square grid paper. It shows convincingly that just moving a point along a line in consecutive unit distances, following very simple rules, can produce a challenging game with subtle mathematical principles and surprises.

A Grasshopper-n problem

Given a line of integral length "n," the object is to start jumping from point 0 in successive jumps of consecutive lengths: 1, 2, 3, ... -n along the line, so as to make as many jumps as possible on the line and finish the **nth** jump at the end point of the line, at point **"n."** **On a line of length "n" if this can be achieved the line has a solution, if not, the line of length "n" has no solution.**

The moves along the line can be in any direction but they are not allowed to leave the line. For greater lengths of **n**, more than one sequence of moves is possible. In competition games between two or more players, scores can be given according to who ended the game nearest to the end point **n**.

We can see that apart from the trivial **n = 1** solution, the first solution (completed n jumps, ending at point n) was achieved on a line of four units in length: **n = 4**.

1. Can you find out the next three lengths n = ? for which solutions are possible?

2. Can you find out how many solutions exist for the first 40 length from n = 1 to n = 40?

3. Can you discover the general rule for which lengths n are solutions possible. We shall call the resulting infinite number sequence 'the grasshopping number sequence': 1, 4, ...

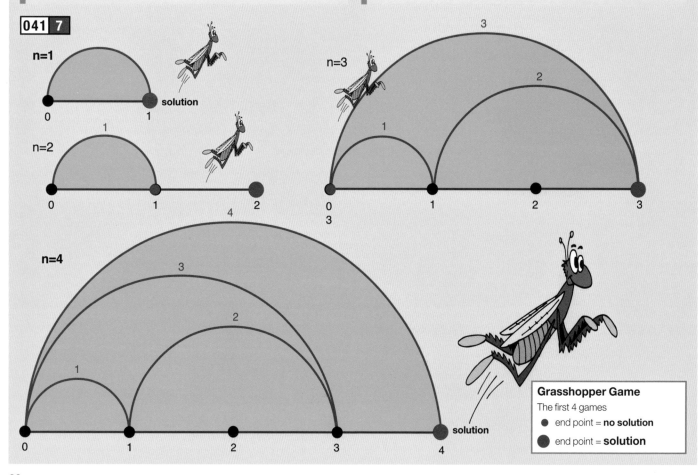

041 **7**

n=1   solution

n=2

n=3

n=4   solution

Grasshopper Game
The first 4 games
● end point = **no solution**
● end point = **solution**

GRASSHOPPING

How many solutions exist for the first 40 lengths? The first two solutions are marked

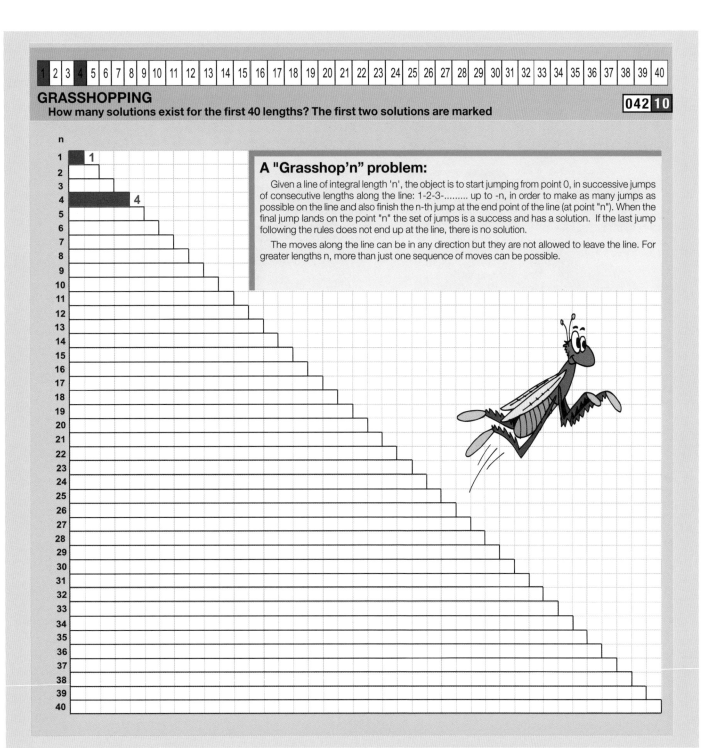

A "Grasshop'n" problem:

Given a line of integral length 'n', the object is to start jumping from point 0, in successive jumps of consecutive lengths along the line: 1-2-3-......... up to -n, in order to make as many jumps as possible on the line and also finish the n-th jump at the end point of the line (at point "n"). When the final jump lands on the point "n" the set of jumps is a success and has a solution. If the last jump following the rules does not end up at the line, there is no solution.

The moves along the line can be in any direction but they are not allowed to leave the line. For greater lengths n, more than just one sequence of moves can be possible.

FROM FLOWER TO FLOWER

The power of graphs-

The garden is filled with flowers as shown. Mr. Bee entered at the bottom right flower. He visited each flower at least once, never leaving the flowers, crossing from flower to flower only along the overlapping boundaries between two flowers just once in a continuous line. Finally, at the end of his journey he will be meeting Mrs. Bee, who will be landing and awaiting him on a flower. Can you identify on which flower they will meet?

EULER'S THEOREM
The Birth of Graph theory

Leonhard Euler was a Swiss mathematician who lived from 1707 to 1783. He carried out more mathematical research than anyone else in history. At that time the German town of Konigsberg had seven bridges and it was said that the people of the town had never been able to solve the problem of how to go for a walk, cross each bridge once only, and return home. Euler solved the problem by replacing the map with something that looked simpler – a Graph or Network.

Given this figure composed of lines joining points, is it possible to traverse the figure in one continuous path, without taking your pencil from the paper and without going over any line twice?

Euler showed that there would have to be at most two places where an odd number of lines meet: and if a return to the start is required, there would have to be no places where an odd number of lines meet. The reasoning is simple – once it is understood. A continuous journey will pass each junction exactly as often as it leaves it – except at the start and finish. The problem of the Konigsberg bridges is then solved by noting that it is equivalent to traversing such a network of lines, which has four junctions with an odd number of lines. So no solution can exist. Euler's problem is really one of topology, a branch of mathematics that deals with properties of figures that are preserved by continuous deformations. Two networks are topologically equivalent if one can be distorted to give the other. If a network can be traversed by a single curve, so can any topologically equivalent network. Another topic arising from Euler's work is graph theory, the study of networks formed by lines connecting points. Not bad for a recreational math puzzle!

EULER'S THEOREM

1. A graph has an Eulerian circuit if and only if it is connected and all of its vertices are even.

2. A graph has an Eulerian path if and only if it is connected and has either no odd vertices or exactly two odd vertices. If two of the vertices are odd, then any Eulerian path must begin at one of the odd vertices and end at the other.

THE SEVEN BRIDGES OF KONIGSBERG

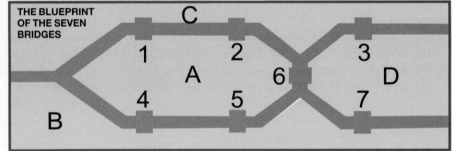
THE BLUEPRINT OF THE SEVEN BRIDGES

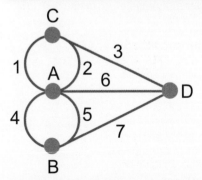
EULER'S GRAPH OF THE SEVEN BRIDGES
The bridges are the seven lines

SEVEN BRIDGES PROBLEM

A famous problem concerns the "Seven Bridges of Konigsberg." It is said the town's people were never able to solve the following problem: Could they go for a stroll, crossing each bridge only once? This topological problem is equivalent to traversing a network of lines, which has four points with an odd number of lines emanating from three points. Therefore no solution can exist (Euler's theorem).

At right is a schematic diagram of the seven bridges of Konigsberg with a topologically equivalent graph (dual graph), whose traversal is tantamount to solving the problem.

LEONHARD EULER (1707–83)

Euler was a Swiss mathematician and one of the most prolific mathematicians ever to have lived. He studied at the University of Basel to become a Protestant minister, like his father, but his love of mathematics led him to change his studies. He was encouraged by Johann Bernoulli, who was a friend of his family. Euler got his first job at the mathematical-physical division of the St.Petersburg Academy of Science, where he was surrounded by a group of eminent scientists and mathematicians, such as Daniel Bernoulli, Christian Goldbach, and others. He was later appointed to the senior chair of mathematics. Euler had 13 children, claiming that he made his greatest mathematical discoveries while holding a baby in his arms. His contribution to mathematics is enormous, particularly in number theory, differential equations, calculus of variations, and other fields. His reputation was very high and in 1741 he was invited by Frederick the Great to the Academy of Science in Berlin, where he wrote: "I can do just what I wish – the King calls me his professor and I think I am the happiest man in the world." He spent 25 years in Berlin, writing about 400 articles before returning to St. Petersburg at the age of 59, becoming completely blind after an illness. He produced there nearly half of his total work, in spite of blindness, relying on an extraordinary memory.

After his death, the Academy continued to publish Euler's works for 50 years or so.

EULERIAN PATHS

A continuous path that visits each edge of a graph exactly once is called an Eulerian path, and an Eulerian path that is also a circuit (i.e. finishes back at the start point) is called an Eulerian circuit. Can you find an Eulerian path or circuit for the above graph?

EULER'S THEOREM – POSSIBLE – IMPOSSIBLE TRACES – TRAVERSABILITY OF GRAPHS

If a network has more than two odd vertices, it does not have an Eulerian path or a an Eulerian circuit.

If a network has two or less odd vertices, it has at least one Eulerian path.

Euler answered the questions of traversability by using the concept of valence and connectedness. The valence of a vertex in a graph is the number of edges meeting at that point. A graph is said to be connected if for each pair of its vertices there is at least one path of edges connecting the two vertices. A route that covers every edge in a graph only once and which starts and ends at the same vertex is called an ***Eulerian circuit***. If the route does not end at the starting vertex it is called an ***Euler's path***. There are two obvious questions to ask about Eulerian circuits:

1. Is there a way to tell by calculation and not by trial-and-error if a particular graph has an Eulerian circuit?

2. Is there a method, other than trial-and-error, for finding an Eulerian circuit when one exists?

Now we can state the famous Euler's theorem, giving a simple general answer to our problems:

If a graph is connected and has all valences even, than it has an Eulerian circuit.

The secret rule for tracing any puzzle of this kind is that you only have to check how many lines are going in or out from every intersection point. If there are more than two intersection points from which an odd number of lines emanate, then the pattern is impossible to trace.

If we make an apparently innocuous change in Euler's problem and ask instead: When is it possible to find a route along the edges of a graph that visits each vertex once and only once in a loop or simple circuit? Then we have a ***Hamiltonian circuit***, which visits each vertex in a graph. Note that in a Hamiltonian circuit some of the edges can be left untraversed. Though different, the concepts of Eulerian and Hamiltonian circuits are similar in that both forbid reuse – in the Eulerian circuit it is of edges, in the Hamiltonian circuit it is of vertices. It is far more difficult to determine Hamiltonian circuits in a graph than Eulerian circuits.

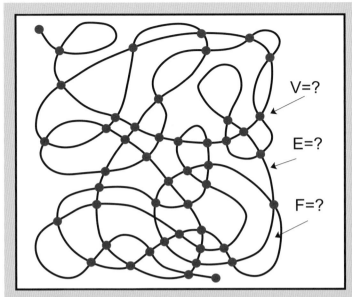

V=?

E=?

F=?

THE FIVE REGULAR POLYHEDRA

Solid	Vertices (V)	Edges (E)	Faces (F)	V - E + F
Tetrahedron	4	6	4	2
Cube	8	12	6	2
Octahedron	6	12	8	2
Icosahedron	12	30	20	2
Dodecahedron	20	30	12	2

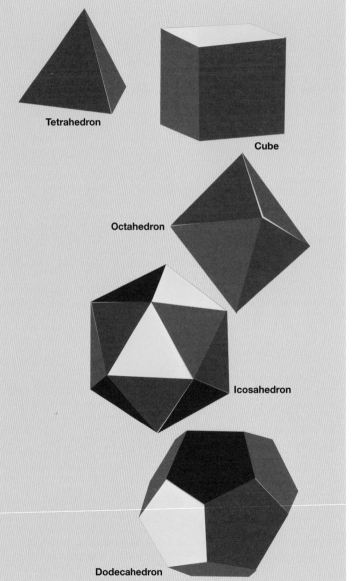

Tetrahedron

Cube

Octahedron

Icosahedron

Dodecahedron

EULER'S FORMULA

I have drawn quite a complex random doodle above. To make it really random, I did it by placing the pen on paper, closed my eyes, and without lifting my pen drew the line careful not to leave the page. You can try to make your own. The purpose of this exercise is to show that even such random doodles can contain hidden patterns of enormous mathematical significance. Can you discover:

1. How many intersection points (V)?

2. How many edges (E)? An edge is a segment connecting two points.

3. How many regions (F)?

We can, of course, count each of these, as long as it takes, but can we count any two and come to know the third characteristic without counting?

The insight that **V - E + F = 2** is always 2, is called the **Euler characteristic or Euler's Formula, one of the most beautiful and important expressions of mathematics**.

It is a great insight about any connected doodle that we can make in the plane. But it is not only that. It can also be shown that all the regular solids have the same relationship of the vertices, edges, faces expressed in the Euler characteristic.

The Euler characteristic remains true on a sphere as well.

The Euler characteristic is a restriction proving that only five combinations of faces, vertices, and edges can form regular solids.

73

TRAVELING SALESMAN PROBLEM
Hamiltonian Paths and Circuits

Eulerian paths and circuits (see pages 71-72) were concerned with finding paths that cover every edge of a graph. Hamiltonian paths and circuits deal with problems of visiting all of the vertices of a graph, without concern for whether or not all edges have been covered. These types of problems were first studied by the Irish mathematician Sir William Rowan Hamilton, who was especially interested in problems of finding a circuit that goes through every vertex exactly once and returns to the starting vertex, which are today called Hamiltonian circuits. Those paths which do not return to the starting vertex after visiting every vertex are called Hamiltonian paths. A related problem to Hamiltonian circuits is the *Traveling Salesman Problem*:

The problem of finding a Hamiltonian circuit in a complete weighted graph for which the sum of the weights of the edges is the minimum.

A **complete graph** is a graph in which every pair of vertices is connected by exactly one edge. A **weighted graph** is a graph for which a number, called a **weight**, is assigned to each edge of the graph (which can be a distance or else). The sum of all weights is called the **weight of the circuit**.

The solution to the traveling salesman problem is the **circuit of minimum weight**. In most problems there is a particular vertex as the starting vertex. Can you find the circuit of minimum weight for the weighted graph on five points starting at point B?

To give an idea of the difficulty of the problem, imagine a mailman visiting each house in a city. For a city with only two houses, the problem is easy, there are just two routes. For a city with four houses there are 24 possible routes (4! = 4 x 3 x 2 x 1 = 24). But for a city with 20 houses, about 2.4 billion billion routes should be possible, and obviously it would not be an easy problem to find the shortest route.

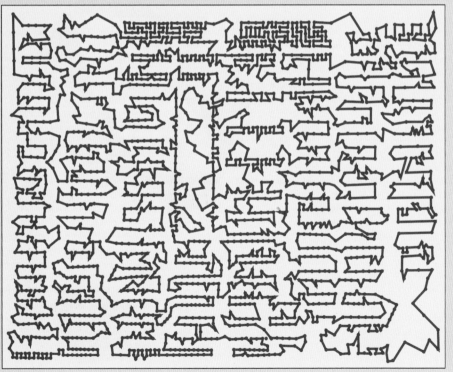

TRAVELING SALESMAN PROBLEM

The largest Traveling Salesman problem, visiting 3,038 cities, was solved by David Applegate, Robert Bixby, Vadek Chvatal, and William Cook in 1990. The solution took one and a half years of computer time. In computer science problems some problems are classified as "practically impossible," since it would take a prohibitively long time to solve them by the fastest program which could be written. Such a typical problem is that of the classic "Traveling Salesman" problem. Suppose a salesman must visit n different cities and the object is to find the optimal route which would minimize the total distance he has to travel. When the number of cities is small, the problem can be solved by trying all the alternatives, but it becomes very difficult with larger numbers.

MARYLIN MINIMALLY

A continuous line drawing of Marylin created via the traveling salesman problem (opposite page) by Robert Bosch and Adrianne Herman, of the Dep. of Mathematics, Oberlin College

TSP ART
(Travelling Salesman Problem Art)

Famous mathematical problems may often inspire and create art. A beautiful example is the TSP Art of Robert Bosch and Adrianne Herman, of the Dep. of Mathematics, Oberlin College, and Craig S. Kaplan, from the University of Waterloo, based on the classic Traveling Salesman Problem (see opposite page), which is a well-studied problem in computer science. Given a collection of cities (points) on a map, the salesman must make a tour of the cities, visiting each once, and returning to the city from which he started. Of all the possible ways, he must find the one requiring the minimum total distance.

SMILEY – TSP ART

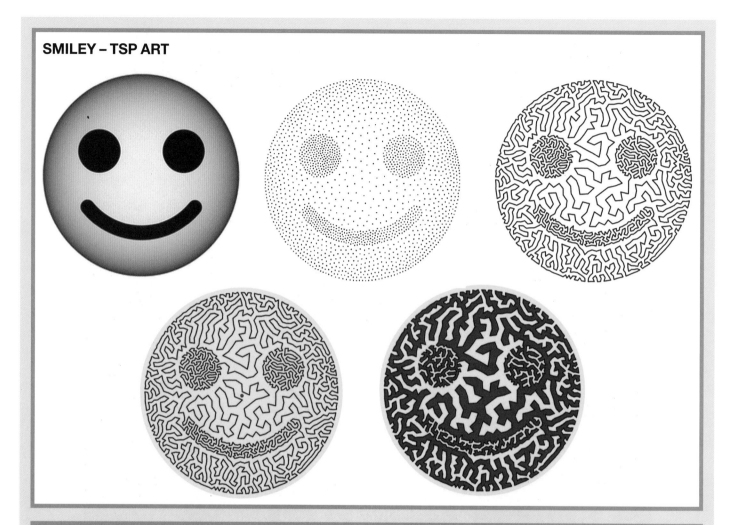

TSP ART

How to do it: Smiley 2006

1 - Select an image

2 - Lay out the dots (cities) according to an algorithm corresponding roughly to the density of the image.

3 - Connect the dots according to a computer program that finds a **TSP Art** tour, which is not the true optimal solution, but is beautiful aesthetically. In our example, there are 2006 dots. Finding an optimal tour, the solution to the traveling salesman problem is extremely difficult for this number of dots. There are no less than 2005 possible different TSP Smiley 2006 tours!

4-5 - The TSP tours are guaranteed to be closed simple curves.

The **Jordan Curve Theorem** states that any simple closed curve in the plane separates the plane into two regions, a part that is inside the curve, and a part that is outside. It is not always easy to determine whether a point is inside or outside a **TSP** tour. Is the red point inside or outside? This question is addressed in simple form in the Inside-Outside? puzzle (page 54).

CONNECTED GRAPHS

A path to all points

Connectedness is a basic and important concept in mathematics, referring to various properties, meaning "all in one piece." In this sense graphs can be connected or disconnected. A connected graph on a number of points "n" is a graph in which there is a path from any point to any other point in the graph. The number of different unlabeled connected graphs from n=1 to n=4 are shown.

Their number is: **1, 1, 2, 6, ...**

Can you work out and draw all the different unlabeled connected graphs for n=5 points? There are 21 of them.

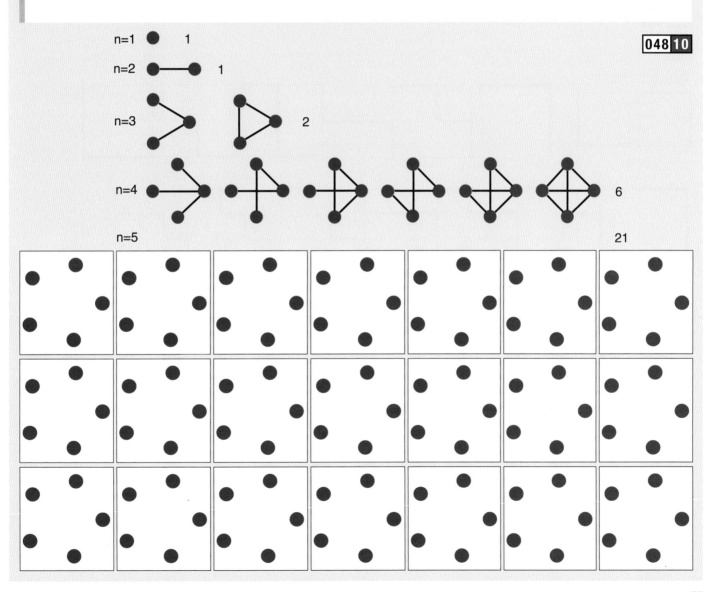

STAIRCASE PARADOX

In the progression sequence, how long will the length of the staircase ultimately become if we divide the squares infinitely? How many stairs will the staircase have in the 10th generation and in the 100th?

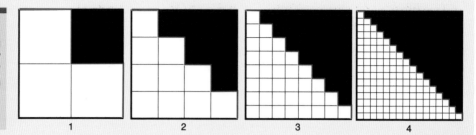

049 8

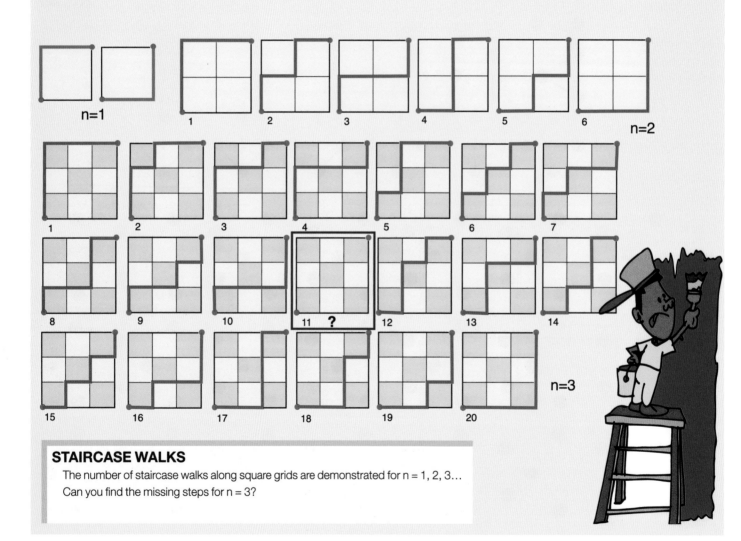

n=1

n=2

n=3

STAIRCASE WALKS

The number of staircase walks along square grids are demonstrated for n = 1, 2, 3…

Can you find the missing steps for n = 3?

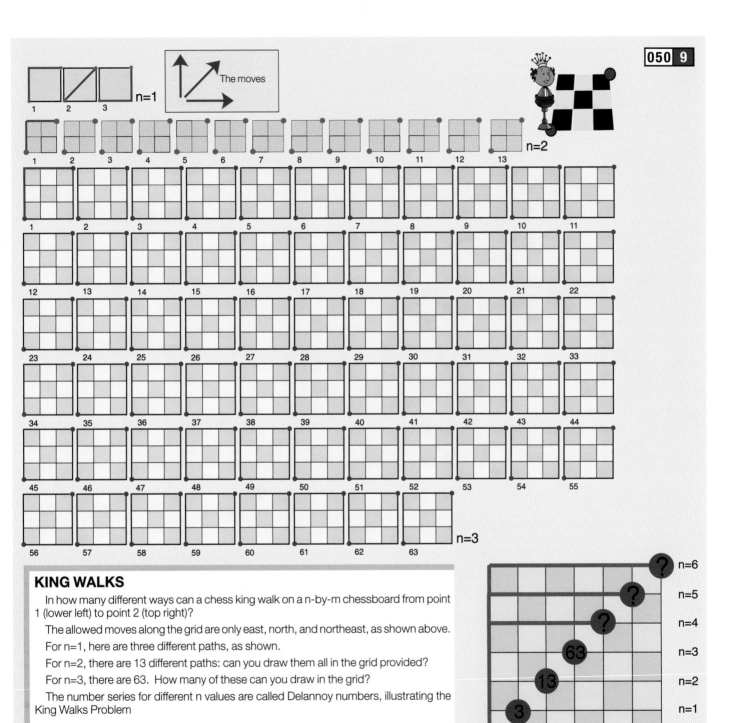

KING WALKS

In how many different ways can a chess king walk on a n-by-m chessboard from point 1 (lower left) to point 2 (top right)?

The allowed moves along the grid are only east, north, and northeast, as shown above.

For n=1, here are three different paths, as shown.

For n=2, there are 13 different paths: can you draw them all in the grid provided?

For n=3, there are 63. How many of these can you draw in the grid?

The number series for different n values are called Delannoy numbers, illustrating the King Walks Problem

EDGE COLORING GRAPHS 1

Edge coloring of a graph involves the coloring of the edges of a graph such that adjacent edges receive different colors.

051 5

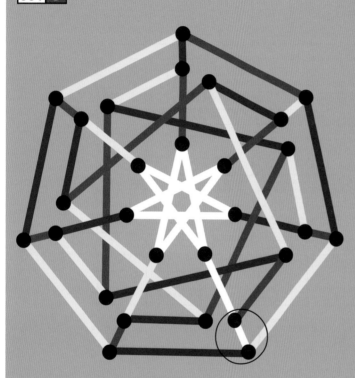

The problem of edge coloring of graphs arises in a great variety of scheduling applications, typically associated with minimizing the number of noninterfering rounds needed to complete a given set of tasks. For example, consider a situation were we need to schedule a given set of two-person interviews. We can construct a graph whose vertices are the people with the edges representing the pairs of people whom you want to interview. An edge coloring of the graph defines the schedule. The colors represent the different time periods, with all meetings of the same color happening simultaneously.

The minimum number of colors needed to edge color a graph is called its **edge-chromatic number** or **chromatic index**.

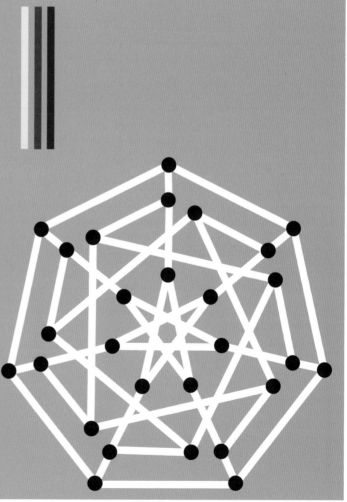

COXETER GRAPH

Puzzle: What is the smallest number of colors needed to color the edges of the graph so that no two edges of the same color share a vertex in common?

Are three colors sufficient?

In the sample game above three colors were not sufficient. Can you do better?

Game: Players alternate coloring lines. The first player unable to color a line loses the game.

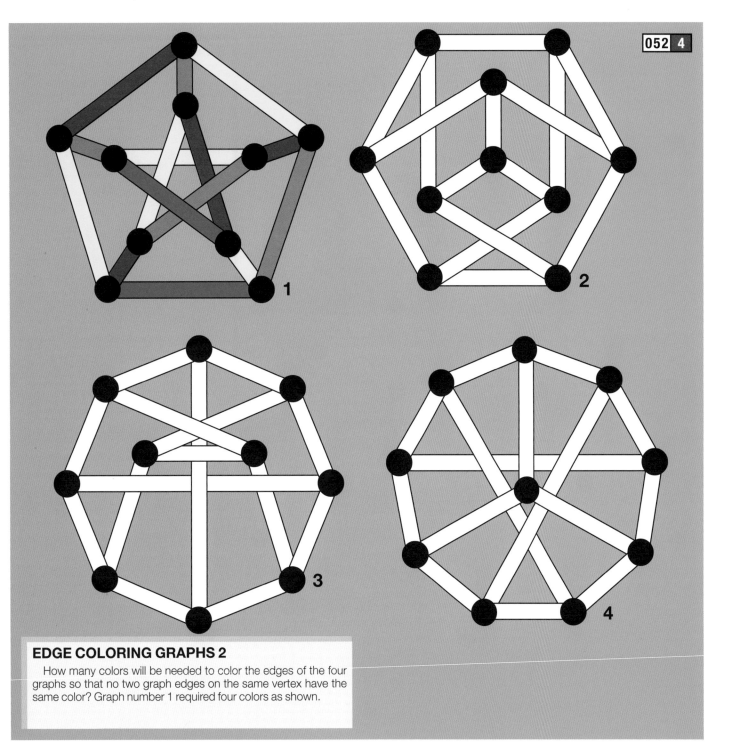

EDGE COLORING GRAPHS 2

How many colors will be needed to color the edges of the four graphs so that no two graph edges on the same vertex have the same color? Graph number 1 required four colors as shown.

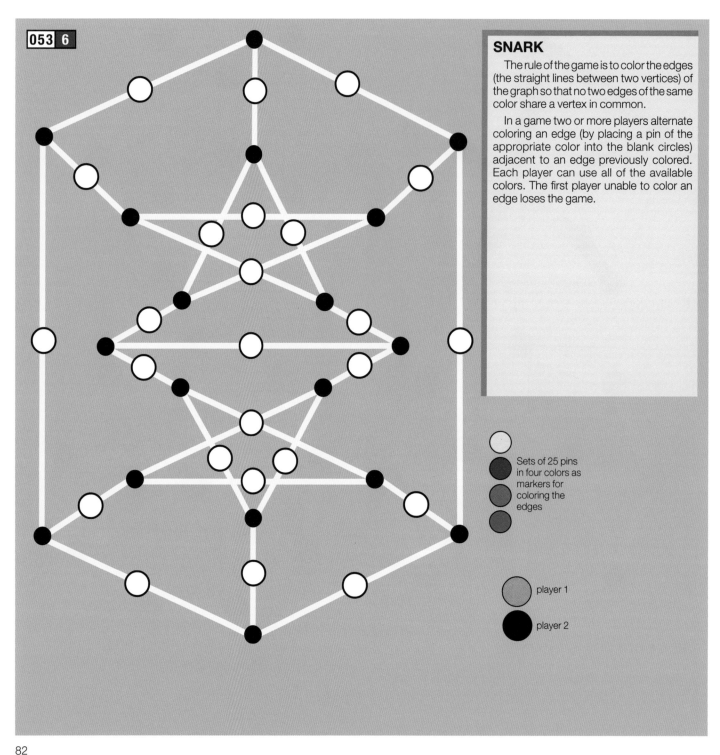

SNARK

The rule of the game is to color the edges (the straight lines between two vertices) of the graph so that no two edges of the same color share a vertex in common.

In a game two or more players alternate coloring an edge (by placing a pin of the appropriate color into the blank circles) adjacent to an edge previously colored. Each player can use all of the available colors. The first player unable to color an edge loses the game.

Sets of 25 pins in four colors as markers for coloring the edges

player 1

player 2

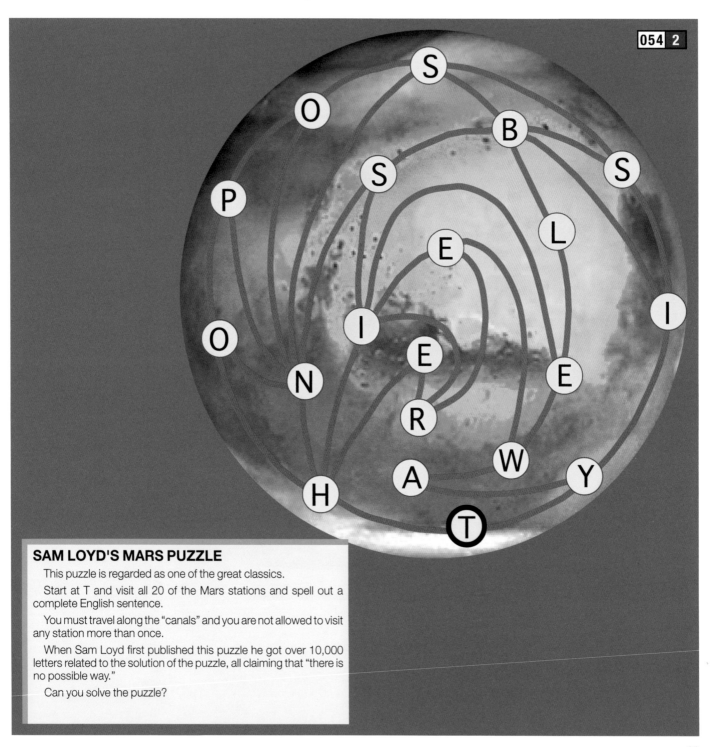

SAM LOYD'S MARS PUZZLE

This puzzle is regarded as one of the great classics.

Start at T and visit all 20 of the Mars stations and spell out a complete English sentence.

You must travel along the "canals" and you are not allowed to visit any station more than once.

When Sam Loyd first published this puzzle he got over 10,000 letters related to the solution of the puzzle, all claiming that "there is no possible way."

Can you solve the puzzle?

LADYBUG MINIMAL CROSSING

Two Ladybugs landed on my cocktail glass, one outside, exactly in the middle of the glass, the other exactly opposite but inside the glass.

The height of the glass is 14 cm and the width 10 cm.

What is the shortest route the outside ladybug must take to reach its friend on the inside?

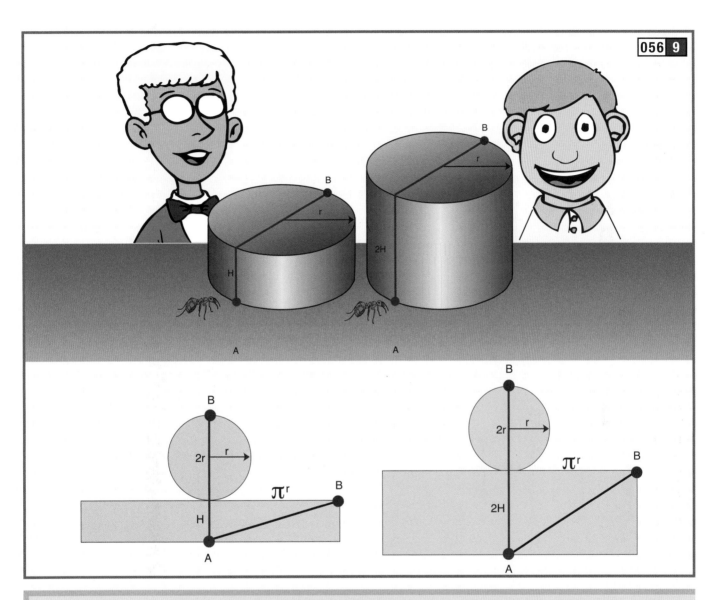

ANTS ON A TIN CAN

Two friends, Mike and John, have two tin cans, both of the same radius with one of double height. They try to solve the following problem: An ant starts its journey on the cans, starting from point A and crawls to the most distant point B. What is the shortest path for the ant to follow to reach point B? Mike concludes that the shortest path for the ant is to crawl up along the side and then cross along the diagonal on the top. He shows his conclusion on the planar nets of the cylinders (red line). John disagrees. According to him, the ant can reach point B just by crawling along the rectangular side of the net, connecting the two points A and B by a straight line, which on the tin will be part of a corkscrew line (blue line). Whose answer is the right solution?

TREE GRAPHS – TOPOLOGY

A mathematical tree is a graph, or a network of points and lines in which there is exactly one path between every pair of nodes (points). It is a *connected graph*, it comes in one piece, and is free of cycles. A cycle, or circuit in a graph, is a path that closes on itself.

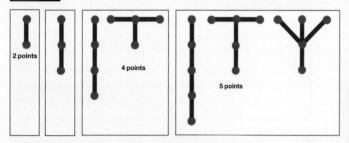

2 points

4 points

5 points

TREE GRAPHS ON 1 TO 5 POINTS

One tree graph connects two and three points; two connect four points; and three connect five points as shown. How many different possible tree graphs connect 6 and 7 points?

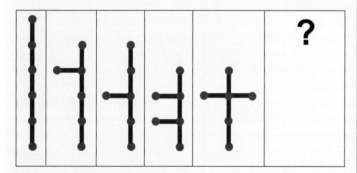

?

TREE GRAPHS ON 6 POINTS

How many tree graphs on 6 points are there? Five are shown, but how many more can you find?

Can you arrange the complete set of tree graphs on 6 points to cover a square 6-by-6 pegboard without any overlapping of their nodes and lines?

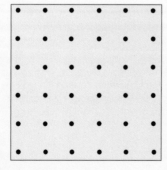

**SIX POINT TREE
GRAPHS PEGBOARD**

TOPOLOGY

In mathematics, understanding the properties of surfaces is called ***topology***, which literally means the "logic of place," because it was first used to describe the landscape in geography. Folding is an extreme case of surfaces changing shape. Topology is the study of continuity of connectedness. It has become a cornerstone of modern mathematics. In topology we are concerned with those properties of a figure that remain unchanged under continuous deformation, called ***topological invariants***. Under continuous deformation means when the shape is bent, twisted, stretched, and compressed. Topology is often called rubber-sheet geometry. While other geometries study rigid shapes, angles, length, curvature, topology deals with total flexibility.

Examples of properties that are *not* topological include the angles of a triangle: by deforming a triangle it is possible to make the angles change. Similarly, the lengths of the sides of a triangle are not topological properties. Indeed, being a triangle is not a topological property: by introducing a bend in one side of a triangle, it can be continuously deformed into a quadrilateral, etc. In fact, to topologists, a triangle is the same as a square, a parallelogram – even a circle. Clearly little traditional geometry survives from the topological viewpoint.

So what properties *are* topological, what properties remain unchanged?

The fact that a triangle has an *inside* and an *outside*, and that it is impossible to pass from one to the other without crossing an edge of the triangle, is a topological property. No matter how a triangle is deformed in the plane, it will still possess an inside and an outside. The fact that a car tire's inner tube has a hole in the middle is a topological property; even a very distorted tube retains its hole. Many topological properties have to do with the way objects are or are not connected up. Whether or not a loop or a string is knotted is a topological property. The basic concepts of topology include many ideas we learn as infants: insideness and outsideness, right- and left-handedness, linking, knotting, connectedness and disconnectedness.

Most topological experiments are based on *transformations*, that is, changes in the shape of a surface without any breaking. Two figures are said to be ***topologically equivalent*** if one can be continuously deformed into another. So a sphere and a cube are topologically equivalent. and the figure 8 and letter B are topologically equivalent (each has two holes). A fundamental problem in topology is to classify objects into classes of topologically equivalent things, on which principle many of the best puzzles are based.

Topological ideas are crucial to the understanding of graphs. What matters is not the precise position of the edges and nodes, but rather the way they connect up. For example, a graph is connected if it is "all in one piece," that is, there's a continuous path from any node to any other node. The precise shape of the edges is irrelevant; all that matters in topology is the connectedness of the graph. Similarly, if a graph contains a circuit – a closed loop with distinct edges – it is topologically equivalent to any other graph possessing a loop.

During the last 50 years or so, topology has been applied to problems in practically every field of science.

Diagram legend:
- 20
- 25
- 30
- 35
- 40
- 45
- 50

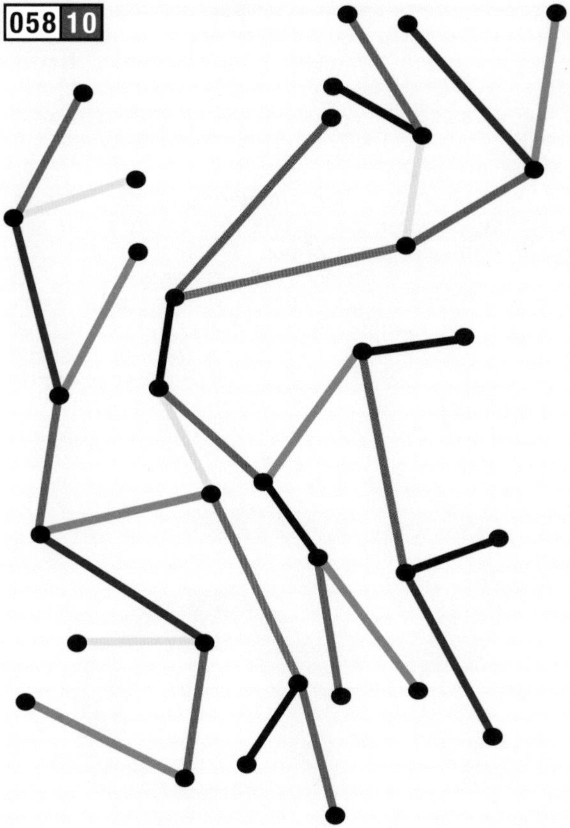

TREE GRAPH – THE LONGEST ROUTE

The schematic diagram shows the road network between a set of towns. Mathematically, it is called a **tree graph**. The colors of the roads indicate how long they are to the nearest 5 miles.

1. Can you find the longest possible distance between any two towns, without taking any U-turns?

2. Generally, this kind of problem can challenge even the most advanced computers, especially if the number of towns increases. Can you imagine a simple way to demonstrate which path through the network is the longest without resorting to any math?

TREE GRAPHS

One of the most beautiful formulas in combinatorics concerns the number of labeled trees.

A connected graph without a cycle is a tree. The number of nodes in a tree graph minus one gives the number of edges. A *connected* graph is one in which it is possible to move between any pair of vertices by moving along the edges of a graph. If a line is removed in a tree graph, the graph ceases to be connected. On the other hand, if a new link between two verices is added, a cycle is created. This will be visualized by the number of *labeled* tree graphs for 1, 2, 3, and 4 vertices shown.

The beautiful **Cayley's theorem** states that there are

$$n^{n-2}$$

different labeled trees on "n" vertices. which, for example, for 5 points gives 125 labeled trees.

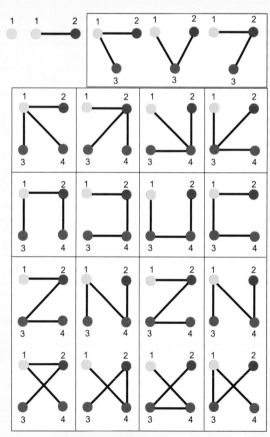

Number of labeled trees of order 1, 2, 3, and 4

87

TOPOLOGICAL EQUIVALENCE

There are branches in mathematics in which the ideas of length, angle, and area don't mean anything and they don't really feature at all. One of these branches is **Topology**, which is sometimes known as **rubber-sheet geometry**.

Two objects are topologically equivalent if one object can be continuously deformed to the other.

Deformation means to do anything to an object except tearing it, such as to stretch it, bend it, shrink it, expand it, etc. To visualize such deformations we have to imagine that the object is made of infinitely flexible rubber. Some of the results of such deformations can be quite counterintuitive. For example, a square is topologically equivalent to a circle, but not to a figure, such as an 8. All the regular polyhedra can be in this way deformed into spheres and therefore are *topologically equivalent*.

Surfaces of three-dimensional bodies, such as spheres or doughnuts, are called two-dimensional manifolds. Three-dimensional manifolds are surfaces belonging to four-dimensional bodies. The Poincare conjecture is one of the best-known problems devised by Henri Poincaré (1854–1912) and it deals with the problem of topological equivalence.

Poincaré made a bold claim: **Three-dimensional manifolds on which any any loop can be shrunk to a single point are topologically equivalent to a sphere.** His attempts to provide a proof were unsuccessful. Ever since, mathematicians have worked hard on proving Poincaré's conjecture, and have succeeded in proving that it holds true for 4, 5, 6, and all higher-dimensional manifolds. But the original conjecture for three-dimensional manifolds remained unproved unti 2003, when it was solved by Grigory Perleman, a Russian mathematician.

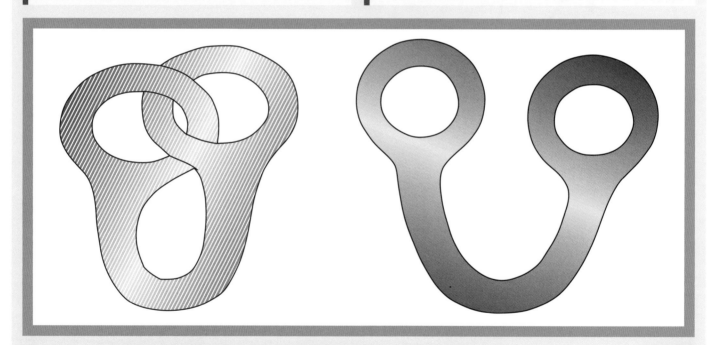

TOPOLOGICAL EQUIVALENCE TRANSFORMATION

Can the three-dimensional object on the left be smoothly deformed into the one on the right?

If this is possible, the two objects are topologically equivalent, and that means it is possible to unlink it without cutting or breaking it.

RAMSEY THEORY

Frank Ramsey and Paul Erdös stated that "complete disorder is an impossibility." Any structure will necessarily contain an orderly substructure, Ramsey Theory aims to figure out how complex a structure must be to guarantee a certain substructure. Stargazers have experienced the validity of Ramsey Theory by finding patterns in the sky. Given large enough numbers, stars will produce patterns from a perfect rectangle to the Big Dipper. The original classic example of Ramsey Theory is the **Party Problem**.

The appearance of disorder is really a matter of scale: a mathematical structure can be found if you look widely enough. British mathematician Frank Plumpton Ramsey (1902–30), who, despite his short life, made considerable contributions to economics and philosophy, wanted to find the smallest set of objects that would guarantee that some of those objects would share certain properties. For example, the smallest number of people that will always include two people of the same sex is three. If there are only two, you might have a man and a woman; since the third person would be either a man or a woman, adding him or her guarantees at least two of one sex.

Or take this question: Can a complete graph have its edges colored using only two colors, so that no three edges of the same color form a triangle? Ramsey proved some general theorems on this question, but instances with four, five, or six nodes are simple enough to analyze using pencil and paper. The Party Problem is based on Ramsey's work. To appreciate how elegant graphs are for solving this sort of problem, imagine listing all possible combinations of acquaintanceship among six people – a total of 32,768 – and having to check if each combination included the desired relationship. A more advanced Ramsey problem would be to imagine a party in which there must be a foursome in which everyone is a mutual friend or everyone is a mutual stranger. How large must the party be? Ramsey's work demonstrated that 18 guests are necessary. If you draw a complete graph with 18 nodes, no matter how you color the lines using two colors, you will inevitably create a quadrilateral formed by connecting four points (persons) in one of the colors. The party size required to ensure at least one fivesome of mutual friends or strangers is still unknown. The answer lies between 43 and 49!

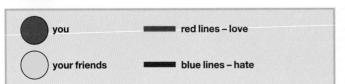

●	you	▬▬▬	red lines – love
○	your friends	▬▬▬	blue lines – hate

THE PARTY PROBLEM
Ramsey game I

Imagine you are sitting at a table with five guests. Assuming that any two people either love or hate each other, you may be intrigued to hear that the group includes at least three people who either all love or hate each other. This was proven by Frank Ramsey and called the Party Problem, which states that any party of six people will always include one or the other of these two groups. With five or fewer people this does not always happen (see illustrations below). How could you prove the Party Problem for six people?

1. You could write down all the possible combinations. For the first member of a pair there are six choices, which leaves five choices for the second of the pair for a total of 30 choices. The order of the choices doesn't matter, then the number of possibilities is 30/2, down to 15. Thus for the two possible relationships (love-hate) the total number of possibilities is 2^{15} or 32,768, quite a big number to count.

2. The general solution was provided by Ramsey. The Ramsey Theory gives answers for groups of any number of people in the party. Also, instead of having just two relationships (love or hate) we can have any number of mutually exclusive kinds of relationships.

Ramsey game II

In a party of you and three friends, any two of you either love or hate each other. Can you invite three or four friends to a party, avoiding groups of three, who all love or hate each other? One by one, color the lines of the graphs in either two colors: red or blue. How many lines can you color, before you are forced to create a triangle of one of the colors, formed by connecting three of the outside numbered points.

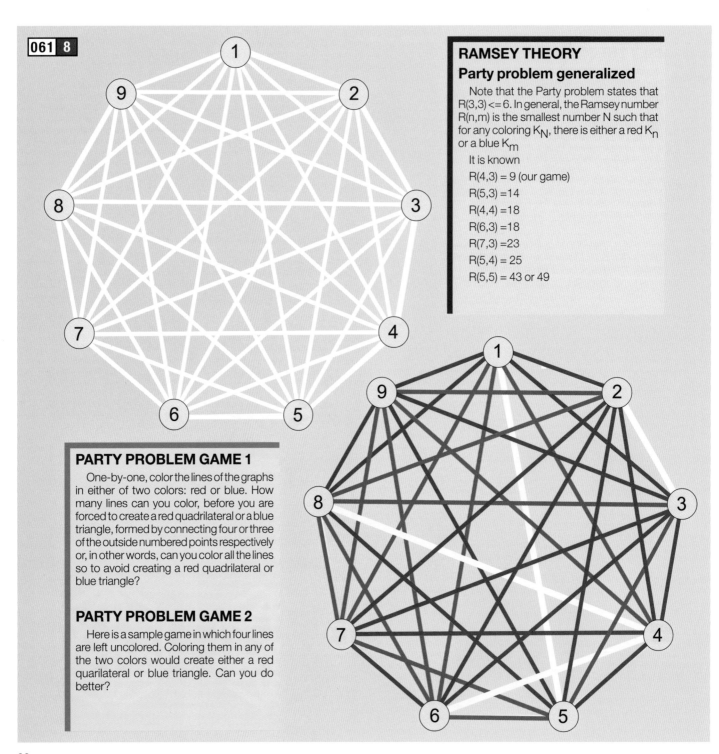

RAMSEY THEORY

Party problem generalized

Note that the Party problem states that $R(3,3) <= 6$. In general, the Ramsey number $R(n,m)$ is the smallest number N such that for any coloring K_N, there is either a red K_n or a blue K_m

It is known

$R(4,3) = 9$ (our game)

$R(5,3) = 14$

$R(4,4) = 18$

$R(6,3) = 18$

$R(7,3) = 23$

$R(5,4) = 25$

$R(5,5) = 43$ or 49

PARTY PROBLEM GAME 1

One-by-one, color the lines of the graphs in either of two colors: red or blue. How many lines can you color, before you are forced to create a red quadrilateral or a blue triangle, formed by connecting four or three of the outside numbered points respectively or, in other words, can you color all the lines so to avoid creating a red quadrilateral or blue triangle?

PARTY PROBLEM GAME 2

Here is a sample game in which four lines are left uncolored. Coloring them in any of the two colors would create either a red quarilateral or blue triangle. Can you do better?

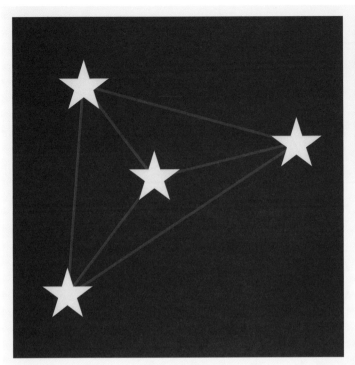

Convex Quadrilateral

Looking at a starry sky, how many stars do you have to select to guarantee a convex quadrilateral when you connect them with straight lines? The four stars selected as shown won't do.

What is the smallest number of points one can place in the plane in a general direction (no three of which lie on a straight line), which will always determine a convex polygon of 4 sides?

Happy Ever After

Esther Klein and George Szekeres proved the theorem for a convex quadrilateral (polygon of four sides). They got engaged and were married, and because of this Erdös named the it the Happy End Problem.

062 9

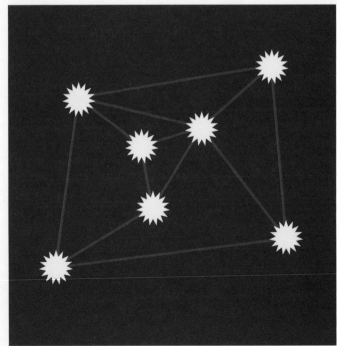

CONVEX PENTAGON

Looking at a starry sky, how many stars do you have to select to guarantee a convex pentagon when you connect them with straight lines? The seven stars selected as shown won't do.

E. Makai proved the theorem for a convex pentagon.

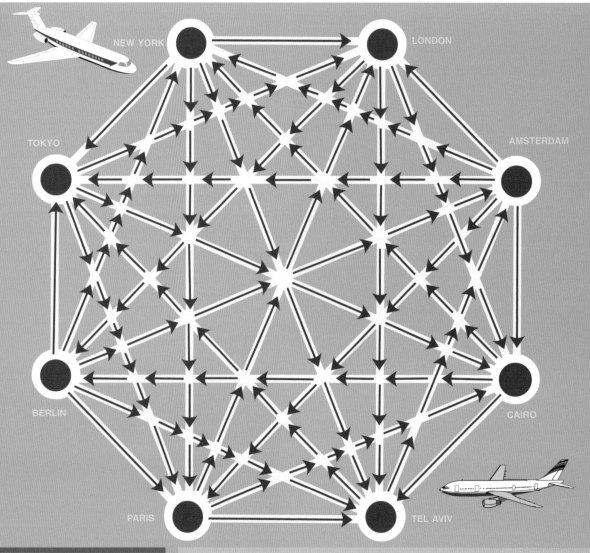

WORLD TRIP

Can you choose any of the cities and plan a journey that visits all the cities following the directions indicated by the arrows on each line and never retracing the same line?

For example what will be the order of the trip from New York to Paris visiting all cities?

ARROW GRAPHS

When an arrow is added to each line of a complete graph it becomes a digraph or directed graph.

A complete graph is a graph in which every every pair of vertices is joined by a line. A complete digraph, like our graph on eight points is called a tournament. An astonishing property of a complete digraph is that no matter how the arrows are drawn, every tournament will have a Hamiltonian path, which is a route that visits every vertex once (see page 74). It should be noted that some edges may not be visited during the trip while completing a Hamiltonian path.

EARLY COMPUTER ART

The Cybernetic Serendipity Exhibition

The first exhibition of computer graphics took place in 1965. As others followed, the most noteworthy was the Cybernetic Serendipity Exhibition in London in 1968. The catalog of this exhibition is still the richest and most comprehensive survey of information on the early state of the new art form.

Ours is an age of technology, in which human labor is taken over increasingly by the computer not all of them purely utilitarian. The earliest computer drawings used mathematical curves and figures, demonstrating a beauty which has been explored in art from the earliest times. A few of these early experiments from the Cybernetic Serendipity Exhibition are reproduced here.

Since the 1960s, computer graphics has not only developed into an art medium but also into an important tool in pure mathematics. The most interesting examples are discoveries of new surfaces that would have been impossible to visualize solely with the mind's eye.

FRIENDLY FLOWERS OF SPACE AND TIME
by Lloyd Summer

VERIFYING STAR
by D.K. Robbins

SINE CURVE MAN
by Prof. Charles Csuri

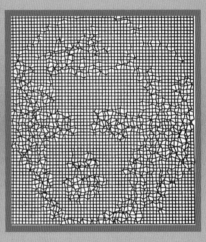

MONROE IN THE NET

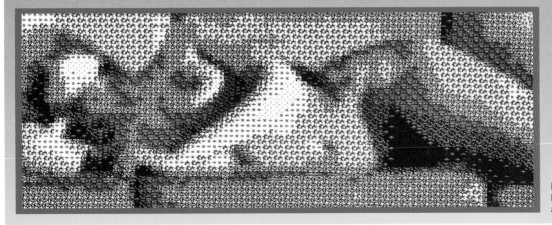

NUDE
by K.C. Knowlton
and L.D. Harmon

FROM LISSAJOUS FIGURES TO HARMONOGRAMS

The French physicist Jules Antoine Lissajous (1773–1838) discovered Lissajous figures in 1815. He would use sounds of different frequencies to vibrate mirrors attached to tuning forks. A beam of light reflected from the mirrors would trace pleasing patterns based on the sound frequencies. A similar set up is used today in laser shows.

Classic Victorian harmonographs that drew Lissajous figures usually consisted of two coupled pendulums, oscillating at right angles to each other, one pendulum carrying a pen and the other the paper. The resulting families of Lissajous curves ended in a point when the pendulums are damped by friction. Dozens of early harmonographs were patented. Their designs limited the size of the drawings and did not allow any artistic expression, but were fascinating and popular as science toys in Victorian times.

In the late 1950s the author of this book patented a novel Harmonograph based on a completely original design concept, which enabled truly beautiful artistic creations of a giant size. The "Harmonograph of Moscovich," as it was patented worldwide, and its unique Harmonogram creations aroused enormous interest at the Cybernetic Serendipity Exhibition in London in 1968, which was one of the most important early art exhibitions of computer art and digital installations of the new medium in the art world. The Harmonograph was later taken to Washington, D.C. and San Francisco. As a consequence of its acclaim at the Cybernetic Serendipity Exhibition, and winning medals at the Geneva Inventions fairs during the 1970s and 1980s, the author was invited with his Harmonograph and its creations to participate at many art exhibitions and several one-man shows. Such as the International Design Center in Berlin, Museum of Modern Art in Mexico City, Didacta exhibitions in Basel and Hannover, the Israel Museum in Jerusalem, and many others.

In 1980, Peter Pan Playthings, a UK toy manufacturer, launched a small toy version of the Harmonograph, which got great TV and press coverage and was marketed successfully until 1985. Presently the Harmonograph is one of the major interactive permanent exhibits at the TECHNORAMA, the Swiss national Science Museum in Winterthur, Switzerland. Hila Moscovich, the artist daughter of the author, is presently creating unique and original harmonograms, which are highly acclaimed by art lovers and collectors worldwide .

LISSAJOUS' OPTICAL HARMONOGRAPH
Lissajous set up projecting moving Lissajous curves and patterns by vibrating tuning forks, mirrors, and pin-point light sources.

VICTORIAN HARMONOGRAPH TOY

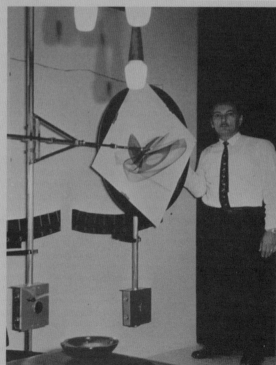

THE "HARMONGRAPH OF MOSCOVICH"
The first prototype of the world-patented harmonograph from 1958 with a Harmonogram on its revolving board.

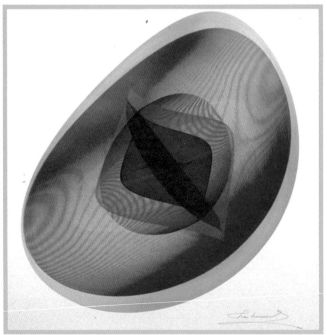

HARMONOGRAMS by Ivan Moscovich

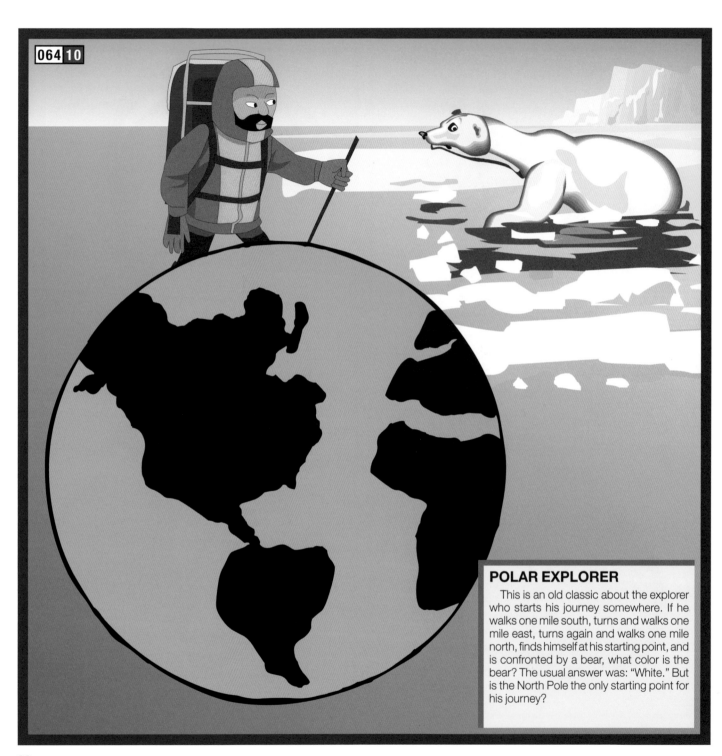

POLAR EXPLORER

This is an old classic about the explorer who starts his journey somewhere. If he walks one mile south, turns and walks one mile east, turns again and walks one mile north, finds himself at his starting point, and is confronted by a bear, what color is the bear? The usual answer was: "White." But is the North Pole the only starting point for his journey?

SERPENT

Copy, cut out, and assemble the ten parts of the serpent into a closed configuration. This won't be as easy as it seems. You will get lots of different convoluted open serpents, but it is a lot harder to make the serpent eat its own tail. Among the many different possible arrangements, only one produces the closed loop. A trial-and-error approach might take a long time, so a little thinking is in order. Here is a hint to get you started: each of the parts of the puzzle contains the key to its solution.

When you have discovered the secret of the serpent, its solution will be very easy for you and this will astound your friends.

NOTE ON OUROBOROS

Ouroboros, the mythical serpent of ancient Egypt and Greece, is represented with its tail in its mouth, continuously devouring itself and being reborn. A Gnostic and alchemical symbol, Ouroboros expresses the unity of all things, material and spiritual, which never disappear but perpetually change form in an eternal cycle of destruction and creation. It was the inspiration for the symbol used to denote infinity – ?.

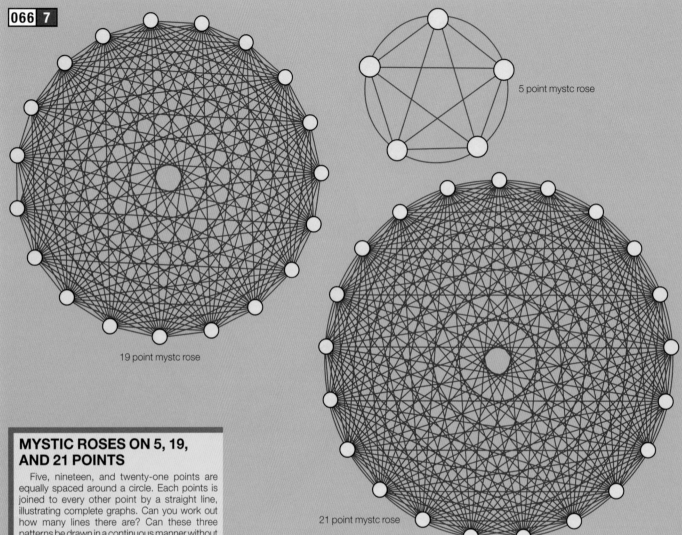

5 point mystc rose

19 point mystc rose

21 point mystc rose

MYSTIC ROSES ON 5, 19, AND 21 POINTS

Five, nineteen, and twenty-one points are equally spaced around a circle. Each points is joined to every other point by a straight line, illustrating complete graphs. Can you work out how many lines there are? Can these three patterns be drawn in a continuous manner without lifting pencil from paper or retracing any lines?

Rather than joining every point to every other, one variation of the mystic rose pattern involves starting at point 1, then visiting various points around the circle, skipping the same number of points at each step. Fo example, if you skip 6 points on a 21-point rose, you would draw an equilateral triangle before ending back at point 1.

In the 21-point mystic rose, will the line close if 14 points are missed? How many vertices will the line cover? And if you miss 12 points?

MYSTIC ROSES

Mystic roses are circle designs in which a set of points is evenly spaced along the circumference of a circle, and each point is connected to every other point by straight lines. As the number of points along the circles increases, the number of lines increases dramatically and the resulting pattern has a pleasing symmetry.

In 1809, the French mathematician Louis Poinsot asked what was the number of lines needed to draw mystic roses of various sizes, and whether a specific n-point mystic rose can be drawn by a continuous line without lifting the pen from the paper or retracing any of the lines.

Can you draw a five-point mystic rose by one continuous line? One on four points?

CIRCLE THEOREMS

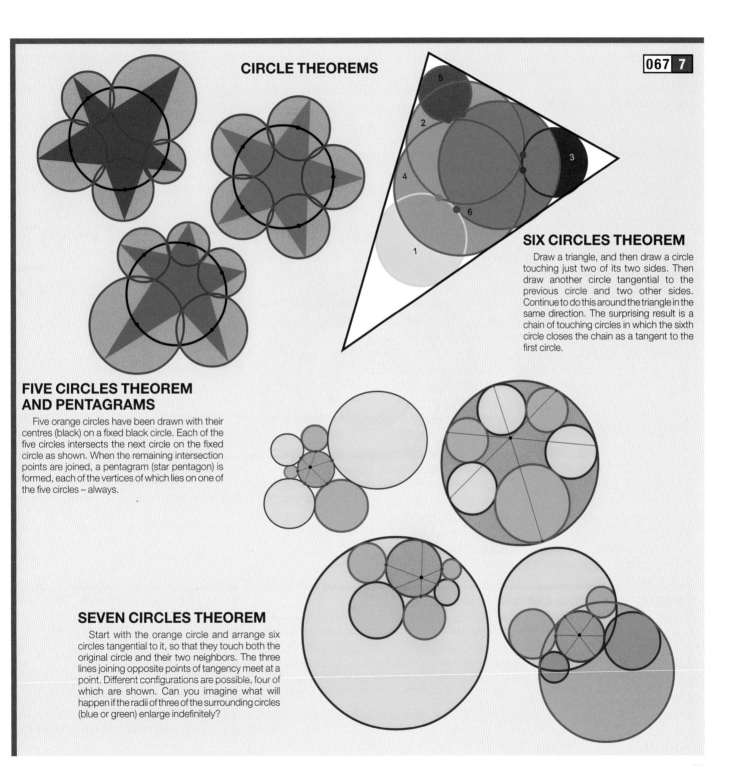

SIX CIRCLES THEOREM

Draw a triangle, and then draw a circle touching just two of its two sides. Then draw another circle tangential to the previous circle and two other sides. Continue to do this around the triangle in the same direction. The surprising result is a chain of touching circles in which the sixth circle closes the chain as a tangent to the first circle.

FIVE CIRCLES THEOREM AND PENTAGRAMS

Five orange circles have been drawn with their centres (black) on a fixed black circle. Each of the five circles intersects the next circle on the fixed circle as shown. When the remaining intersection points are joined, a pentagram (star pentagon) is formed, each of the vertices of which lies on one of the five circles – always.

SEVEN CIRCLES THEOREM

Start with the orange circle and arrange six circles tangential to it, so that they touch both the original circle and their two neighbors. The three lines joining opposite points of tangency meet at a point. Different configurations are possible, four of which are shown. Can you imagine what will happen if the radii of three of the surrounding circles (blue or green) enlarge indefinitely?

99

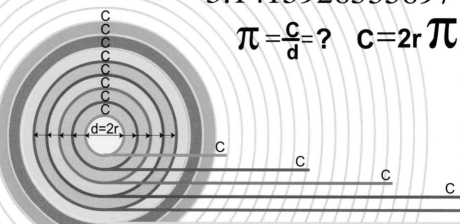

THE AMAZING NUMBER $\pi = 3.1415926535897$

$$\pi = \frac{c}{d} = ? \quad C = 2r\,\pi$$

$$\frac{\pi}{4} = 1 - \frac{1}{3} + \frac{1}{5} - \frac{1}{7} + \frac{1}{9} - \cdots\cdots\cdots\cdots$$

NUMBER PI AND A CIRCLE'S CIRCUMFERENCE

Pi is no ordinary number. It is special and comes up in the most unexpected places. Like the extraordinary connection between Pi and the **odd numbers**. What on Earth have circles got to do with the odd numbers? Its history goes back about four thousand years and its study reveals the inherent beauty of mathematics. The symbol denoting it is a letter of the Greek alphabet. It was introduced by none other than Leonhard Euler, the great Swiss mathematician. Because the circle plays such an important role for so many things in mathematics, science, and everyday life, it is well worth knowing, but what is pi "exactly"?

Pi represents the ratio of the circumference of a circle to its diameter. Pi is always the same number, no matter how big a circle is.

This ratio is one of the most fascinating number constants in the long history of mathematics.

.... If the Pythagorean theorem is the most beautiful result in the whole of geometry, then the next best known must surely be the equations for the circumference and area of a circle, and the number Pi.

PI BY ARCHIMEDES' METHOD

Archimedes' method for estimating pi relied on inscribed and circumscribed regular polygons (polygons with sides of equal length) on a circle having a diameter of one unit (or a radius of half a unit). The perimeters of the inscribed and circumscribed polygons served respectively as lower and upper bounds for the value of pi. Archimedes had to develop geometric constructions and using this method on a 96-sided regular polygon, he was able to determine that pi was between 3 10/71 and 3 1/7 or between

3.14084 and 3.14285.

If Archimedes took the average value between these limits, he would have obtained pi= 3.141845 with an astonishing accuracy of 99.99 %.

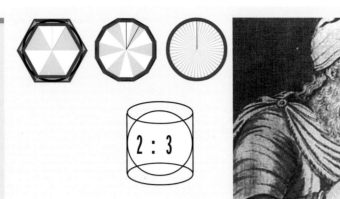

ARCHIMEDES (287–212 B.C.)

Archimedes is considered one of the three greatest mathematicians of all time, along with Newton and Gauss. In his own time, he was known as the Wise One, the Master, and the Great Geometer. His works and inventions brought him fame that lasts to this very day. He was one of the last great Greek mathematicians. Born in Syracuse in Sicily, Archimedes was the son of Phidias the astronomer. Archimedes proved to be a master at mathematics and spent most of his time contemplating new problems to solve, becoming at times so involved in his work that he forgot to eat. Most of Archimedes fame comes from his relationship with Hiero II, the king of Syracuse. He seemed to make a hobby out of solving the king's most complicated problems. At one time, the king ordered a gold crown and gave the goldsmith the exact amount of metal to make it with. When Hiero received it, the crown had the correct weight but the monarch suspected that some silver had been used instead of gold. Since he did not know how to prove it, he brought the problem to Archimedes. One day while considering the problem, the Wise One got into his bathtub and recognized that the amount of water that overflowed the tub was proportional the amount of his body that was submerged. This observation is now known as Archimedes' Principle and gave him the means to solve the problem ingeniously (s. page 16). He invented the entire field of hydrostatics with the discovery of the Archimedes' Principle.

Another time, Archimedes stated "Give me a place to stand on and I will move the Earth." King Hiero II, who was absolutely astonished by the statement, asked him to prove it. Archimedes, who had been studying the properties of levers and pulleys, built a machine by means of which he could single-handedly lift a ship from a distance away.

However, his greatest invention was integral calculus. To determine the area of sections bounded by geometric figures such as parabolas and ellipses, Archimedes broke the sections into an infinite number of rectangles and added the areas together. This is known as integration. He also anticipated the invention of differential calculus as he devised ways to approximate the slope of the tangent lines to his figures.

In 212 B.C., Marcellus, a Roman general, decided to conquer Syracuse, attacking from both land and sea. King Hiero persuaded Archimedes to develop weapons to defend the city, which he did. The Roman legions were routed by huge catapults hurling 500-pound boulders and giant cranes with claws that lifted and dropped the ships onto the rocks. The Romans fled and Marcellus was forced to lay siege to the city, which fell after eight months. The story goes that while Archimedes was drawing figures in the dust a Roman soldier demanded he come with him. Archimedes responded, "Don't disturb my circles!" The enraged soldier pulled out his sword and killed the Great Geometer. On his tombstone is inscribed a figure of a sphere inside a cylinder and the 2:3 ratio of the volumes between them – the discovery that he considered his greatest achievement.

THE VALUE OF PI

The history of pi is virtually the history of mathematics itself. The ancient Egyptians and the Babylonians knew about it, but they could figure its value only as a bit bigger than 3. In 225 B.C., the Greek mathematician Archimedes inscribed and circumscribed a circle with a 96-sided polygon and found that the ratio lies between 3 1/7 and 3 10/71. Ptolemy in 150 A.D. found a value of 3.1416, which is sufficiently accurate for most practical purposes. Modern supercomputers have calculated pi to 1.24 trillion decimal places.

Pi is a number that cannot be written as a repeating decimal or a finite decimal, it is irrational, it cannot be written as a fraction (the ratio of two integers). It is also transcendental, because it cannot be the solution of an equation based on five operations – addition, subtraction, multiplication, division, and square root extraction. The proof of its transcendence by Lindeman in the 19th century also proved the impossibility of squaring the circle, thus ending the search for solution of the most famous problem in Antiquity. Its digits are assumed to be random and they seem to be, at least for the first few hundred billion digits, but the actual proof is not in the reach of present-day computers. Every possible pattern eventually occurs in pi. Pi does contain an endless variety or remarkable patterns that ar the result of chance.

Pi crops up in all sorts of unexpected places in mathematics besides circles (normal distribution, prime number theory, probability, river meanders). Pi appears in the formulas engineers use to calculate the force of magnetic fields, and physicists use it to describe the structure of space and time.

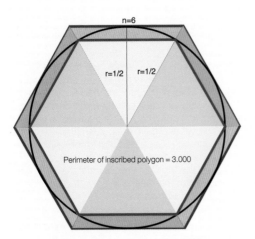

n=6

r=1/2   r=1/2

Perimeter of inscribed polygon = 3.000

Perimeter of circumscribed polygon = 3.464

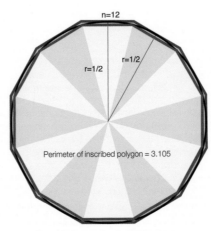

n=12

r=1/2   r=1/2

Perimeter of inscribed polygon = 3.105

Perimeter of circumscribed polygon = 3.215

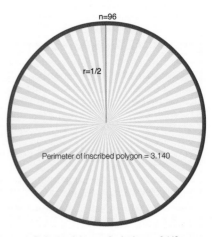

n=96

r=1/2

Perimeter of inscribed polygon = 3.140

Perimeter of circumscribed polygon = 3.142

Memory trick: Can you remember the value of pi up to seven decimal places?

The trick is to remember the sentence **"May I have a large container of coffee"**. The number of letters in each word corresponds to the numbers in pi.)

CONWAY'S GROUPING OF PI DECIMALS

Separate the decimals of pi into groups of ten. Will ever be such a group containing all the ten digits from 0 to 9 (0, 1, 2, 3, 4, 5, 6, 7, 8, 9) ?

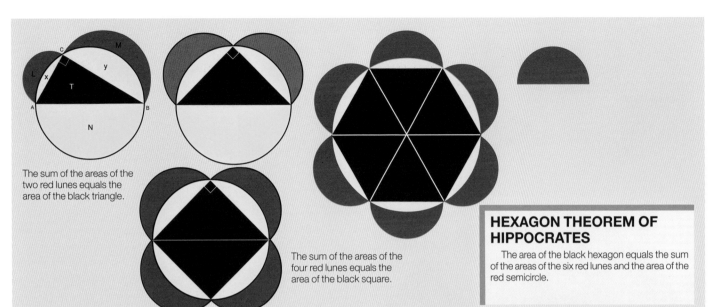

The sum of the areas of the two red lunes equals the area of the black triangle.

The sum of the areas of the four red lunes equals the area of the black square.

The area of the black hexagon equals the sum of the areas of the six red lunes and the area of the red semicircle.

CRESCENTS (LUNES) OF HIPPOCRATES
An early attempt to square the circle

The Greek geometer Hippocrates (about 430 B.C.) from the Aegean island of Chios (not to be confused with Hippocrates of Cos, the famous father of medicine) used a principle of give-and-take and applied it to several forms of curved shapes whose areas could be described in surprisingly simple terms. He was the first to be able to show that areas of lunes (areas bounded by circular arcs) can be equal to the area of a rectilinear figure, such as a triangle or a square. Hippocrates' works are lost, but he must have tackled the problem in a similar way as described here.

In a section devoted to the famous Pythagorean theorem, we have seen that in its extended generalized form, the Pythagorean relationship holds for any set of similar figures placed on the three sides of a right-angled triangle, as long as they are placed in corresponding orientation. This holds for circles as well. Hippocrates used semicircles as a set of similar polygons as his starting point. He made the surprising discovery that certain curvelinear areas are calculable, that is, that squares having the same area can be constructed. His discovery aroused enormous interest, since it was believed that if the area bounded by two circular arcs can be calculated, it must also be possible to square the circle, that is, to construct a square with the area equal to that of a given circle, which is bounded by only one circular arc – a goal that was never fulfilled.

Hippocrates constructed overlapping semicircles on the sides of a right-angled triangle. Can you make a guess at what will be the combined areas of the two red crescents?

A square is inscribed in a circle. Four semicircles are drawn on the four sides of the square, describing four moon-shaped crescents. Can you guess what will be the total area of the four red crescents?

It is a curious fact that although the circle cannot be squared some other figures bounded by circular arcs often can, which still arouses false hopes in many a "circle squarer." Hippocrates of Chios, the most famous geometer of his time, found the solution to such a problem, while trying to square a circle – a truly remarkable feat at the time.

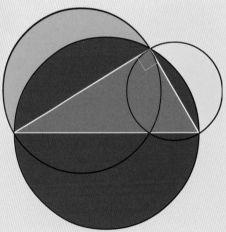

PYTHAGOREAN THEOREM
Applied to Circles

Pythagorean theorem applied to circles leads to an interesting result. We have seen that any triangle can be circumscribed by a unique circle, the circumcircle. What if the triangle is right angled? In a right triangle the diameter of the circumcircle coincides with the hypotenuse. Consequently, in any right triangle, the sum of the areas of the circles built on the two legs is equal to the area of the circumcircle.

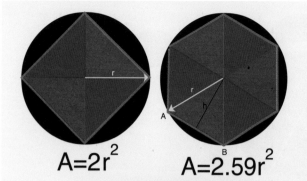

$A=2r^2$

$A=2.59r^2$

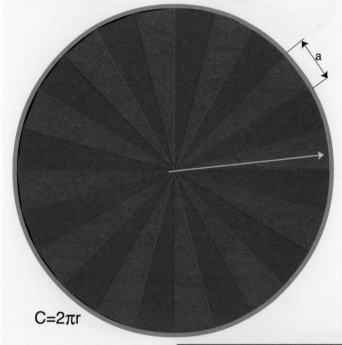

$C=2\pi r$

CIRCLE AREA AND NUMBER PI

The problem of determining the area of a circle was a great mathematical challenge that Archimedes (287–212 BC) attempted to solve. He tried to solve it by the "squaring the circle" method, i.e. looking to find the square (polygon) that has the same area as a circle of a given radius. His method leading to the exact formula is demonstrated.

The circle of radius "r" is divided into a great number of near isosceles triangles with sides "r" and bases "a" (small circular arcs approximating straight lines), which can be arranged to form a parallelogram as shown. The more sectors the circle is divided into the clearer the sectors resemble triangles, the triangles becoming smaller and smaller, and the figure approaches the form of a rectangle. The height of each triangle is roughly the same as the radius of the circle r. The circumference of the circle = 2 x r x pi. Each color of triangle covers half of the circle's circumference, so the length of the rectangle is half this, that is, pi x r. Hence: area of circle = area of the rectangle (as shown) = height x width = r x (pi x r) = pi x (r squared), which is the famous formula we know today.

Note that this is an approximation only. The method actually works only if the base of each triangle ("a" in the diagram) is infinitely small.

AREA OF A CIRCLE:

$$A = \pi r \times r = \pi r^2$$

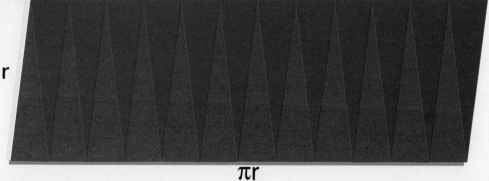

r

πr

BUFFON NEEDLE EXPERIMENT
Georges-Louis Leclerc, Comte de Buffon (1707–88)

Buffon's Needle is among the oldest problems in the field of geometrical probability. It is one of the most startling examples of number pi showing up in strange places. Buffon, in his 44-volume encyclopedia *Historie Naturelle*, described everything known about the natural world. In the appendix he included the problem (completely unrelated to natural history) of the needle experiment. In his *Les Epoques de la Nature*, he daringly suggested that the planet was much older than the 6,000 years proclaimed by the Church. He became the most important natural historian of his time, having great influence across a number of scientific fields. At the age of 20, Buffon discovered the binomial theorem, and later introduced differential and integral calculus into probability theory.

n throws	matches falling on a line m	pi = 2n/m
10	5	4
20	7	3.3333
30	5	3.5294
40	6	3.4782
50	7	3.3333
60	6	3.3333
70	6	3.3333
80	6	3.3333
90	8	3.2148
100	8	3.1746

BUFFON NEEDLES AND THROWING DARTS

If a needle is dropped from a considerable height on our game board that has drawn upon it parallel lines so that the distance between them is equal to the length of the matchstick or needle shown, what is the chance that the matchstick or needle will fall touching a line?

If a needle or matchstick of length L is dropped on a board that is ruled with equally spaced lines at a distance $d >= L$, then the probability that the needle comes to cross a line is exactly $P = 2L/Pi\,d$.

Lazzarini in 1901 dropped a needle of $L = 5/6d$ some 3,408 times and got pi correctly to six decimals.

length of the matchstick or needle

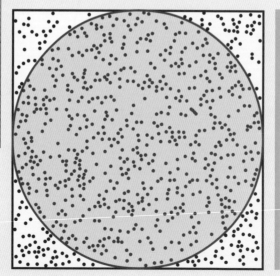

A random pattern of 800 dart throws

THROWING DARTS
Circle area approximation

Another way to approximate the area of the circle would be by the Monte Carlo method of throwing darts into a square's area. The Monte Carlo method uses random numbers and probability to solve problems. If random samples are uniformly scattered along the surface of a square in which a circle is inscribed, the proportion of hits in the circle approximates to the ratio of the area of the circle to that of the square. To get a satisfactory approximation a great number of random samples is required.

In our experiment 800 darts were thrown and the area of the circle was obtained with a 96 percent accuracy.

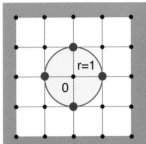

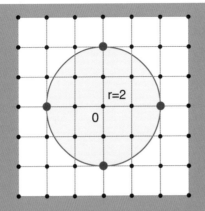

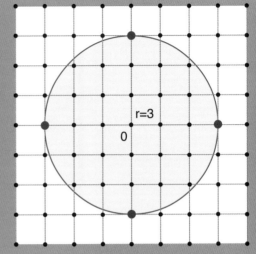

CIRCLE LATTICE POINTS

Schinzel's Theorem

The number of lattice points on the circumference of circles centered at (0,0) with radii from 1 to 4 are shown. Can you find the number of lattice points for a circle with radius 5, with its center situated at point (0,0)? And for a circle with radius 25?

Lattice points are regular arrays of points (more informally known as grids or meshes), usually square arrays, i.e., points with coordinates (x,y) where x and y are integers. In the plane, point lattices can have unit cells in shapes other than squares, rectangles, hexagons, etc. The circles can also be centered at other points than the center.

In general, **Schinzel's Theorem** shows that for every positive integer n, there exists a circle in the plane having exactly n lattice points on its circumference.

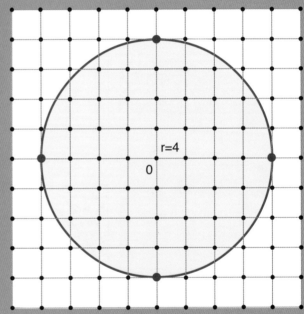

circle radius	0	1	2	3	4	5	6	7	8	9	10	11	12	25
number of lattice points	1	4	4	4	4									?

The number of lattice points on the circumference of circles centered at (0,0)

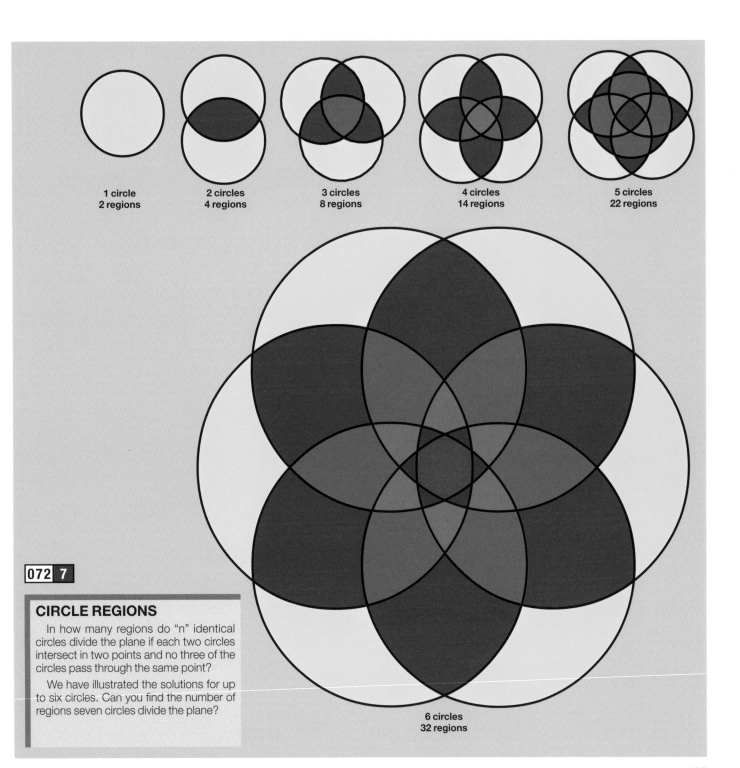

1 circle
2 regions

2 circles
4 regions

3 circles
8 regions

4 circles
14 regions

5 circles
22 regions

072 7

CIRCLE REGIONS

In how many regions do "n" identical circles divide the plane if each two circles intersect in two points and no three of the circles pass through the same point?

We have illustrated the solutions for up to six circles. Can you find the number of regions seven circles divide the plane?

6 circles
32 regions

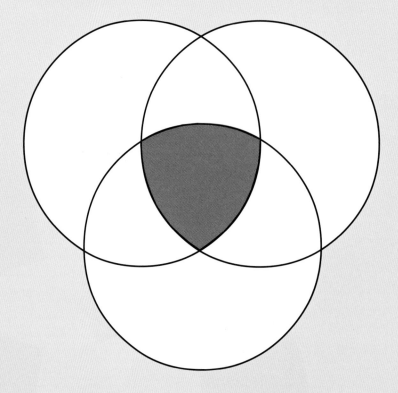

TRIPLE CIRCLES OVERLAP

Each of the three identical circles passes through the centers of the other two.

Is the area of the overlap (shaded) greater or smaller than one-fourth of the area of a circle?

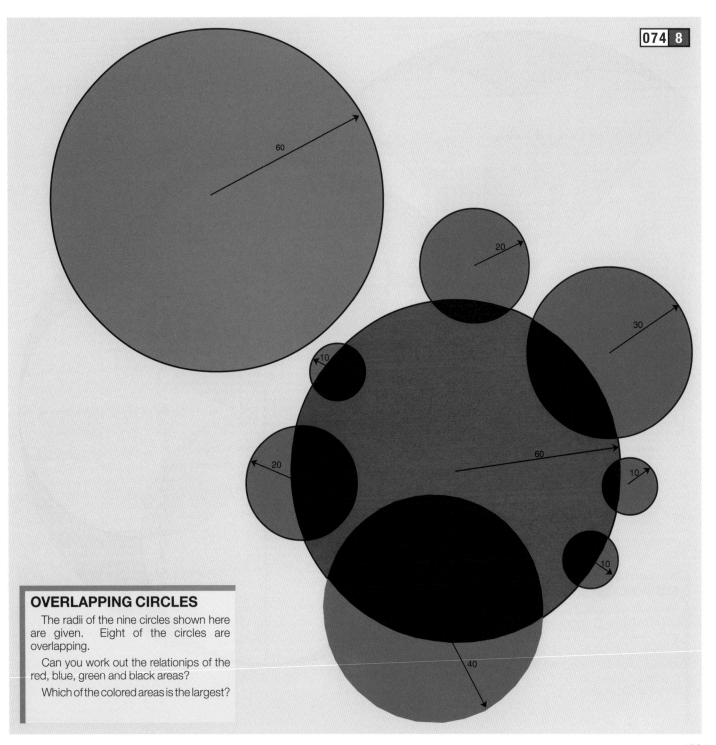

OVERLAPPING CIRCLES

The radii of the nine circles shown here are given. Eight of the circles are overlapping.

Can you work out the relationips of the red, blue, green and black areas?

Which of the colored areas is the largest?

109

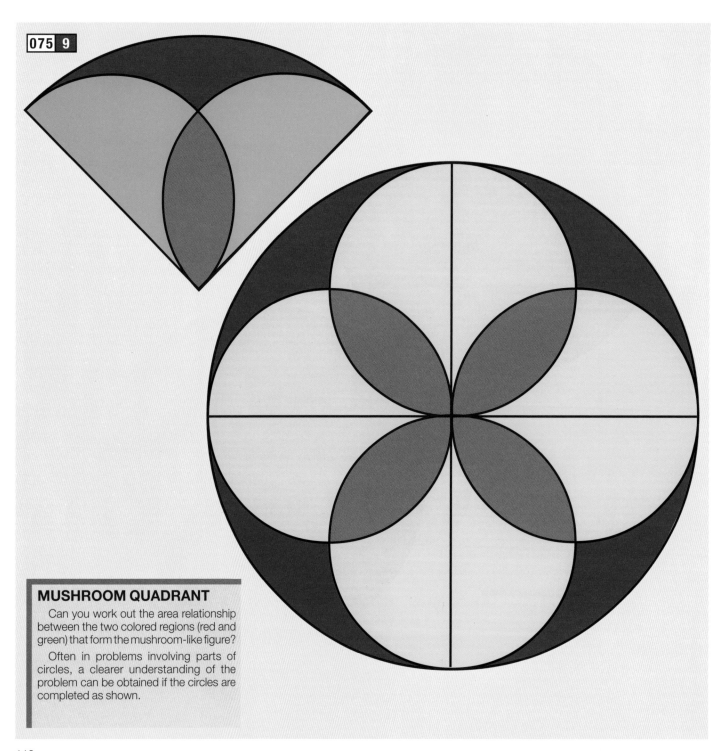

MUSHROOM QUADRANT

Can you work out the area relationship between the two colored regions (red and green) that form the mushroom-like figure?

Often in problems involving parts of circles, a clearer understanding of the problem can be obtained if the circles are completed as shown.

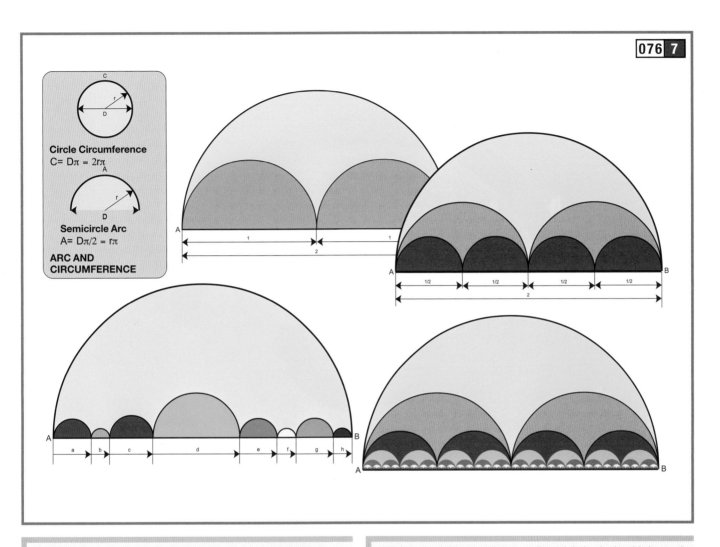

Circle Circumference
C = Dπ = 2rπ

Semicircle Arc
A = Dπ/2 = rπ

ARC AND CIRCUMFERENCE

SEMICIRCLES PARADOX AND NUMBER PI

The enormous interest in pi is greatly due to the fact that pi pops up in many unexpected places that leaves us truly perplexed. One such instance is the interesting geometric paradox involving inscribed smaller semicicles extended from one end of a larger semicircle's diameter to the other. Several examples are demonstrated, in which the number of inscribed semicircles increases progressively. The following may seem quite counterintuitive and may not appear to be true, but it is!

The sum of the arcs lengths of the smaller semicircles is equal to the arc length of the large semicircle.

The sum of the arcs of the small semicircles in the third sample equals the arc length of the large semicircle, which is one half of the diameter (AB) times pi as shown:

pi(a)/2 + pi(b)/2 + pi(c)/2 + pi(d)/2 + pi(e)/2 + pi(f)/2 + pi(g)/2 + pi(h)/2)
= pi/2 (a + b + c + d + e + f + g +h) = = pi/2 (AB line).

But what happens when we endlessly increase the number of small semicircles along the diagonal of the large semicircle, as in the fourth example?

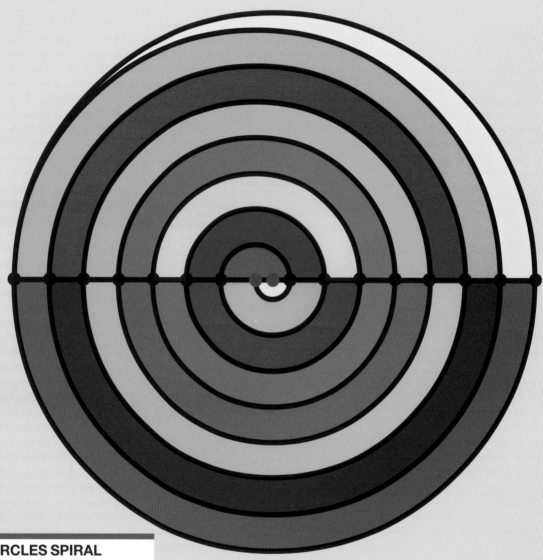

SEMICIRCLES SPIRAL

The spiral was created by a series of successively larger semicircles. The two red points are at a distance "r" from each other and are alternately the centers of the semicircles. Using pi it's possible to measure the length and area of the spiral.

Can you do it?

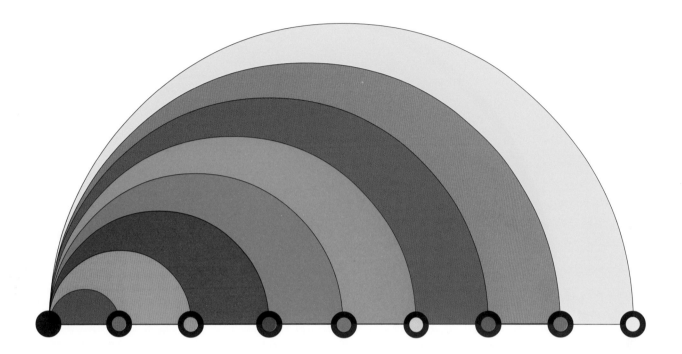

SEMICIRCLES CHAIN PUZZLE

Can you attach the eight semicircles to the 16 pins on the straight line without any two or more semicircles crossing?

Each semicircle is attached to two pins and the semicircles are not allowed to share the pins. A pin is allowed to attach the semicircles on both sides of the line.

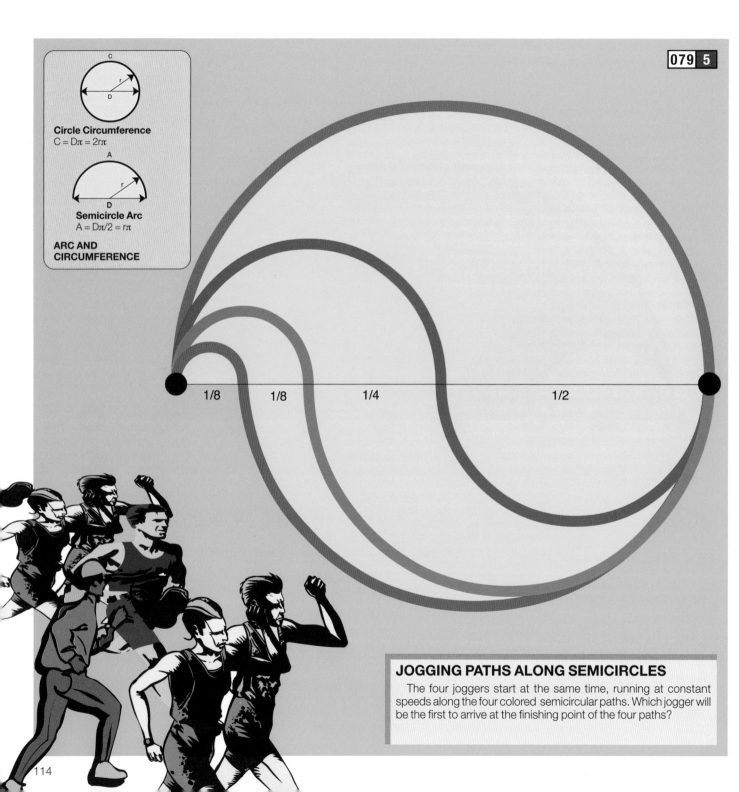

Circle Circumference
$C = D\pi = 2r\pi$

Semicircle Arc
$A = D\pi/2 = r\pi$

ARC AND CIRCUMFERENCE

1/8   1/8   1/4   1/2

JOGGING PATHS ALONG SEMICIRCLES

The four joggers start at the same time, running at constant speeds along the four colored semicircular paths. Which jogger will be the first to arrive at the finishing point of the four paths?

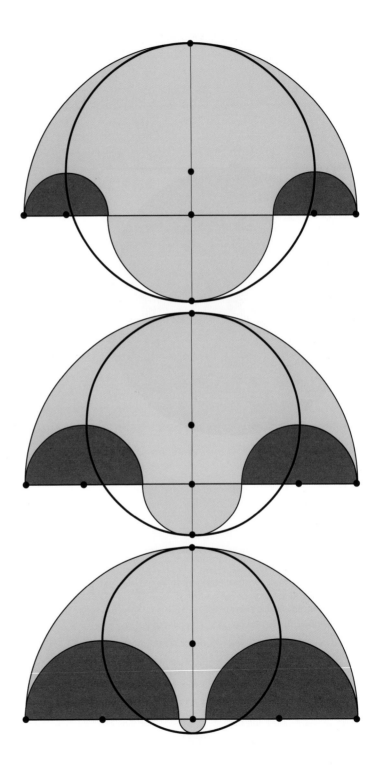

SALINON OF ARCHIMEDES

The salinon is a geometric figure studied by Archimedes. Its area (blue) is enclosed by four semicircles along the diameter of the big semicircle. The two semicircles on the sides of the diameter are equal and inside the big semicircle, while the middle semicircle is on the opposite side. The area of the salinon is equal to the area of the circle along the line perpendicular to the middle of the diameter, with its endpoints on the two opposing semicircles, as shown in three examples with different sizes of the inside semicircles.

Can you prove these relationships?

Note that in the third example, where the middle semicircle almost disappears, we are approaching a special case of salinon, where the fourth semicircle has a diameter of zero. You will recognize that this is the Arbelos previously described. It is truly astonishing that Archimedes could have discovered these relationships without the tools of modern mathematics.

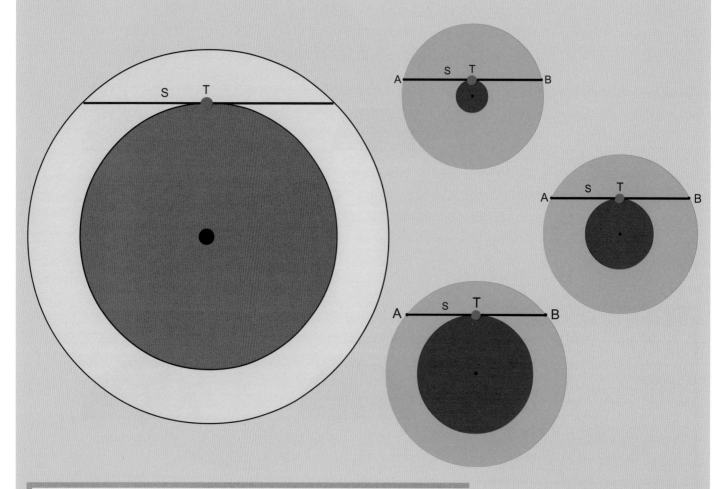

CIRCLE RINGS

A chord of length S of the big circle is tangent to the smaller circle, touching it in one point T. The problem is to find the area of the four rings (blue) formed between the circumference of the small circle and the large one in each diagram.

Do you think there is enough information given to solve the problems?

Yes, there is! And it will sound even more counterintutive to discover that the rings in all the circles shown actually have the same area.

The area of the ring depends only on the length of the chord, S, and the chords in the four samples are of the same length. Can you check that?

A hint: The Pythagorean theorem can be of help.

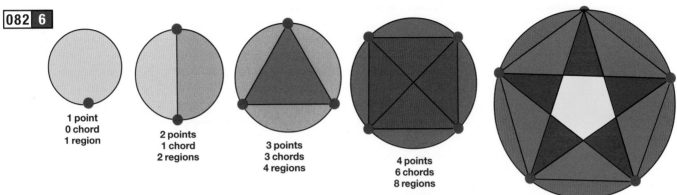

1 point
0 chord
1 region

2 points
1 chord
2 regions

3 points
3 chords
4 regions

4 points
6 chords
8 regions

5 points
10 chords
16 regions

CIRCLE CUTTING CHORDS

If **"n"** points are placed on the circumference of a circle and joined by chords (a line joining two points on the circumference of a circle is called a chord).

1. How many chords will be resulting?

2. In how many pieces will the circles and the polygons formed by the points be dissected into?

From one to seven points are placed on the circumferences of seven circles, showing the number of chords and the number of pieces dissected by the chords, except for the circle with seven points.

Can you work out how many chords will result from seven points when they are all interconnected, and in how many pieces will the seven-point circle and the heptagon be divided?

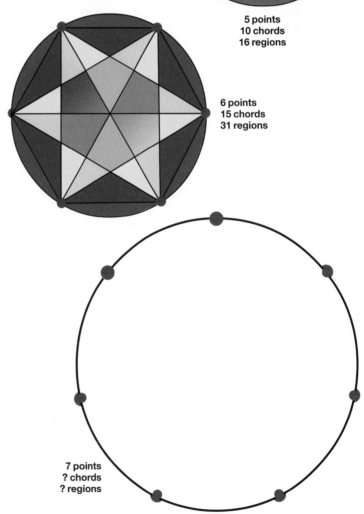

6 points
15 chords
31 regions

7 points
? chords
? regions

number of:								
points	1	2	3	4	5	6	7	8
chords	0	1	3	6	10	15		28
circle pieces	1	2	4	8	16	31		99
polygon pieces	0	0	1	4	11	25		91

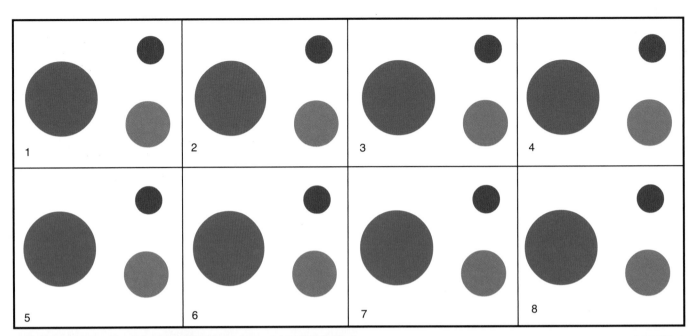

APOLLONIUS' THEOREM

In how many different ways can a fourth circle be added to any three given circles so that the three circles all touch the circumference of the fourth added circle?

We can reveal that there are only eight different possibilities. Can you add the fourth circle in each case?

What is the largest number of identical circles that can touch a single circle? Or identical spheres?

This is one of the classic problems of Greek antiquity. It relates to the general problem about the maximum number of mutually touching circles in a flat plane. It is called Apollonius' Problem because it was solved by one of the greatest Greek mathematicians Apollonius of Perga (c. 260–170 BC). His original treatise *Tangencies*, which was written about 200 BC, has been lost. There exist many solutions today.

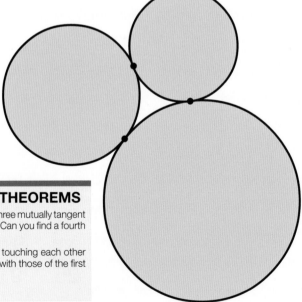

DESCARTES AND BEECROFT'S TOUCHING CIRCLES THEOREMS

A special case of Apollonius' touching circles theorem is to determine a circle touching three mutually tangent circles. It is called Descartes' Circle Theorem. Three mutually touching circles are shown. Can you find a fourth circle that touches the three circles? How many different solutions can you find?

Philip Beecroft extended Descartes' Theorem with his theorem: If any four circles are touching each other mutually, another set of four circles may be found whose mutual contacts shall coincide with those of the first four. Harold S. Coxeter elegantly proved Beecroft's theorem.

CIRCLE AND SPHERE PACKING

Circle packing is an arrangement of circles inside a given boundary without overlap. Generalized to spheres in the plane or space it is sphere packing. In 1940, L. Fejes Toth proved that hexagonal packing is the densest possible plane packing of circles or spheres. Its packing density is about 0.90, that is, 90% of the space can be used. A sphere (ball) is perhaps the simplest solid shape that one can imagine. It has no corners or edges. Every spot on the outside of a ball is exactly the same distance from the center of every other spot.

Kepler found that there are two basic ways to arrange circles or spheres in a plane. In a **square** lattice or in a **hexagonal** lattice (like in a honeycomb). These two arrangements can be stacked in space in several ways. There can be an endless number of random packings in between. Square layers can be stacked so that the spheres are vertically above each other, or the spheres in each layer nestle into the gaps between four spheres in the layer below.

With hexagonal layers there are also two possibilities, aligned or staggered, but staggered layers of hexagonally packed spheres lead to the same arrangement as staggered layers of square packed ones. If the spheres in these arrangements are allowed to expand, they form three-dimensional shapes. The cubic lattice forms cubes; the hexagonal lattice hexagonal prisms; and for the face-centered cubic lattice, Kepler's rhombic dodecahedron – the tightest possible packing.

The efficiency of a packing is measured by a number, its density (i.e. the proportion of space that is filled with spheres): The results in plane:

1. Square lattice: 0.7854

2. Hexagonal lattice: 0.9069

In three-dimensional space:

3. Cubic lattice: 0.5236

4. Hexagonal lattice: 0.6046

5. Face-centered cubic lattice: 0.7404

6. Dense random packing: 0.64

The problem of the close packing of spheres is closely related to geometric solids, which can be fitted together to completely fill space. Kepler tried to obtain such solids by imagining that each packing sphere expands to fill the intermediate space.

Kepler's insight found a fundamental connection between the formation of a snowflake, the construction of a honeycomb by bees, and the growth of a pomegranate. According to his theory, the regular, symmetric patterns that arise in each case can be described and explained in terms of "space-filling" geometric figures, such as his own discovery, the rhombic dodecahedron, which is a solid figure having 12 identical rhombic faces.

The rhombic dodecahedron, which can be packed to fill space, is the key to the sphere-packing problem.

PACKING CIRCLES OR SPHERES

There are two ways of filling the plane with circles or spheres.

CUBIC SPHERE PACKING

In square layers, corresponding spheres are stacked vertically above each other. The density is about 0.52

HEXAGONAL SPHERE PACKING

There are two ways to add a hexagonally packed layer.

(Above left) Spheres in the third layer are directly above those in the first.

(Above right) Face-centered cubic packing, with a density of about 0.74, which is the densest regular packing of spheres.

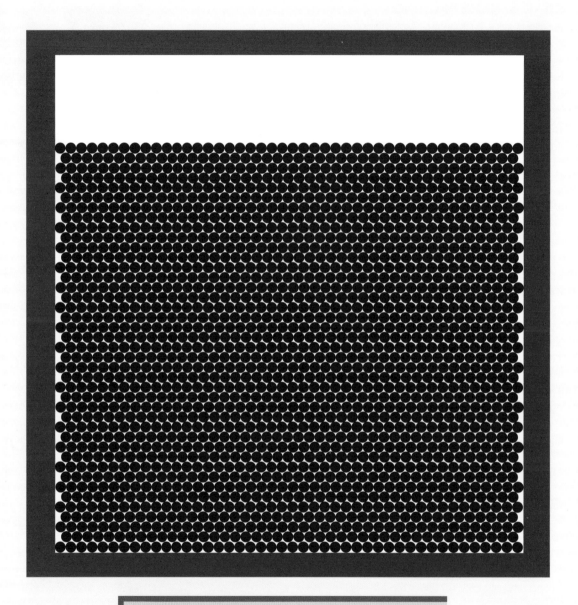

SPHERE PACKING BOX

A hermetically sealed box in which are enclosed thousands of small identical steel balls is in an ordered arrangement as shown. What will happen if the box is repeatedly shaken?

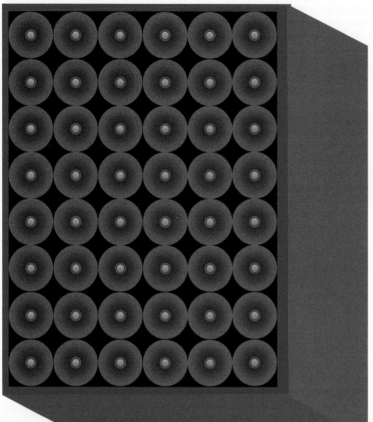

PACKING SPHERES IN A CUBE

You have a supply of spheres of 25 mm diameter. Twenty-seven of them are packed in cubic packing in a cube box just a bit larger than the width of three spheres, specifically with sides of 78 mm. Is it possible to rearrange them to fit in another five spheres to make a total of 32?

PACKING BOTTLES

You have a crate in which 48 identical bottles of wine are tightly packed. How would you repack them to make space for additional bottles of the same size? How many more bottles can you tightly pack into your crate?

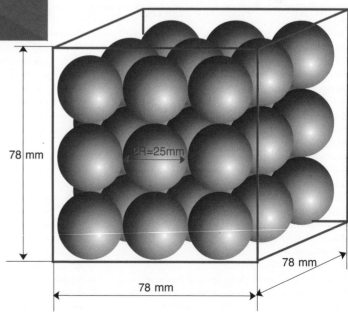

78 mm

2R=25mm

78 mm

78 mm

n=1 d=1

n=2 d=0.585

n=3 d=0.508

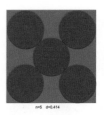

n=4 d=0.5

n=5 d=0.414

n=6 d=0.375

n=7 d=0.348

n=8 d=0.341

n=9 d=0.333...

n=10 d=0.294...

PACKING CIRCLES IN UNIT SQUARES

What is the size of the largest circle or set of circles that can be packed in a unit square? The first ten consecutive cases are shown here.

PACKING 11 AND 13 IDENTICAL CIRCLES IN UNIT SQUARES

Can you find the patterns of how 11 and 13 identical circles can be packed in unit squares?

The unit squares are given for circles equivalent to the size of coins: a US Quarter Dollar; a Euro; and a Pound Sterling. These are shown in different colors.

The object is to pack 11 and 13 of each coin into the squares of their corresponding colors: the large green square for the Pound; the slightly larger blue square for the Euro; and the largest red square for the Quarter Dollar.

If you want to do this puzzle on separate paper, without coins, the dimensions you need are:

a) the diameter of the coins (in millimeters):
- Quarter = 24mm
- Euro = 23mm
- Pound = 22.5mm

b) the dimensions of the side of each of the green, blue and red squares for the 11 circles and the 13 circles boards (also in millimeters):
- Red (n = 11) = 85mm
- Blue (n = 11) = 81mm
- Green (n = 11) = 79.5mm

- Red (n = 13) = 101.52mm
- Blue (n = 13) = 97.42mm
- Green (n = 13 = 95.31mm

$ US Quarter 11 x

€ Euro 11 x

£ UK Pound 11 x

11 circles - d=0.283

$ US Quarter 11 x

€ Euro 11 x

£ UK Pound 11 x

13 circles - d=0.267

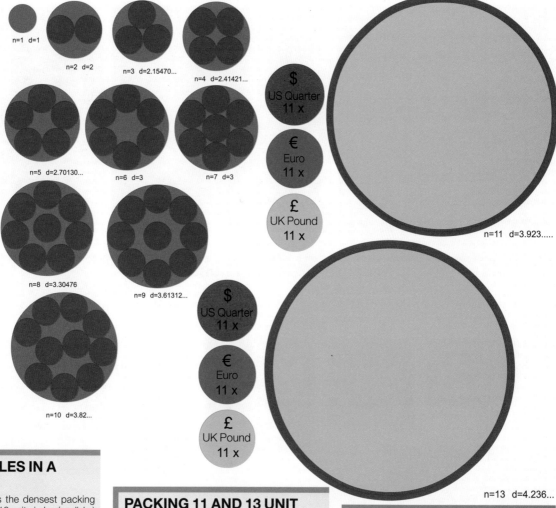

n=1 d=1

n=2 d=2

n=3 d=2.15470...

n=4 d=2.41421...

n=5 d=2.70130...

n=6 d=3

n=7 d=3

n=8 d=3.30476

n=9 d=3.61312...

n=10 d=3.82...

$ US Quarter 11 x

€ Euro 11 x

£ UK Pound 11 x

n=11 d=3.923.....

$ US Quarter 11 x

€ Euro 11 x

£ UK Pound 11 x

n=13 d=4.236...

PACKING CIRCLES IN A CIRCLE

The illustration shows the densest packing possibilities of 2 through 10 unit circles (or disks) into the smallest containing circles. The numbers below each example are the minimum diameters of the outside circle in relation to the inside unit circles.

Proving that a particular pattern is optimal is a very difficult mathematical problem. It was only recently that Hans Melissen achieved the proof of the optimal solution (the optimality) for 11 circles/disks, and most numbers higher than this are not proven.

PACKING 11 AND 13 UNIT CIRCLES INTO A CIRCLE

Can you pack 11 and 13 unit circles in the smallest possible circle?

The object is to pack 11 and 13 of each circle, representing coins (a US Quarter Dollar; a Euro, and and a UK Pound) into the circles of their corresponding color.

If you want to do this puzzle on separate paper, without coins, the dimensions you need are:

a) the diameter of the coins (in millimeters):
- Quarter = 24mm
- Euro = 23mm
- Pound = 22.5mm

b) the dimensions of each of the green, blue and red circles for the 11 circles and the 13 circles boards (also in millimeters):
- Red (n = 11) = 95mm
- Blue (n = 11) = 91mm
- Green (n = 11) = 88mm

- Red (n = 13) = 102mm
- Blue (n = 13) = 99mm
- Green (n = 13) = 96mm

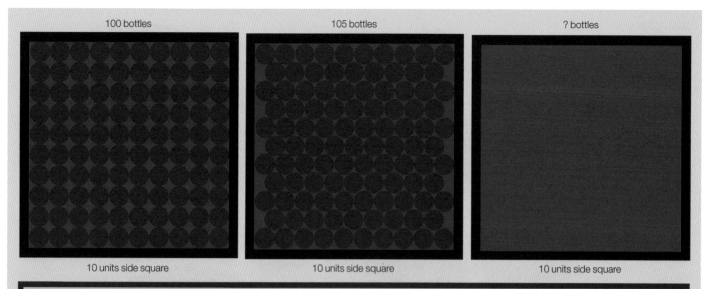

100 bottles — 10 units side square

105 bottles — 10 units side square

? bottles — 10 units side square

PACKING BOTTLES IN SQUARES – GENERAL PROBLEM

Bottles are shown packed in square crates, containing 4, 9, 16, 25, 36, 49, 64, 81, and 100 bottles. Can you repack the bottles in each box into smaller square crates? Combinatorial problems like these are quite recent and their answers are often surprisingly difficult but elegant.

PACKING 100 BOTTLES IN A SQUARE CRATE

If the diameter of the bottle is 1 unit, you can easily pack 100 bottles in a square crate with sides of 10 units. You can do better by packing the bottles in a hexagonal array, in which case you can pack 105 as shown. But can you do even better?

089 10

124

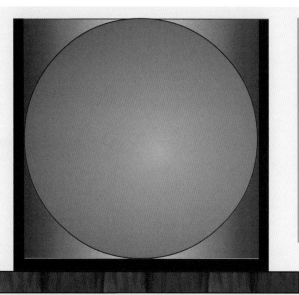

NOTES ON SPHERES

Because of its uniform curvature the sphere is considered the most perfect three-dimensional form. We began life as simple, floating spheres. Our own spherical origin echoes the starting shape from which virtually all living things emerge. A sphere, or ball, is perhaps the most basic symmetrical solid shape that one can imagine. It has no corners or edge. Every spot on the outside of a ball is exactly the same distance from the center as every other spot.

The sphere appears to reign as dominant shape on the astronomical scale and the atomic infinitesimal scale as well. Stars and planets are subject to the constant pull of their own gravity, which makes them to take on nearly spherical shapes. This fact is visualized to astronauts in orbit when any spilled liquid quickly forms into little floating balls.

SPHERE-CYLINDER VOLUME AND SURFACE AREAS

You have a thin-walled glass sphere filled with water fitting exactly into a cylindrical box, the width and height of which match the diameter of the sphere. If you break the glass sphere and pour the water into the cylinder, how much of the cylinder's volume will be filled with water? Which object has more surface area, the sphere or the cylinder?

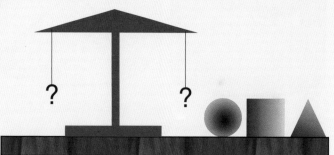

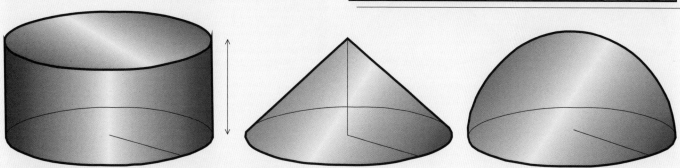

SPHERE CYLINDER CONE VOLUMES

We can see a cylinder, cone, and a hemisphere of identical heights and widths. Can you guess the relationships of their volumes and surface areas?

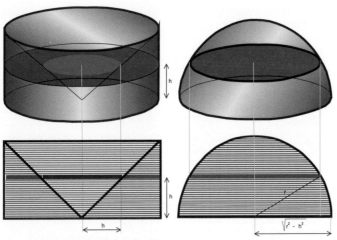

Area of the red rings = $\pi (r^2 - h^2)$ = Area of the red circles = $\pi (r2 - h2)$

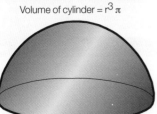

Volume of cylinder = $r^3 \pi$

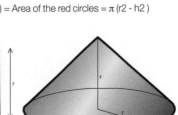

Volume of cone = $1/3\, r^3 \pi$

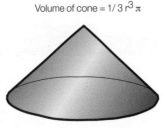

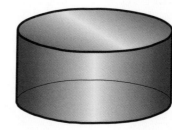

Volume of hemisphere = Volume of cylinder - Volume of cone = $r^3 \pi - 1/3\, r^3 \pi = 2/3\, r^3 \pi$

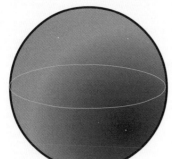

Volume of sphere = 2 volumes of hemisphere = $4/3\, r^3 \pi$

SPHERE CYLINDER CONE 2 VOLUMES

The area of the red rings in the cylinder is the same as the area of the red circle in the hemisphere. Cavalieri's principle (on the next page) helps us to conclude that the hemisphere and the cylinder minus the cone have the same volume. Archimedes proved that the volume of a sphere is two-thirds that of the smallest cylinder containing it, and that its surface area is the same as that of the hollow cylinder. He considered his discovery of these relationships as one of his greatest accomplishments.

CAVALIERI'S PRINCIPLE

Bonaventura Francesco Cavalieri (1598–1647) was an Italian mathematician and a student of Galileo. He discovered what became known as Cavalieri's principle, which states that if two solids have the same height and, if their cross sections are parallel and at equal distances from their bases are always equal, then the two solids have the same volume.

Cavalieri's principle works with plane figures as well as three-dimensional ones as demonstrated below. The basic principle was originally invented by Zu Changzhi, a Chinese astronomer (429–500), but Cavalieri developed the method which was a significant step towards establishing the basic idea of integral calculus.

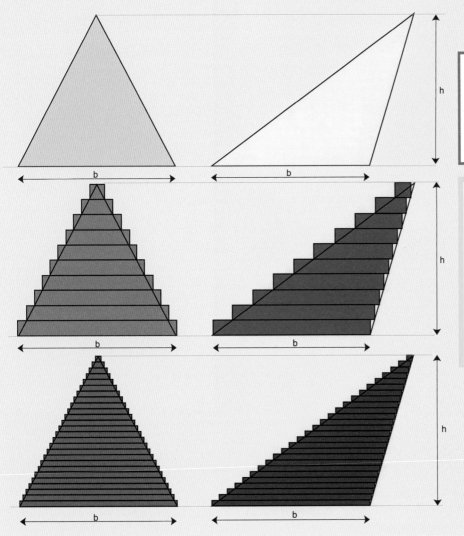

CAVALIERI'S PRINCIPLE

For two triangles

The two triangles have the same base and height. Therefore their areas are the same. Cavalieri's principle, with the triangles approximated by rectangular slices visualizes this relationship, since each rectangular slice remains the same and the slices are only shifted. By increasing the number of slices, more and more accurate approximations of the areas are obtained.

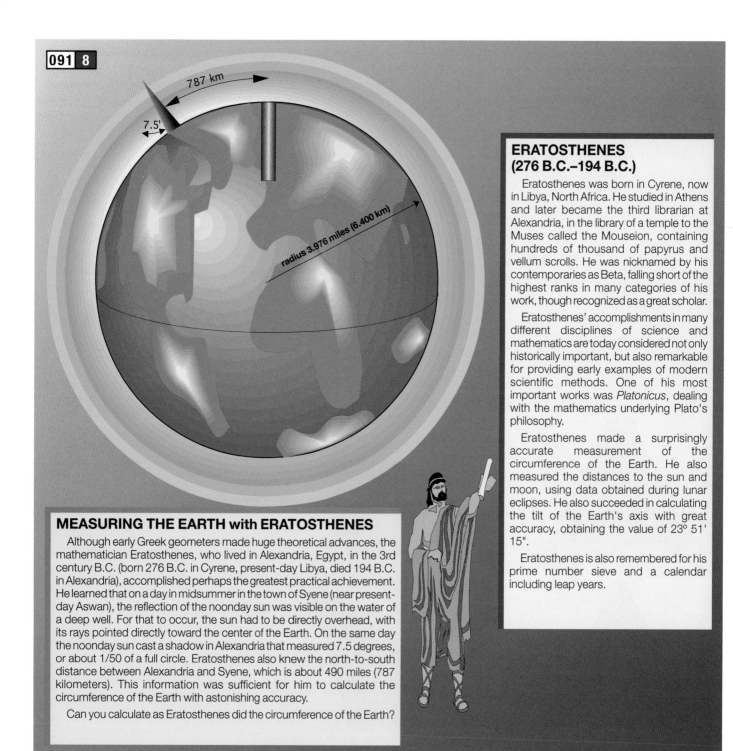

787 km

7.5'

radius 3.976 miles (6.400 km)

ERATOSTHENES (276 B.C.–194 B.C.)

Eratosthenes was born in Cyrene, now in Libya, North Africa. He studied in Athens and later became the third librarian at Alexandria, in the library of a temple to the Muses called the Mouseion, containing hundreds of thousand of papyrus and vellum scrolls. He was nicknamed by his contemporaries as Beta, falling short of the highest ranks in many categories of his work, though recognized as a great scholar.

Eratosthenes' accomplishments in many different disciplines of science and mathematics are today considered not only historically important, but also remarkable for providing early examples of modern scientific methods. One of his most important works was *Platonicus*, dealing with the mathematics underlying Plato's philosophy.

Eratosthenes made a surprisingly accurate measurement of the circumference of the Earth. He also measured the distances to the sun and moon, using data obtained during lunar eclipses. He also succeeded in calculating the tilt of the Earth's axis with great accuracy, obtaining the value of 23° 51' 15".

Eratosthenes is also remembered for his prime number sieve and a calendar including leap years.

MEASURING THE EARTH with ERATOSTHENES

Although early Greek geometers made huge theoretical advances, the mathematician Eratosthenes, who lived in Alexandria, Egypt, in the 3rd century B.C. (born 276 B.C. in Cyrene, present-day Libya, died 194 B.C. in Alexandria), accomplished perhaps the greatest practical achievement. He learned that on a day in midsummer in the town of Syene (near present-day Aswan), the reflection of the noonday sun was visible on the water of a deep well. For that to occur, the sun had to be directly overhead, with its rays pointed directly toward the center of the Earth. On the same day the noonday sun cast a shadow in Alexandria that measured 7.5 degrees, or about 1/50 of a full circle. Eratosthenes also knew the north-to-south distance between Alexandria and Syene, which is about 490 miles (787 kilometers). This information was sufficient for him to calculate the circumference of the Earth with astonishing accuracy.

Can you calculate as Eratosthenes did the circumference of the Earth?

ROPE AROUND THE EARTH

One of the most amazing and counterintuitive paradoxes is the "Rope around the Earth" puzzle created by Ernest Dudeney. For this puzzle we shall assume the Earth is a perfectly smooth sphere and the equator is exactly 40,000 kilometers. A rope is placed around the equator forming a closed, circular loop. Then the rope is cut and exactly one meter of rope is added and closed again in a loose loop this time. Let's now imagine lifting the rope all around the Earth so that it is again forming a perfect closed circle, which is everywhere at an equal distance from the surface of Earth. How far will the rope be from the surface of the Earth?

$\sqrt{R^2 - 3^2}$

R-3

3 R

6

HOLE IN A SPHERE PARADOX

Marilyn vos Savant, famous from her Monty Hall problem in her "Ask Marilyn" column in Parade magazine, reported this challenging problem. If you bore a perfect 6-inch long cylindrical hole through the center of a 6-inch diameter solid sphere, what is the volume of the remaining sphere? To bore a 6-inch long hole in a much bigger sphere you must have a very thick drill which will remove two caps of the sphere and a big part of its volume, leaving only a curved cylindrical ring, like a napkin-ring. The accompanying drawings may give you visual clues to the answer. Now imagine that a giant drill bores a 6-inch hole through the Earth? What will be left of it?

COCKTAIL AT LARGE

Visually estimate, but do not calculate, which is greater, the circumference of the cocktail glass or its height?

REULEAUX TRIANGLE

Curves of Constant Width

Which plane figure has the smallest possible area for a given diameter? Is it the circle?

The circle has a constant width, which is its diameter. Are there other curves than the circle that have the same property, i.e. *curves of constant width*?

Such a figure can easily be constructed. Draw an equilateral triangle. Then, with each of the three corners as centers, draw the circular arc passing through the other two corners. You obtain a curve named the Reuleaux Triangle, named for the man who discovered it in 1875. The width of this curve in every direction is equal to the side of the equilateral triangle or, the distance across from the triangle's vertex to the opposite arc. This is also the distance between two parallel lines tangent to the figure, which will stay the same as the curves revolve, One of the many astonishing properties of the Reuleaux triangle is that its ratio of the perimeter to its width is also equal to pi as with the circle.

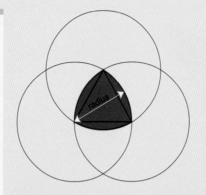

REULEAUX TRIANGLE

The triangular curved shape (a Reuleaux triangle) is revolving inside the fixed square frame. A point on its circumference will describe a near-perfect square. No wonder the shape has been used for a patented drill boring square holes.

REULEAUX POLYGONS

The three cocktail glasses stand on a horizontal platform resting on three wheels, one of which is a circle and the other two irregular shapes as shown. What will happen to the glasses when the platform starts moving and the three wheels start to turn?

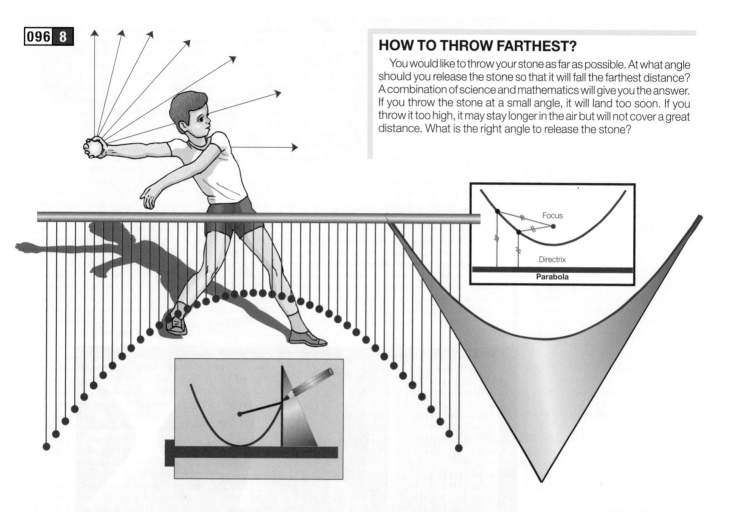

HOW TO THROW FARTHEST?

You would like to throw your stone as far as possible. At what angle should you release the stone so that it will fall the farthest distance? A combination of science and mathematics will give you the answer. If you throw the stone at a small angle, it will land too soon. If you throw it too high, it may stay longer in the air but will not cover a great distance. What is the right angle to release the stone?

Focus

Directrix

Parabola

PARABOLA

The suspended weights hanging from the horizontal rod are forming a parabola, a curve which is one of the conic sections. The parabola is a limit between ellipse and hyperbola. What will be the shape of the curve formed by the suspended weights when the angle of the rod changes to 20 degrees to the horizontal?

A parabola is defined as the path or locus of a point which moves so its distances from a fixed point (focus) and a fixed line (directrix) are equal. Using this definition, one of the ways of drawing a parabola is using a T-square, triangle, tacks, and a pieces of string. The string is the same length as the vertical side of the triangle and is tacked to the focus and the triangle. Placing the pen against the string and

keeping it against the triangle as the triangle is sliding along the T-square, which is the directrix, the pen will draw a parabola as shown. A parabola can be drawn as the envelope of two lines by connecting opposite points by straight lines as shown.

A parabola is one of the curves found in nature. It is the trajectory of a body in motion under the influence of gravity, as discovered by Galileo in the 17th century and later proven by Newton. When we throw a ball in the air its path follows a parabola. A spout of water takes the same shape. A parabola's shape has some interesting physical properties making it ideal for mirror reflectors in headlights, dishes of radiotelescopes, and for the shape of whispering galleries.

HYPERBOLIC PARABOLOID

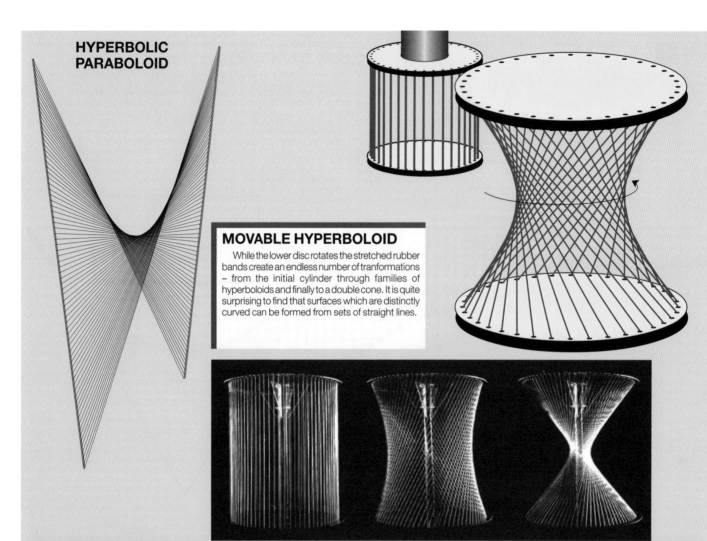

MOVABLE HYPERBOLOID

While the lower disc rotates the stretched rubber bands create an endless number of tranformations – from the initial cylinder through families of hyperboloids and finally to a double cone. It is quite surprising to find that surfaces which are distinctly curved can be formed from sets of straight lines.

BEAUTIFUL SURFACES

Ruled Surfaces

Many complex three-dimensional surfaces can be often created by simple constructional methods. A group of such surfaces are called ruled surfaces, or saddle surfaces, because they can be formed by families of straight lines. The geometry of ruled surfaces was named "hyperbolic" by Klein in 1871. The sum of angles of triangles in such surfaces always add up to less than 180 degrees. If the triangles are very small, then its angles are nearly two right angles.

A surface is a geometric magnitude having no dimensions. A **ruled surface** is one which can be generated by a straight line, which moves. A ruled surface may be a plane, a **single curved** (developable) surface or a **warped** (not developable) surface. A cylinder, for example, is a ruled surface of parallel straight lines. A **hyperbolic paraboloid** Is a ruled surface in which all sections parallel to one coordinate plane are hyperbolas and all sections parallel to another coordinate plane are parabolas. It is a surface shaped like a saddle made from a set of straight lines, using a simple method of curve stitching in space as shown.

A **hyperboloid** may be generated by revolving a parabola about its axis, or by revolving a straight line about another straight line so located that the two lines are not in the same plane. The hyperboloid falls into both categories: that of surfaces of revolution and of warped surfaces. The hyperboloid cannot really be appreciated, fully understood and admired, until we can see it from all possible angles. The stretched rubber strings forming the surface demonstrate convincingly that the surface elements are straight lines and that the surface is generated by revolving a properly oriented line about an axis.

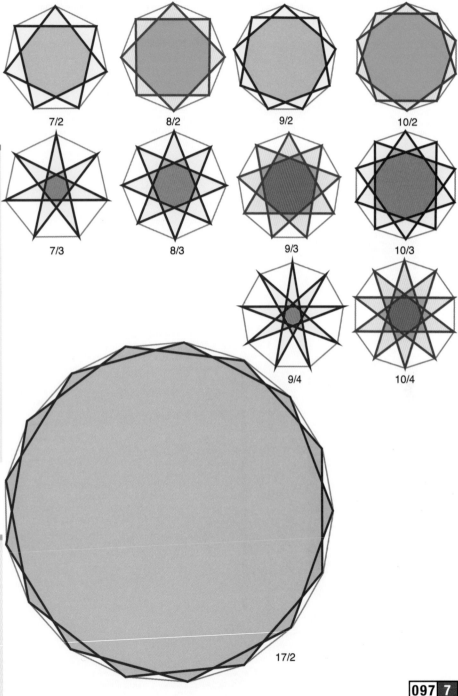

5/2 6/2 7/2 8/2 9/2 10/2

7/3 8/3 9/3 10/3

9/4 10/4

17/2

REGULAR STAR POLYGONS

Regular polygons and star polygons can be subdivided into the following subgroups:

1. **Simple regular polygons:** convex polygons with all their diagonals inside the polygon.

2. **Regular star polygons:** non-convex polygons, whose sides are diagonals of the convex polygons.

3. **Regular star figures:** or compound polygons of identical regular polygons.

Star polygons have featured in art since antiquity. We have already seen the pentagram with its association with the golden ratio, which was given occult significance by Pythagoras and his followers. A regular star polygon is a self-intersecting equilateral equiangular polygon.

A star polygon is created by connecting one vertex of an n-sided regular polygon to another non-adjacent vertex and continuing until the initial vertex is reached again: n is the number of sides of the regular polygons and x is the number of steps to be repeated. The Schlafli symbol n/x denotes a star polygon.

STAR HEPTADECAGONS

How many regular star polygons and star figures (compound polygons) can you find in a regular heptadecagon? The first star heptadecagon Fig. 17/2 is shown.

At age 19 Gauss discovered a beautiful construction of a 17-sided regular polygon using only a compass and straightedge, and it is said this convinced him to devote his life to mathematics, which was a fortunate decision for the the future of the science.

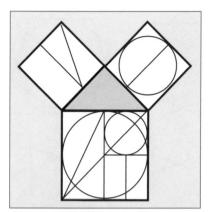

the structure: The Pythagorean Theorem

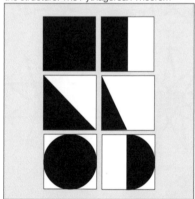

the six shapes

the three sizes and colors

SHAPE FAMILY UNIVERSE
A Pythagorean world of fun

"Family of Shape" is a program for pre-school and primary school children.

My experience has convinced me that through play, fun, and simple guided games and visual activities, very young children can discover for themselves many of the basic ideas underlying all later school mathematics. I have devised the "Family of Shape" programme to provide children and their nursery school teachers the ideas' materials for them.

It is designed mainly for children in nursery schools, continuing into the first two years at infant schools, or first schools. But its usefulness does not end there. In one inner-city New York school, it has been welcomed enthusiastically and used by children all the way up to sixth grade (age 11). It was extensively used in Leicestershire primary schools, in nursery schools in France, the Middle East, Greece, etc.

In general, children when given a choice of activity have consistently demanded to work with SHAPE FAMILY materials even though they had a vast range of other materials at their disposal.

Its aim is to help children begin to absorb math just as they begin to absorb their mother tongue: by meeting it as an essential and all-pervading part of their environment. In the home the very young child may never heard of grammar and syntax, verbs and nouns, adverbs and adjectives, phrases and sentences. Yet well before he or she begins schools he can speak to make himself understood and hear with understanding.

Similarly, in using the abstract Shape Family universe in his formative years, he need never hear of geometry and arithmetic, scalene triangles and isosceles triangles, proportions and ratios, mathematical demonstrations and mathematical proofs. Yet before his formal schooling begins he will have met with all these things. And he will have laid a firm foundation for his future mathematical education.

(The "Family of Shape" program was produced by Invicta Plastics in collaboration with Aldus House (Doubleday) publishing, during the seventies and eightees.)

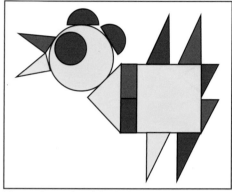

16-part, three-color minimal solution

30-part, three-color maximal solution

20-part, two-color solution

THE SHAPE FAMILY UNIVERSE

Concept and images
copyright © Ivan Moscovich

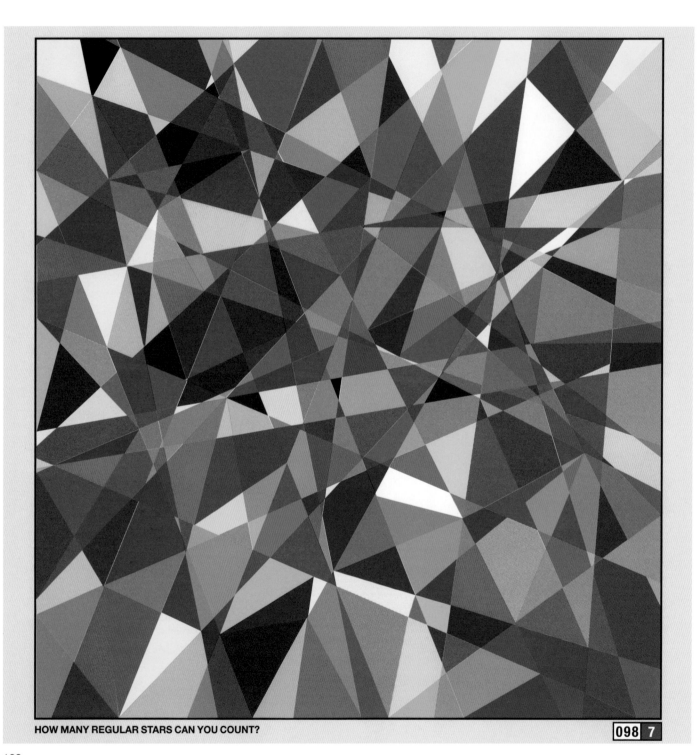

HOW MANY REGULAR STARS CAN YOU COUNT?

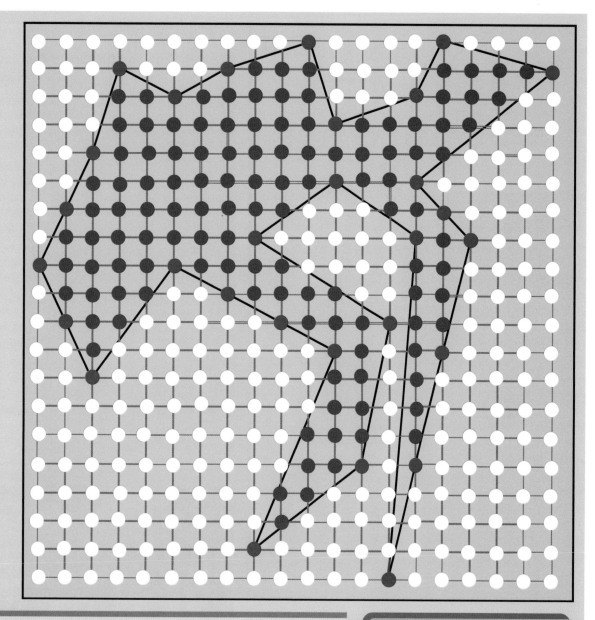

PICK'S THEOREM

Pick's theorem provides an elegant formula for finding the area of simple lattice polygons (polygons without self-intersection). Such polygons have their vertices at points of a square grid lattice, in which the points are spaced at unit distances.

In the square grid lattice the lattice polygon is shown with its vertices in red. Can you work out what is the area of the enclosed polygon in unit squares?

Georg Pick (1859–1943) was born in Vienna. He was killed in the Theresianstadt concentration camp.

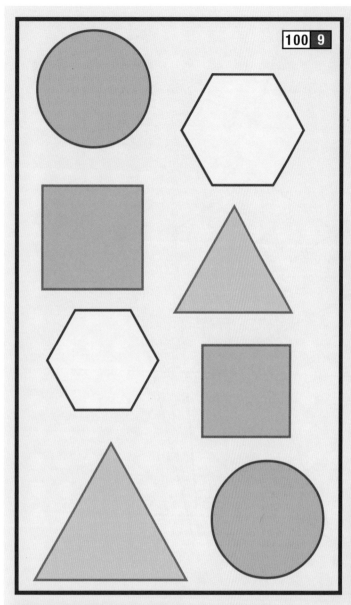

AREA–PERIMETER

Queen Dido and the Island Problem

When a closed line or curve on a piece of paper defines space, they define area, which is two-dimensional space. But even the paper has depth and so a flat piece of paper is really a surface. Beneath a surface is a volume, which is three-dimensional space. The outline of the shape is called the perimeter.

The 5th-century Greek writer Proclus wrote that some landowners estimated land values on their perimeter not on area. How wrong they were! One of the most beautiful ancient stories related to the concepts of area and perimeter is the story of Queen Dido and the foundation of Carthage, called today the "Island Problem," as told by the Roman poet Virgil. Queen Dido was a Phoenician princess who fled from the city of Tyre (in today's Lebanon) with her people by ship to the North African coast at a place which later became Carthage. She wanted to buy land from the local ruler so that she and her people could start a new life. She was told of the condition that she could buy only as much land as she could enclose by the skin of an ox. She, of course, wanted to make the most of this condition and with the help of her people they cut the hide in as thin strips as possible and tied their ends together to form a big closed loop. This must have been a length of about 2,000 meters. They spread this length on the ground enclosing as much area as they could.

The ancient Greeks were aware of the isoperimetric problem and of the isoperimetric property of the circle, i.e. that it is the closed plane curve enclosing the greatest area. Consequently, among all plane shapes with the same area, the circle has the shortest perimeter.

EQUAL AREAS AND PERIMETERS

One set of the four shapes (circle, square, triangle, and hexagon) all have the same areas. The other four all have the same perimeters. Can you sort out the two sets – those with equal areas and equal perimeters?

NINE-POINT CIRCLE THEOREM
Points, lines, circles, and a triangle
The nine-point circle, also called Euler's circle, is fascinating because it always passes through nine important points associated with the triangle. Let's first visualize the three triple sets of points of a triangle called Euler points, before we construct the nine-point circle.

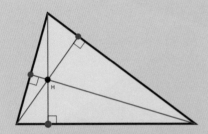

2. The second set of three points
MIDPOINTS OF THE SIDES
Using a compass the three midpoints of the sides are eaily located (Mascheroni construction). The three perpendiculars from the bisector points meet in a point which is the **circumcenter**, the center of the triangle's circumscribed circle or circumcircle, the unique circle that passes through its three vertices. Its radius is called the **circumradius**, R. Can the orthocenter be outside the triangle?

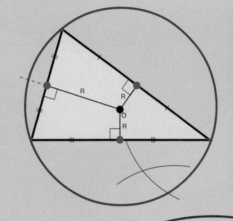

1. The first set of three points
BASES OF THE ALTITUDES
Take a triangle and draw from its three vertices perpendiculars to the opposite sides. Each of the three points on the sides is called a **perpendicular foot**, and the lengths of the lines are the altitudes of the triangle. The three **altitudes** meet in a point called the orthocenter. Can the **orthocenter** be outside the triangle?

101 8

NINE-POINT CIRCLE
The beauty of the nine-point circle of a triangle is that it always passes through the three triplet points. The center of the nine-point circle is called the Kimberling center, and it is the midpoint of the line between the circumcenter and the orthocenter.

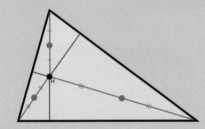

3. The third set of three points
MIDPOINTS FROM VERTICES TO ORTHOCENTER
The last set of triple points are inside the triangle, at midpoints of the segments that join the vertices and the orthocenter. Can the orthocenter be outside the triangle?

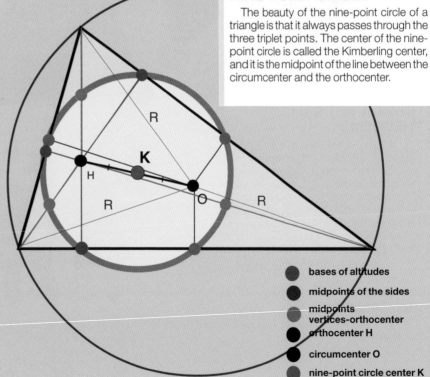

● bases of altitudes
● midpoints of the sides
● midpoints vertices-orthocenter
● orthocenter H
● circumcenter O
● nine-point circle center K

CHVATAL ART GALLERY THEOREM

In this strangely shaped art gallery consisting of 25 walls, revolving security cameras were installed at every corner. In the example shown, 24 cameras (red dots) have been installed. However, cameras are expensive to install and maintain. What is the minimum number of cameras required so that every square inch of the gallery is covered by at least one camera?

ART GALLERY

Another art gallery has 14 walls and several revolving security cameras. What shape should the gallery be for one single revolving security camera to be able to cover every square inch of the area?

TRISECTION

Remember, the ancient Greeks introduced problems that require figures to be constructed by the use of compass and straightedge alone (s. page 30). Three famous problems left by them resisted the efforts of many mathematicians over the centuries to solve them.

Duplicating the cube (constructing a cube double the volume of a given smaller cube).
Squaring the circle (constructing a square equal in area to a given circle) and
Trisecting the angle (dividing a given angle into three equal parts).
None of these problems are solvable by using a compass and unmarked straightedge.

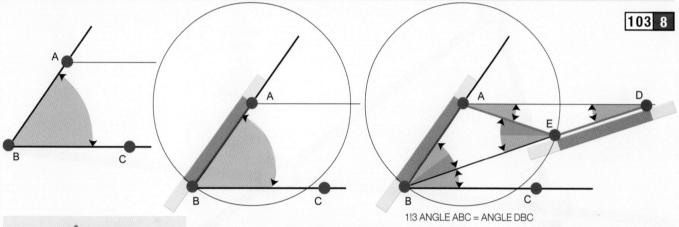

1!3 ANGLE ABC = ANGLE DBC

ANGLE TRISECTION

It *is* possible to trisect an angle, just not with a compass and a straightedge, which was proven by Wantzel in 1836. The simplest method is using a *marked* straightedge (Archimedes' trisection) visualized above There are many other methods as well. The angle trisection protractor shown at left is a linkage mechanism which can be designed using a compass and a straightedge and can be used to trisect a given angle or, in fact, triple one.

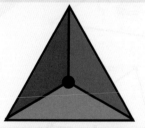

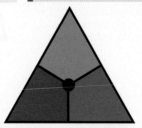

TRISECTING TRIANGLE

It is easy to trisect an equilateral triangle into three identical parts as shown above. It is more difficult to find the smallest number of pieces into which you can dissect an equilateral triangle with straight lines which can be put together to create three identical shapes, when the cuts may not pass through the center of the triangle.

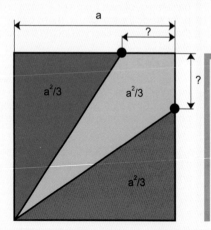

a

?

?

$a^2/3$ $a^2/3$

$a^2/3$

TRISECTING SQUARE AREA

The two lines trisect the square area into three parts of identical areas. Where whould the two points have to be placed to achieve such a dissection?

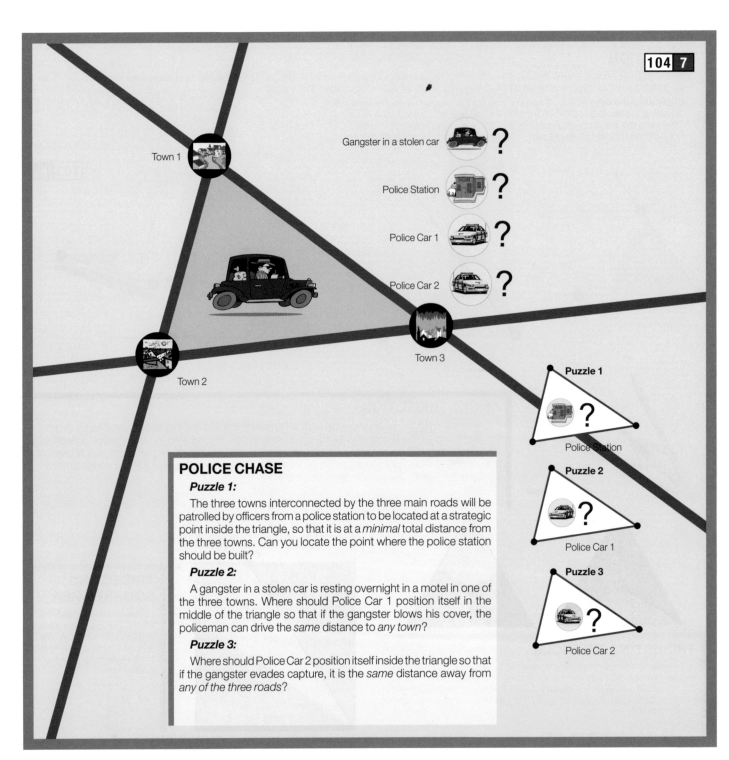

Town 1

Town 2

Town 3

Gangster in a stolen car ?

Police Station ?

Police Car 1 ?

Police Car 2 ?

Puzzle 1
Police Station

Puzzle 2
Police Car 1

Puzzle 3
Police Car 2

POLICE CHASE

Puzzle 1:
The three towns interconnected by the three main roads will be patrolled by officers from a police station to be located at a strategic point inside the triangle, so that it is at a *minimal* total distance from the three towns. Can you locate the point where the police station should be built?

Puzzle 2:
A gangster in a stolen car is resting overnight in a motel in one of the three towns. Where should Police Car 1 position itself in the middle of the triangle so that if the gangster blows his cover, the policeman can drive the *same* distance to *any town*?

Puzzle 3:
Where should Police Car 2 position itself inside the triangle so that if the gangster evades capture, it is the *same* distance away from *any of the three roads*?

MANDALA

Pythagoras described geometry as **visual music**. **Visual harmony** can be created by applying **angle** and **shape** combined in ways that are in unison with universal laws of mathematics. Mandalas are geometrical designs made through uniform divisions of the circle, which have for thousands of years evoked the relations of form, movement, space, and time – as visual representations of the universe and creation. Mandalas symbolize an expanded way of thinking, transcending language and the rational mind.

The word **mandala** comes from the Sanskrit and means **sacred circle**. The most famous and revered of all the Hindu madalas is the **Shri Yantra**, or **Yantra of Creation**, an ancient symbol of the universe. It has a deep mathematical beauty that arises from the nine diverse interlocking triangles creating 43 smaller triangles that define the Shri Yantra.

MANDALA
Puzzle 1

The 9 overlapping triangles create 43 smaller triangles of different sizes. The nine triangles are numbered and co-lored according to their orientation and size. In what con-secutive order must the triangles be removed one by one to create the quick-est descending se-quence of all the remaining red trian-gles?

To achieve this must all the 9 tri-angles be removed?

Puzzle 2

How many trian-gles of all sizes are there altogether if you include combi-nations of red and white shapes?

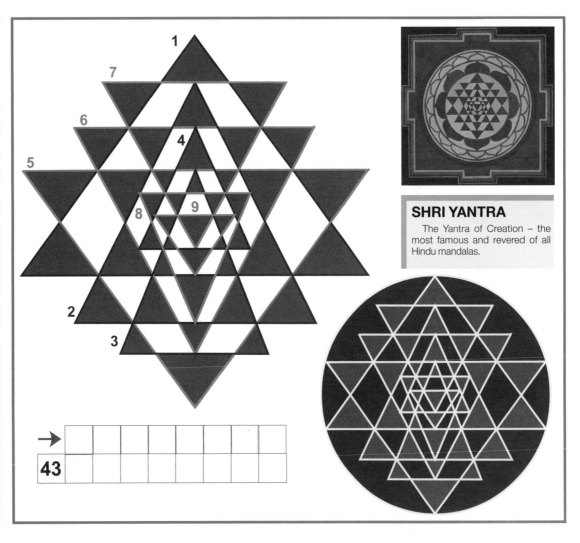

SHRI YANTRA

The Yantra of Creation – the most famous and revered of all Hindu mandalas.

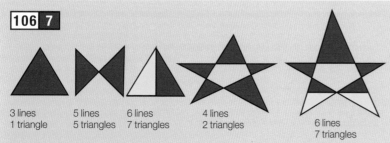

3 lines
1 triangle

5 lines
5 triangles

6 lines
7 triangles

4 lines
2 triangles

6 lines
7 triangles

lines "n" 3 4 5 6 7 8 9 10 11 12 13 14 15 16
triangles 1 2 5 7 11 15 21 25 32 38 47 ? 65 ?

KOBON TRIANGLES

The Kobon triangles combinatorial problem was invented by Kobon Fujimura, a Japanese teacher and puzzle inventor, who posed the question: "What is the largest number of non-overlapping triangles that can be created by n straight line segments in the plane?"

For n = 3, 4, 5, and 6 lines, the maximum number of triangles is 1, 2, 5, and 7 as shown above. The maximum number of non-overlapping triangles for 7, 8, and 9 lines are 11, 15, and 21 respectively, as shown below.

Edd Pegg, Jr. on his MathPuzzle site reported great progress on the problem, among the solutions, Toshitaka'a Suzuki's beautiful 15 lines and 65 triangles solution. The problem becomes very difficult for a greater number of lines, and no general solution has yet been found.

How would the solutions to the Kobon Triangles shown look if we introduced the restriction that the lines must be drawn as a single continuous broken line?

KOBON TRIANGLES

The Seven-Line Problem

An eleven-triangle solution

KOBON TRIANGLES

The Eight-Line Problem

A fifteen-triangle solution

KOBON TRIANGLES

The Nine-Line Problem

A twenty-one-triangle solution

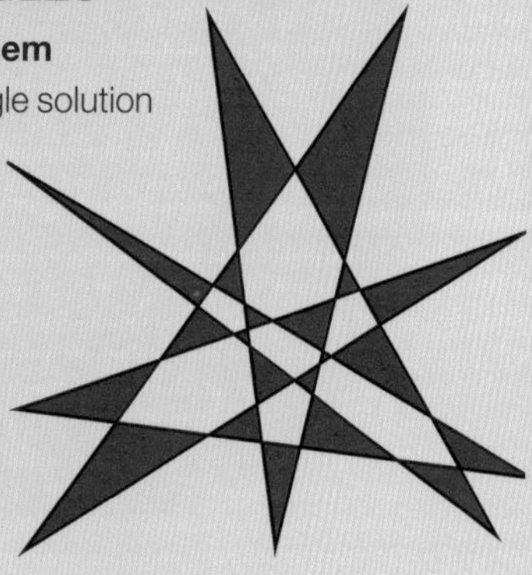

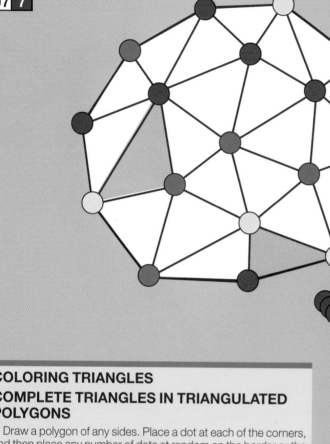

complete triangle

a
b
c

COLORING TRIANGLES
COMPLETE TRIANGLES IN TRIANGULATED POLYGONS

Draw a polygon of any sides. Place a dot at each of the corners, and then place any number of dots at random on the border or the inside. Then, using the dots as corners, divide the polygon into non-overlapping triangles and label their corners in any way, using three colors, red, blue, and yellow.

Coloring the triangles this way there can be ten different types of triangles as shown above. A triangle having at their vertices all three colors is a **complete triangle**. An edge in two colors (red and blue) is a complete edge. In the triangulated polygon above there are two **complete** triangles (having at their vertices three different colors – red-blue-yellow).

We have the same polygon as above only with its boundary vertices colored as before. Can you color the remaining vertices so to have only one complete triangle using any of the trhee colors? Can you color all the vertices of the triangles so as to avoid any complete triangles?

Leaving the borders as they are you can subdivide the inside differently as you wish and try again to solve the problems.

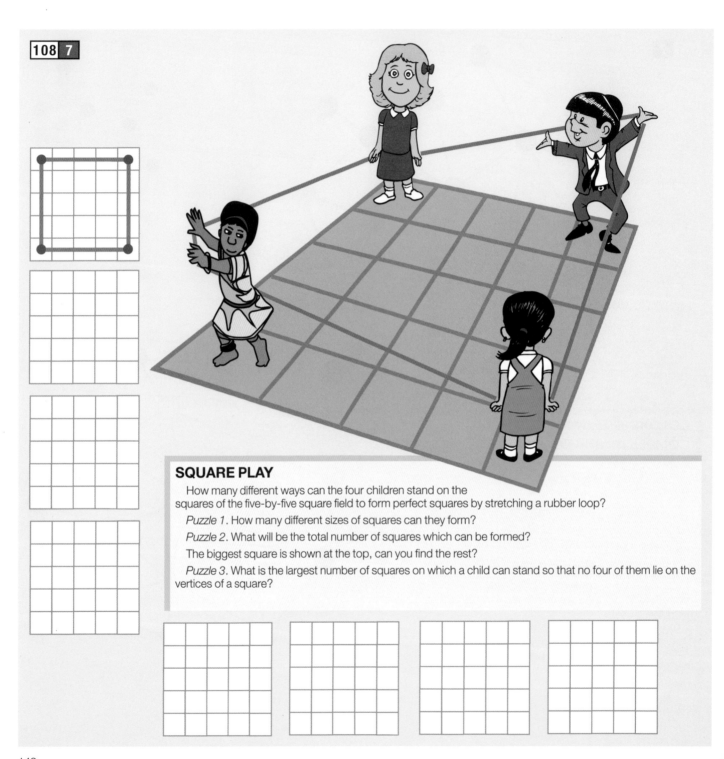

SQUARE PLAY

How many different ways can the four children stand on the squares of the five-by-five square field to form perfect squares by stretching a rubber loop?

Puzzle 1. How many different sizes of squares can they form?

Puzzle 2. What will be the total number of squares which can be formed?

The biggest square is shown at the top, can you find the rest?

Puzzle 3. What is the largest number of squares on which a child can stand so that no four of them lie on the vertices of a square?

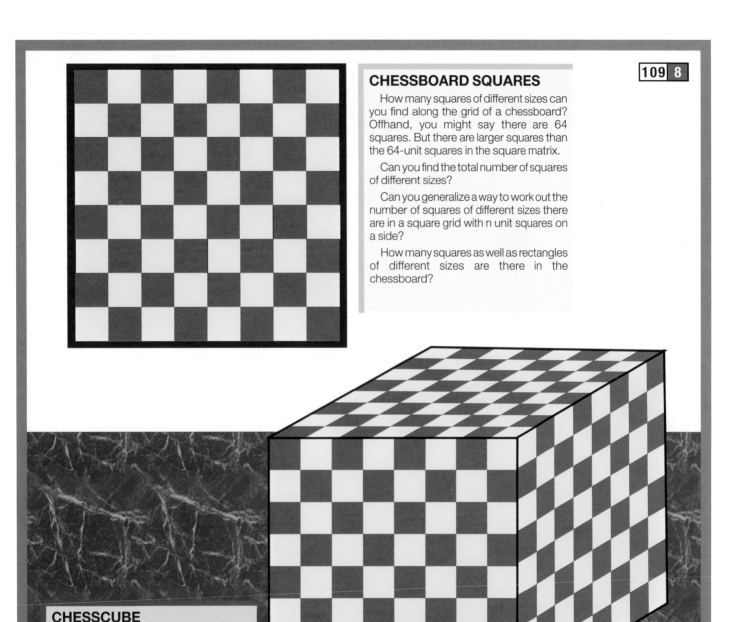

CHESSBOARD SQUARES

How many squares of different sizes can you find along the grid of a chessboard? Offhand, you might say there are 64 squares. But there are larger squares than the 64-unit squares in the square matrix.

Can you find the total number of squares of different sizes?

Can you generalize a way to work out the number of squares of different sizes there are in a square grid with n unit squares on a side?

How many squares as well as rectangles of different sizes are there in the chessboard?

CHESSCUBE

How many cubes of different sizes composed of unit cubes are there in a 3-D chesscube?

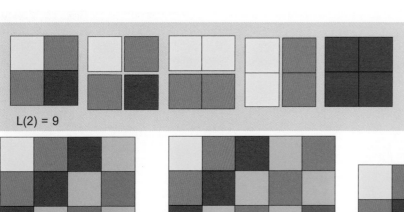

L(2) = 9

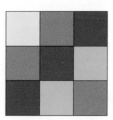

L(3) = ?

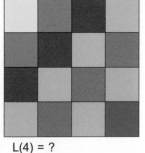

L(4) = ?

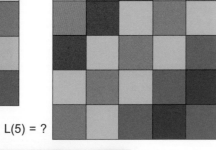

L(5) = ?

L(6) = ?

L(7) = ?

L(8) = ?

SQUARE LATTICE NUMBERS

How many squares and rectangles?

If we extend the Chessboard squares problem to include rectangles of different sizes as well, we obtain the *lattice number* for a square lattice.

Puzzle 1: Can you work out what this number L(n) is for square lattices from n=1 to n=8?

Puzzle 2: In the chessboard, an 8-by-8 square lattice, how many different sizes of squares and rectangles are there?

A SQUARE – BUT WHERE?
What color is the square?

In how many different ways can you arrange in a row the ten numbers, in which some are identical as shown.
n=10; a=1; b=2; c=3; d=4

COMBINATORIAL GEOMETRY $\boxed{112}\ \boxed{7}$

The Beauty of Combinations and Permutations–Counting made easy–Factorials

Combinatorics is a beautiful branch of mathematics and one of the oldest. Combinatorics studies the ways in which numbers and objects can be combined, grouped, ordered, and counted. It has produced many elegant and simple solutions for complex problems, as well as the oldest puzzles. Many fields of science and everyday situations depend on the principles of combinatorics, specifically on **combinations** and **permutations**. Permutations are the rearrangements of numbers or objects into ordered sequences. The number of such possible arrangements in a system may seem small at first, but possibilities rise quickly with the number of elements and soon become impossibly large. The basic instance is simplicity itself:

One object by itself can be arranged in just one way and come in just one order.

Two objects, (call them a and b) can be arranged as **ab** or **ba** for a total of two permutations.

Three objects – a,b, and c – can be arranged in six ways:

abc,   acb,   bac,   bca,   cab,   cba.

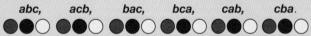

For the general case with **n** number of objects, the way to work out the permutations is to take the objects one at a time. The first object can fall at any of the n possible positions; for each of those possibilities, the second object can fall at one of *n-1* possible places (since it can't occupy the place the first object takes up); for every one of those *n(n-1)* permutations, the third object can fall in one of *n-2* places; and so on.

In general, for *n* objects there are n times as many more permutations as there are in systems with only *n-1* objects. For example, there are four times as many possible permutations in a system with four objects than there are in a system with three–in other words, 24 permutations. There are 5 x 24, or 120, different ways to arrange 5 things and 6 x 120, or 720, ways to arrange six

things. These numbers are called *factorials* and are designated with a !, as in 6!, or six factorial, which equals 720.

Therefore, the general formula for the total number of order of n things, or permutations is:

P =n! = n x (n-1) x (n-2) x (n-3) x .... 3 x 2 x 1

This number becomes very large very rapidly.

What about cases that do not deal not with ordering one group but finding the permutations of **n** things taken **k** at a time? The mathematics here is only a bit trickier. Say you wanted to know how many ordered groups of three can be made from five different elements (such as color, or letters, or something else). You would calculate:

P_k=n!/ (n-k)! = 5!/ (5-3)! = 120/2 = 60

Sometimes we are not concerned about the order of the things (permutations), but are only interested in the constitution (the number of choices) of the sample in question (combinations). A combination is a set of things chosen from a given group, when no significance is attached to the order of the things within the set.

Therefore, the general formula for the total number of combinations is:

C= n!/k!(n-k)! = 5!/3!(5-3)! = 10

which in our specific case of before would produce 10 groups of the elements in each (regardless of the order of the element in each group).

Up to this point we have been dealing with objects which are all different. Sometimes it may happen that there is a number of identical things of 'a' one sort, 'b' of another, etc. In this case the number of permutations is:

$P_{a,b,c}$ = n!/a!b!c!

Most probabilities relating to games and puzzles can be determined by counting the total number of possibilities and the number of outcomes having some desired property. The ratio of these two numbers gives the probability. The formulas for permutations and combinations facilitate and shorten the counting. The values for the number of combinations of **n** elements taken **k** at a time can be obtained from the well-known Pascal's triangle.

PERMUTATIONS, COMBINATIONS, FACTORIALS
CHARLIE'S SHELF

Charlie's shelf can hold four of his favorite toys. He has decided to change their order every morning. Can you help him to work out how many days he will need to arrange the four toys in all possible arrangements (permutations)?

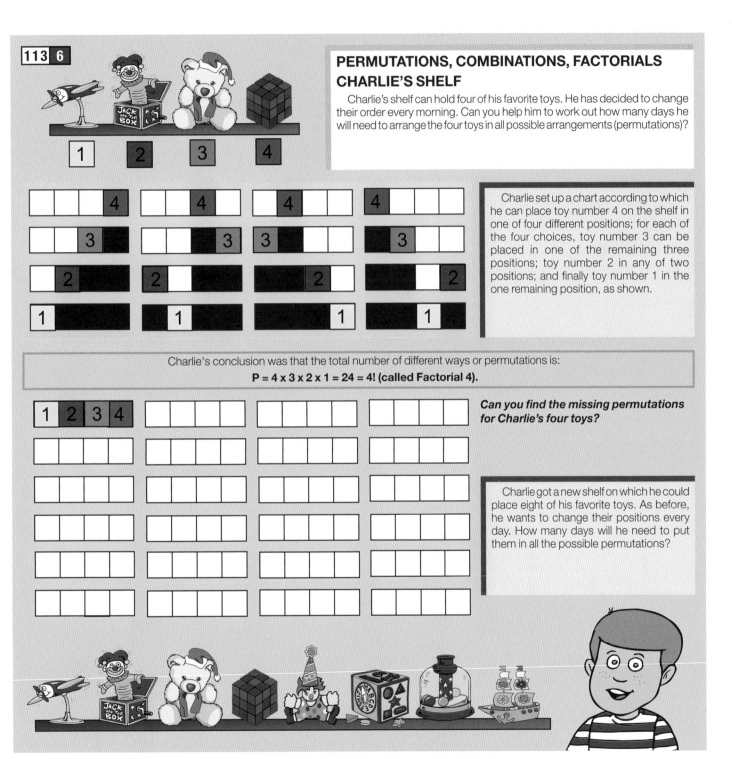

1   2   3   4

Charlie set up a chart according to which he can place toy number 4 on the shelf in one of four different positions; for each of the four choices, toy number 3 can be placed in one of the remaining three positions; toy number 2 in any of two positions; and finally toy number 1 in the one remaining position, as shown.

Charlie's conclusion was that the total number of different ways or permutations is:

P = 4 x 3 x 2 x 1 = 24 = 4! (called Factorial 4).

1 2 3 4

Can you find the missing permutations for Charlie's four toys?

Charlie got a new shelf on which he could place eight of his favorite toys. As before, he wants to change their positions every day. How many days will he need to put them in all the possible permutations?

153

(From the ancient Egyptian "Rhind Papyrus," dated 1850 BC, written by the scribe Ahmes)

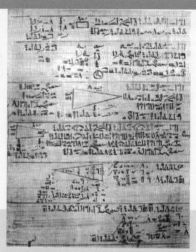

HOUSES, CATS, WHEAT, MICE

Ahmes's puzzle (one of the oldest classic combinatorial puzzles)

Seven houses each have seven cats. Each cat kills seven mice. Each of the mice would have eaten seven ears of wheat. Each ear of wheat would have produced seven unit measures of flour. How many unit measures of flour were saved by the cats?

ST. IVES RIDDLE

Ahmes's puzzle has inspired many variations, among them the St. Ives' riddle. Leonardo of Pisa (Fibonacci) in 1202, published the rhyme in his *Liber Abaci*. Did he have access to the "Rhind Papyrus"?

As I was going to St. Ives,
I faced a man with seven wives.
Every wife had seven bags.
Every bag had seven cats.
Every cat had seven kits.
Kits, cats, bags, and wives,
How many were going to St. Ives?

PIGEONHOLE PRINCIPLE

FIFTY MAILBOXES PUZZLE

The mailman delivers 151 pieces of mail to 50 mailboxes. After all the letters have been delivered, one mailbox has more letters than any other box. What is smallest number of letters it can contain?

NUMBER OF HAIRS PUZZLE

Are there two human beings alive today who have precisely the same number of hairs on their bodies?

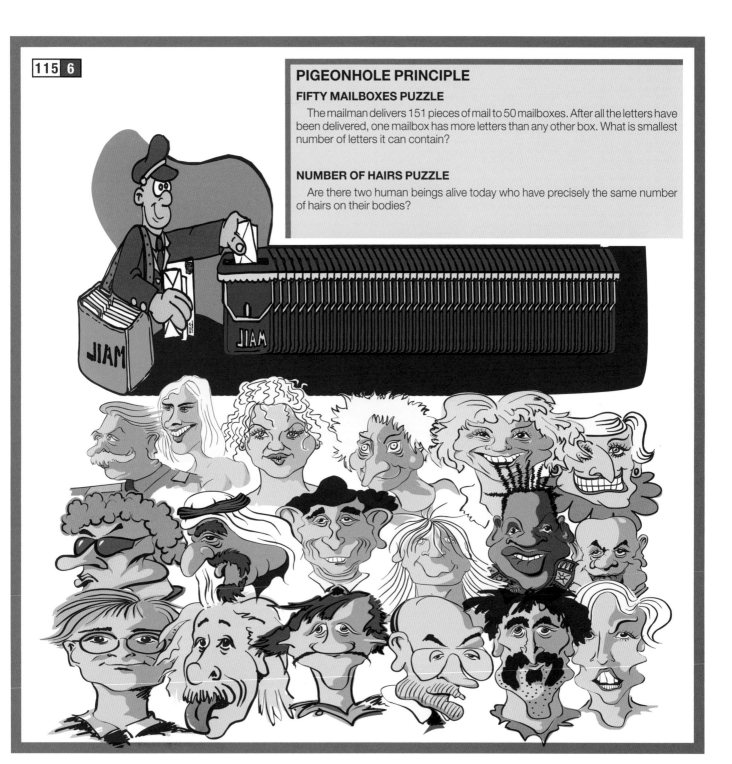

SKYDIVING

Four skydivers are practicing for the big show. Three of them, the red team, are a bit superstitious and always want to jump one after the other. In how many different ways can the four skydivers jump from the plane?

Roman portrait bust, said to be of Flavius Josephus (from *Les Dossiers d'Archeologie*, 2001)

JOSEPHUS' PUZZLE

Flavius Josephus, famous historian, soldier and scholar decided to solve a puzzle to save his life, so the legend says. He was defending the city of Jotaphat, which fell to the Roman general, Vespasian. Josephus and his fighters hid in a cave and decided to commit suicide rather than surrender. This moment of history is the topic of the Josephus' Puzzle, ascribed to him. The group of 41 zealots, including Josephus, agreed to form a circle, and starting from a fixed position every third man counted would be killed, until only one man remained alive, who would then kill himself. Was it pure luck or divine intervention that Josephus was the last man remaining alive? Or did Josephus want to stay alive and was he able to figure out where to place himself when the counting began?

What position in the red circle below had to be occupied by Josephus?

Suppose Josephus wanted to save the lives of his five best friends as well. Where should he place them?

Where would you choose to stand in a circle of 30 people in a similar count in which every ninth person was eliminated (blue circle below)? What about in a circle of 50 people, in which every seventh person was eliminated (yellow circle below)?

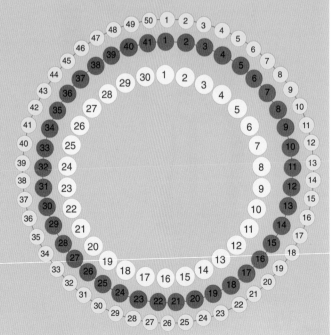

The Josephus problem or Josephus permutation problem is a theoretical problem occurring in computer science, recreational mathematics, and mathematics in general. It was studied by many great mathematicians, including Leonhard Euler, but the mathematical formula for solving such problems has not yet been found. General solutions are still achieved by trial-and-error...

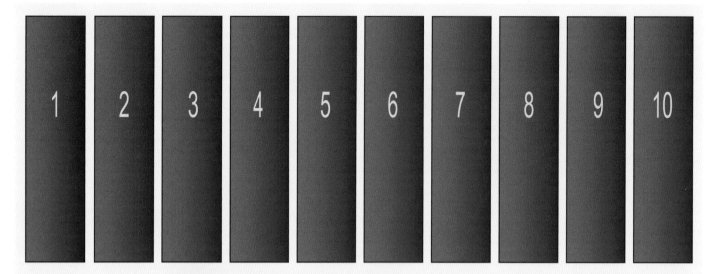

HOTEL DOORS

Ten hotel doors are numbered from 1 to 10; all are closed. The cleaning lady walks by and opens every door. Then a second cleaning lady walks by and closes all the even-numbered doors. Then the repairman walks by and changes the state of every door whose number is a multiple of three. Then another person changes the state of every door whose number is a multiple of four, and so on, until ten people have walked by. Which doors will be open after the tenth person has walked by? Can you also give an intelligent guess as to which doors would be open at the end if there were 100 doors involved in the same procedure?

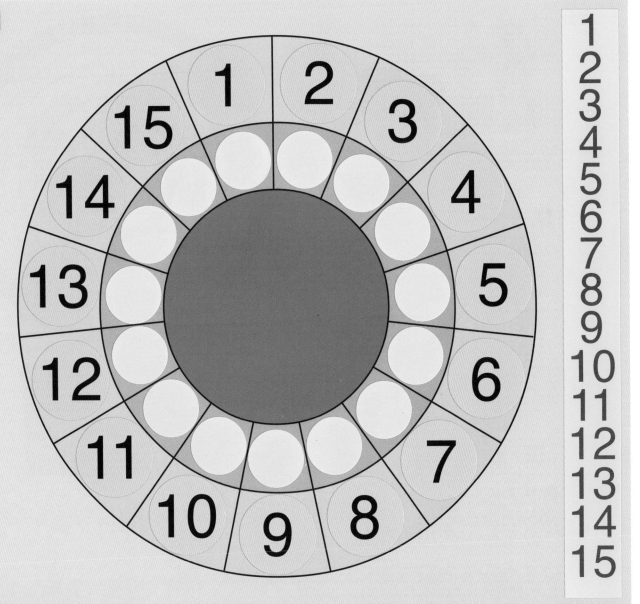

1
2
3
4
5
6
7
8
9
10
11
12
13
14
15

NUMBER CAROUSEL

Fifteen numbers are evenly distributed on the outer carousel as shown. Can you distribute the same numbers in the inner carousel, so that no matter how you revolve the inner carousel, there will always be only one single pair of identical numbers next to each other along any radial line?

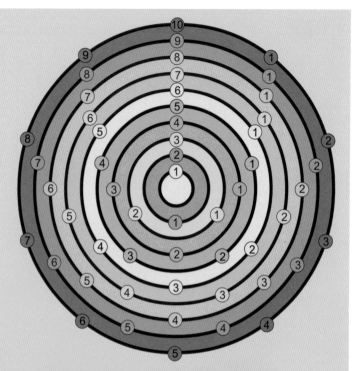

CIRCULAR PERMUTATIONS AND KNIGHTS OF THE ROUND TABLE

There are many problems in recreational mathematics that involve seating arrangements of people, knights, and couples around round tables.

The basic problem asks for the number of different possible arrangements of "n" things distributed along the circumference of a circle.

Can you work out the number of different circular permutations for n, from 1 to 10 as compared to regular linear permutations?

Puzzle 1- What is the number of different **fixed circular permutations**, when the circles are not allowed to be taken out of the plane and flipped over?

Puzzle 2- What is the number of **free circular permutations**, when flipping over is allowed?

n	1	2	3	4	5	6	7	8	9	10	
	1	2	6	24	120	720	5040	40320	362880	3638800	n!

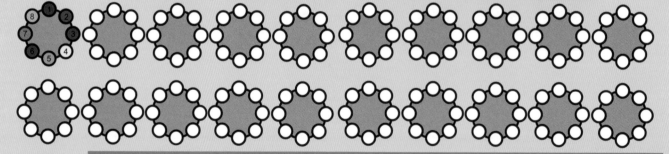

KNIGHTS OF THE ROUND TABLE

What are the different ways eight knights can be seated around the round table so that no one has the same two neighbors more than just once? One arrangement is shown with the knights numbered from 1 to 8. This is not an easy combinatorial problem. There are 21 different arrangements. How many can you identify?

SOCKS IN THE DARK

LOST SOCKS

Imagine you had ten pairs of socks and, as it usually happens, you discover six socks are lost.

The question is, what is more likely:

1. In the best possible scenario, the six lost socks constitute three complete pairs, and you are left with 7 complete pairs?; or

2. In the worst possible scenario, the six lost socks are single socks, in which case you are left with only four complete pairs and six single socks?

MURPHY'S LAW

Edward Murphy stated: "Anything that can go wrong, will, and at the worst possible times".

SOCKS IN THE DARK

In the drawer you have six red, eight yellow, and ten green socks. In complete darkness, how many socks must you pick out to ensure to get a pair of any color?

And how many must you pick out in order to have pair of each color?

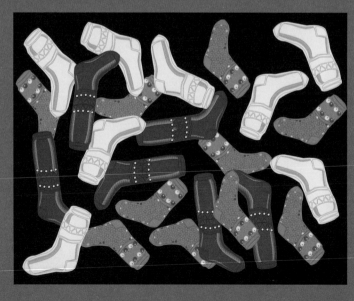

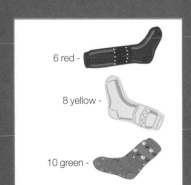

6 red -

8 yellow -

10 green -

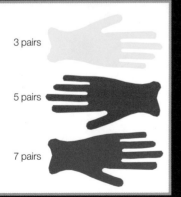

3 pairs

5 pairs

7 pairs

GLOVES IN THE DARK

In the drawer you have three pairs of yellow gloves, five pairs of red gloves, and four pairs of blue gloves.

In complete darkness, how many gloves do you have to draw to ensure to have a complete pair of gloves in one of the colors and proper handedness?

GIRLS AND BOYS IN A ROW

In how many ways can six boys and six girls line up in a row of six so that in as many lines as possible, there is a girl next to at least one other girl and no girl is alone? Any combination is permitted, including all girls.

There are 21 different ways for them to line up. Can you find all the different possible patterns?

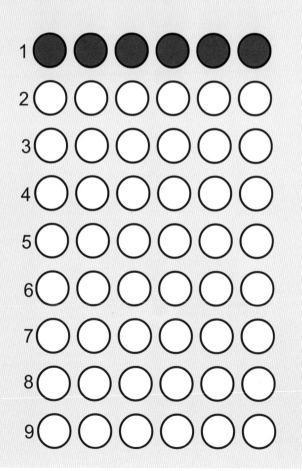

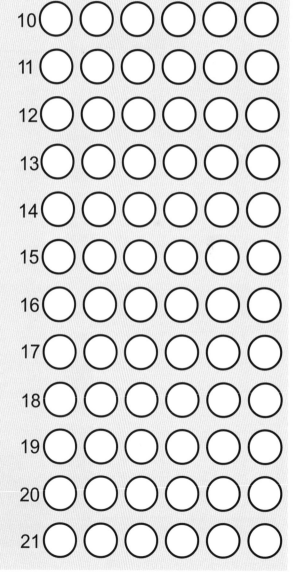

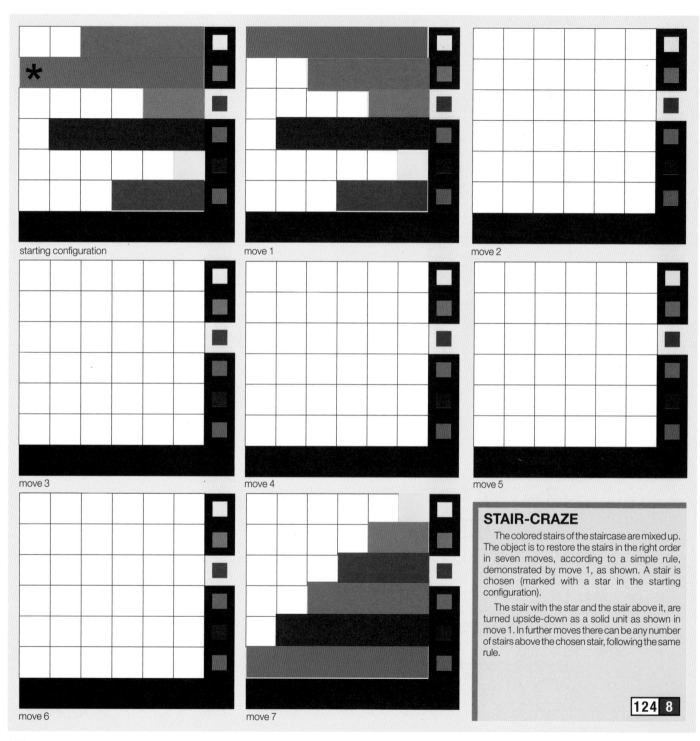

starting configuration

move 1

move 2

move 3

move 4

move 5

move 6

move 7

STAIR-CRAZE

The colored stairs of the staircase are mixed up. The object is to restore the stairs in the right order in seven moves, according to a simple rule, demonstrated by move 1, as shown. A stair is chosen (marked with a star in the starting configuration).

The stair with the star and the stair above it, are turned upside-down as a solid unit as shown in move 1. In further moves there can be any number of stairs above the chosen stair, following the same rule.

124 8

POSI-NEGA MEMORY GAME

Memory games have been around for centuries and one of the most popular kinds has been known for more than a 100 years. In this 'classic' memory game, a set of tiles, or cards, is laid face down on a surface and two tiles are flipped face up over each turn. The object of the game is to turn over a matching pair of tiles on your turn; when you do, you collect the tiles and the person who collects the largest number wins the game.

Such games stimulate observation, concentration and memory and are fun for all ages. A new variation, as a computer game, is increasing their popularity even more.

You can easily create an unusually challenging version of this kind of a game by copying the tiles of the Posi-Nega Memory Game and cutting them into two sets of matching tiles.

The 25 patterns of positive and negative images are based on the same 5-by-5 square matrix.

POSI-NEGA MEMORY GAME

An abstract version of the classical memory game

How long will it take you to pair up the 25 tiles?

One tile does not have a pair. Which tile is the odd-one-out? You can use the grid in which the first pair (numbered 1) have been marked to work out the answer.

The matching pairs in this game are positive-negative reversals of the patterns

125 3

SOLUTIONS

001

FRIENDS MEET

There are exactly eight possibilities for the product of three ages to be 36

Son 1	Son 2	Son 3	Product	Sum
1	1	36	36	38
1	2	18	36	21
1	3	12	36	16
1	4	9	36	14
1	6	6	36	13
2	2	9	36	13
2	3	6	36	11
3	3	4	36	10

Since Ivan could not solve the problem when he knew the sum of the three numbers – the date of the encounter – that meant that the sum had to be 13, for which there are two possibilities. The added information about the youngest son means that one of the possibilities can be eliminated – the 9-year-old and two 2-year-olds – since in this case there is no youngest son. Igor's sons are 1 years old with twins of 6 years old.

002

ROTATING TABLES
ROTATING TABLE WITH THREE POCKETS

Depending on the two chosen pockets essentially there are six different possibilties before the initial first spin, as shown. In all cases the two chosen pockets are the two at the bottom. After the initial spin, the bell will ring in case **1** and **2**, and the game is ended after one spin.

a) If the two glasses are oriented in the same direction, invert both (case **3** and **4**), and after the second spin in both cases the bell will ring.

b) If the two glasses are oriented in different directions (case **5** and **6**), invert the glass that is facing down. After the second spin the bell will ring for case **5**.

c) If the bell doesn't ring after the second spin, it means you are dealing with case 6, and you have to chose two pockets again:

1- If the two chosen pockets show glasses in different orientations--again invert the glass facing down.

2- If the two chosen pockets show glasses in same orientations--invert both glasses.

This will ensure that after the third spin the bell will ring and the game is ended. Thus for the rotating table with three pockets the minimal number of spins to ensure the bell to ring is three.

ROTATING TABLE WITH FOUR POCKETS

A similar procedure will ensure that the bell will be ringing in a minimum number of five spins:

Spin1- Chose a diagonal pair of pockets and orient the glasses the ame way up.

Spin 2- Chose two adjacent pockets. If the glasses are both turned up, leave them, otherwise invert the glass that is turned down. If the bell does not ring, it is certain that there are three glasses with the same orientation.

Spin 3- Chose a diagonal pair of pockets. If one of the glasses is turned down, invert it and the bell will ring after spin 4. If both are turned up, invert one of them.

Spin 4- Chose adjacent pockets and invert the glasses.

Spin 5- Chose a diagonal pair of pockets and invert both glasses. The bell will ring and the game will end after 5 spins.

003

RIDDLE OF THE SPHINX

The answer to the Riddle of the Sphinx is a human.

A human crawls on four limbs as a baby, walks upright on two legs as an adult, and walks with the aid of a cane in old age.

004   005

COUNT FUN

Obviously, there is some difference between the two seemingly random number patterns, since in the second game your performances were so much better. What can it be? There must be something in the arrangement of the numbers in the second game that made them easier to find. It was not something you were aware of while playing the game, but your subconscious was helping you to solve your problems. It discovered the pattern hidden to your conscious and made you more creative. Even now that you know the secret is in the pattern it may not be easy to discover. The numbers in the second grid are grouped in such a way that your eyes follow a repeating pattern: 1 is in the top right quarter, 2 in the bottom left, 3 in the top left, and 4 in the bottom right. This repeats for every four numbers until you get to 90. Your subconscious discovered the secret and made good use of it, while you were not consciously aware of it. This is an impressive demonstration of the power and creativity of your subconscious mind, solving problems while your conscious is not aware of it, and how your mind solves problems in general.

"Order is the shape upon which beauty depends."
Pearl S. Buck

Among the oldest direct evidence of human counting is a baboon's thigh bone marked with 29 notches. The bone is 35,000 years old and was discovered in mountains in Africa.

First test   Second test   Third test
Game One scores

First test   Second test   Third test
Game two scores

006

TRICK HORSES

Confronted with this puzzle many people have a conceptual "block," and are unable to place the riders properly. But the solution is quite simple as you can see.

007

LEONARDO'S MESSAGE

'Those who are inventors and interpreters between Nature and Man, as compared with the reciters and trumpeteers of the works of others, are to be considered simply as an object in front of a mirror in comparison with its image when seen in the mirror, the one being something in itself, the other nothing: people whose debt to Nature is small, for it seems only by chance that they wear human form, and but for this one might class them with the herds of beasts.'

008

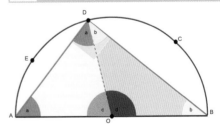

THALES AND HIS THEOREMS
ANGLES IN A SEMICIRCLE

Considering point D on the semicircle: AOD is an isosceles triangle (since OA and OD are radii of the circle) and so is BOD. Therefore the two angles marked a are equal, as well as the two angles marked b, because we know that a triangle's angles add up to 180 degrees.

2a + c = 180
2b + d = 180
c + d = 180

2(a + b) + c + d = 360
2(a + b) + 180 = 360
a + b = 180/2 = 90

Considering different points, such as C and E, you will come to the same results. The angles in the semicircles are right angles.

THE SHADOW AND THE LAMPPOST

A general theorem about angles and triangles enables us to measure the properties of objects that are hard to reach or are too far away. The tip of the lamppost is hard to reach, but its shadow stretches along the ground, and all Jim has to do is measure it with his feet. At that time of the day the shadow of the lamppost is exactly identical to its height. The association between shadows and measurement was part of the ancient Greek world. Hieronymus declared that Thales measured the pyramids based on their shadows, after having observed the moment when our shadows are equal to our own heights (Thales' theorem).

010

The right-hand object for the Top View. The middle object for the Front View.

According to Desargues' theorem, all the intersections among the extensions of the four triangles fall along the side where the triangles come into contact with their shadows. The result of this constraint is that all the other points around it are "freed up": each of them is authorized to be the potential light source, or the projection center.

SHADOW TREES

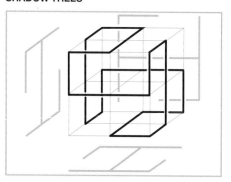

BIANGLES

There is only one biangle of side length 4 units, while there are 4 biangles of side length 5 units

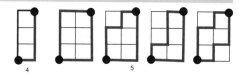

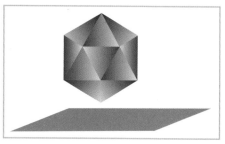

013

FLATLAND CATASTROPHE

Flatlanders may not be able to sense the approach of the giant icosahedral meteorite. Those Flatlanders who won't be removed by the collision into another dimension, will experience the first contact of the icosahedron approaching with its vertex first, as a point growing to a line which will diminish into a point and disappear. An observer from the third dimension would see a sequence of two-dimensional cross-sections of the icosahedron, from a point to pentagons, decagons, or hexagons, depending on the orientation of the icosahedron entering the two-dimensional plane of flatland.

Interesting flatland paradoxes may be associated with this event: the icosahedron travelling through Flatland can remove an object from a sealed chest – without opening the chest and without breaking any of its walls. A chest in Flatland is just a closed two-dimensional figure. Flatlanders can't enter it without opening it, or breaking its walls.

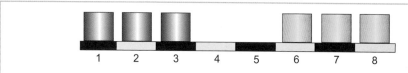

014

FLATLAND GAMES

The second player can always win in Flatland checkers. In flatland chess, the first player can force a win. The only correct opening in flatland chess is to move the knight. In the sample game, yellow moves first.

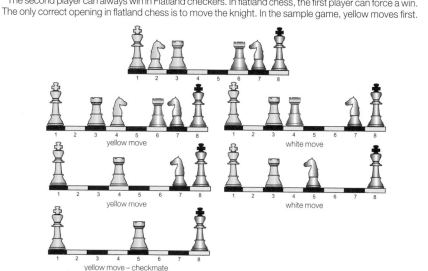

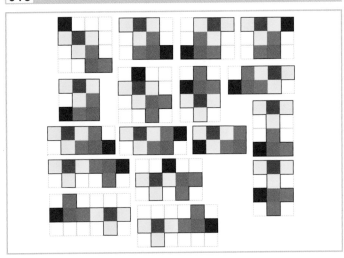

BEAUTIFUL RECTANGLES

In each set of color rectangles there is one in golden ratio proportions.
Did you choose these as the most pleasing?

017

GOLDEN RECTANGLES AND REGULAR POLYHEDRA

1. The sides of the three golden rectangles form a linked Borromean ring.

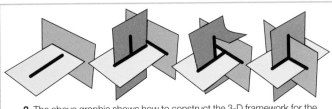

2. The above graphic shows how to construct the 3-D framework for the icosahedron from three golden rectangles.

FIBONACCI RABBITS

Jan	Feb	Mar	Apr	May	Jun	Jul	Aug	Sep	Oct	Nov	Dec
1	**1**	**2**	**3**	**5**	**8**	**13**	**21**	**34**	**55**	**89**	**144**

The sequence of numbers shows the number of rabbit pairs in each month, starting from January (when the first pair was introduced) until December. The total number of pairs at the end of the year is 144. Can you discover the secret pattern behind this number sequence and continue it further?

We shall see a lot more of the "Fibonacci number sequence," as the sequence is today called, because of its mysterious relationships with the golden ratio, spiral, rectangle, and triangle, which are all integral patterns an grows; but the 'how' and the 'why' of it still remain a complete mystery.

And all this from a 13th century puzzle dealing with breeding pairs of rabbits.

The absolutely fascinating property of the Fibonacci sequence is that all we have to know to generate it as far as we wish is to know its first two numbers- 1, 1 - and the process of adding the terms together as the sequence grows. It is an example of a **recurrence sequence**. We use the previous numbers to generate the next number.

We can form similar recurrence sequences using different starting numbers. For example the **Lucas sequence** starts with 2 and 1. The resulting sequence is:

2, 1, 3, 4, 7, 11, 18, 29, 47, 76, 123,..... having little in common with Fibonacci numbers.

Apart from the first three numbers none of the numbers of the Lucas sequence are Fibonacci numbers.

Still. is there any relationship between Fibonacci and Lucas sequence or, for that matter, any other possible recurrence sequence?

The truly astonishing relationship between these will be revealed later.

019

FIBONACCI NUMBERS: PINE CONE

Pine cones show Fibonacci Spirals in two sets of spirals that can be clearly distinguished and counted:

Counterclockwise: 8 spirals.

Clockwise 13 spirals.

The two numbers are neighbours in the Fibonacci Number series.

The reason for this spiral pattern may relate to optimal packing for the seeds of different sizes.

FIBONACCI STAIRCASE AND THE GOLDEN RATIO

The relationships between the Fibonacci number sequence and the Golden ratio: Divide any number in the Fibonacci series by the number before it, and the answer will always be close to 1.618, the Golden ratio.

Phi is the only number that is exactly one away from its reciprocal **1/1.618 = 0.618.**

Every natural number may be expressed as the sum of distinct nonconsecutive Fibonacci numbers in more than just one way.

For example, 232:

1-1-2-1.5-1.666-1.600-1.625-1.615-1.619-1.617-1.618-1.617-1.618-..........

If we take a calculator and look at the list of decimals, we can see that the numbers are getting closer and closer to each other, approaching a limit which is really astonishing.

The truly amazing result is **Phi**, the **golden ratio**. Who could have believed that this innocent-looking line division, which Euclid defined for purely geometrical purposes, and the invented number series, would have such important consequences in nature and the whole of mathematics and science? The golden ratio, or Phi, plays an important role as a fundamental building block in nature.

SNOWFLAKE 3-D STRUCTURES

In the three-dimensional analog of the twodimensional snowflake curve, the growing tetrahedra form a solid which will have an infinite surface area while still enclosing a finite volume. (see in solution 022)

SNOWFLAKE AND ANTI-SNOWFLAKE FRACTALS

It is easy to prove that the area of the curve is finite. The fact that the curve appears to remain within the page of our book is a good indication. Further than that, at no stage of the development will the curve extend beyond the circle circumscribed about the initial triangle. The limit of this infinite construction encloses an area 8/5 that of the original triangle.

Now about the length of this curve. If we suppose that the side of the original triangle is 1 unit long, then the perimeter is 3 units. In construction of the second polygon each segment is replaced by two line segments that altogether are equal to 4/3 its length. Thus, at each stage, the total length is increased by a factor of 4/3. Clearly this is not bounded. A curve of infinite length is the result. An important principle shown by the snowflake and similar so-called pathological curves is that complex shapes can result from repeated applications of very simple rules. These shapes are called fractals.

Are there three-dimensional analogs of the snowflake and similar curves? For example, if tetrahedrons are constructed on the faces of tetrahedrons, will the limiting solid have an infinite surface area? Will it enclose a finite volume?

THREE-DIMENSIONAL ANALOG OF THE SNOWFLAKE CURVE FRACTAL

023

PACKING "2-BY-N" GAMEBOARDS WITH DOMINOS

Interestingly enough, the number of packing dominos in the 2-by-n gameboards follows the Fibonacci number sequence.

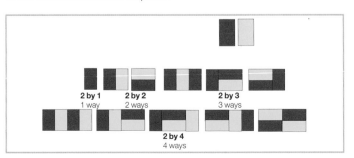

2 by 1
1 way

2 by 2
2 ways

2 by 3
3 ways

2 by 4
4 ways

FIBONACCI PAINTING HOUSES

The five houses painted according to the specified rules. The number of different color patterns follow the Fibonacci number sequence (2, 3, 5, 8, 13 ...), which is another unexpected appearance of this beautiful number sequence. Assuming that the sequence will be consistent for a higher rise house, we can assume that the 12-story house can be painted in 377 different color patterns.

(The Fabulous Fibonacci Numbers by Alfred Posamentier Ingmar Lehmann)

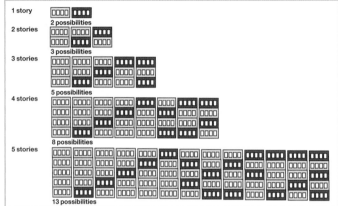

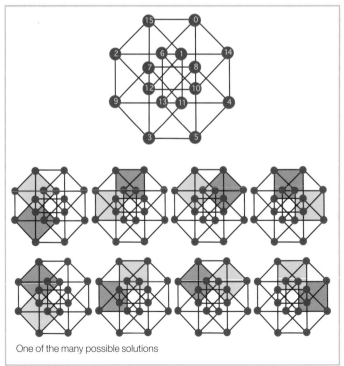

One of the many possible solutions

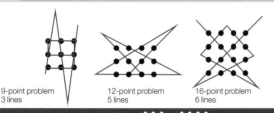

9-point problem
3 lines

12-point problem
5 lines

16-point problem
6 lines

LINES THROUGH DOTS

The classical solutions are shown above, but the problem was pursued to the extreme.

One-line solutions were proposed, by cutting out the dots and glueing them back in a straight line or, by folding the page so that the dots overlap in a single line, etc.

We did not mention any restrictions on how thick the line must be.

So without cutting or folding, a 150-point thick line can solve the three problems easily by one thick line. But when you free your mind of all limitations the creative possibilities to solve the problem are endless.

Your page with the dot problems are on the surface of the Earth which is a sphere. Draw a single line a few times round the glove so that it goes through each sets of dots.

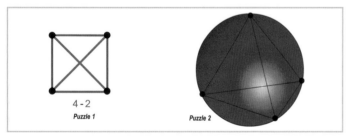

026

4 - 2

Puzzle 1

Puzzle 2

EQUIDISTANT TWO DISTANCE POINTS

The maximum number of equidistant points that can be placed on the sphere is four. The points are placed along the vertices of an inscribed tetrahedron. In general, the maximum number of equidistant point on a plane is three. Only one additional point can be placed in the three-dimensional plane

INSIDE-OUTSIDE?

A simple closed curve (a bent or curved line) is one which does not cross itself. If you imagined it as a loop of string you could always rearrange it as a circle. Such a line divides the plane into two regions: an inside and an outside.

How can you tell whether points in a simple closed curve are inside or outside? One time-consuming way would be to trace or shade everywhere the point you can get to without crossing any line. But there is a much more elegant and shorter way of finding out whether a point is inside or outside a simple closed curve. Draw a straight line from a point in question to the outside of the curve, and then count the number

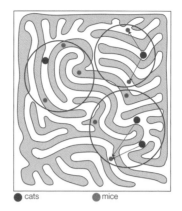

● cats   ● mice

of times the straight line crosses the curve. If it crosses the curve an even number of times, then the point is outside. If it is an odd number of times, then it is inside. This rule is the famous "Jordan Curve Theorem" of mathematics. This rule works in our problem as well, even if some parts of the closed curve are hidden. All inside regions are separated from each other by an even number of lines and any inside region is separated from any outside region by an odd number of lines.

In our puzzle, all cats are outside of the fence and they can catch only three unfortunate mice who also happen to be outside the fence as shown by the arrows

028

MINIMAL DISTANCE CIRCLES – CIRCULAR GOLOMB RULERS

One solutions is shown for each of the eight circles. Because these are circles, there can be many other solutions. To give you an idea of the cominatiorial power of these puzzles, there are no less than 33,033 ways to place five markers on the vertices of the division-15 circle. There are 300 million ways to place 8 markers on the vertices of the 40-agon. And there are more than 1.5 billion ways to place 8 markers on the vertices of the 57-agon.

The beauty of mathematics is that, often, seemingly very difficult problems and puzzles, which have scary titles in textbooks, such as "perfect difference sets" or, "modular golomb rulers", and are explained by complex equations, can, with a bit of patience, logical thinking and some experimention be solved by non-mathematicians too

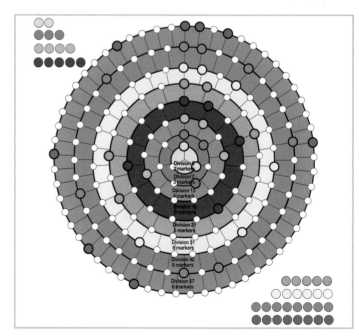

Division 2
2 markers

Division 7
3 markers

Division 13
4 markers

Division 15
5 markers

Division 21
5 markers

Division 31
6 markers

Division 40
8 markers

Division 57
8 markers

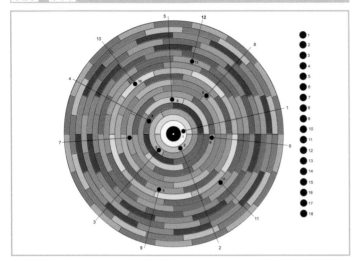

EIGHTEEN-POINT CIRCLE GAME

Shown here is a sample game with a 12-point solution. Can you do better? Surprisingly, it is only possible to place 17 points according to the rules (Berlekamp and Graham 1970, Warmus 1976). Steinhaus (1979) gives a 14-point solution (0.06, 0.55, 0.77, 0.39, 0.96, 0.28, 0.64, 0.13, 0.88, 0.48, 0.19, 0.71, 0.35, 0.82), and Warmus (1976) gives the 17-point solution. Nobody, as yet, has provided an 18-point solution.

No solution needed

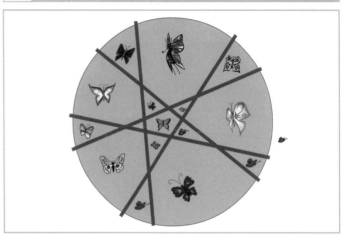

The problem relates to the general question of dividing a closed region of a plane with straight-line cuts.

The maximum number of regions obtained this way using five straight cuts is 16, so yes one could accommodate that 16th butterfly..

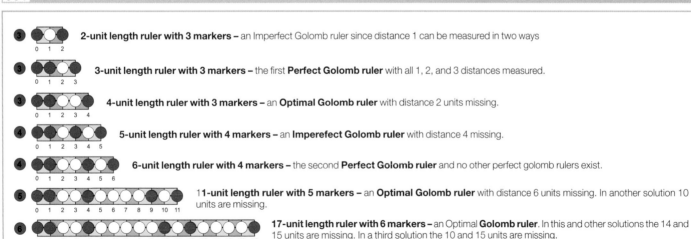

3 **2-unit length ruler with 3 markers** – an Imperfect Golomb ruler since distance 1 can be measured in two ways

3 **3-unit length ruler with 3 markers** – the first **Perfect Golomb ruler** with all 1, 2, and 3 distances measured.

3 **4-unit length ruler with 3 markers** – an **Optimal Golomb ruler** with distance 2 units missing.

4 **5-unit length ruler with 4 markers** – an **Imperefect Golomb ruler** with distance 4 missing.

4 **6-unit length ruler with 4 markers** – the second **Perfect Golomb ruler** and no other perfect golomb rulers exist.

5 **11-unit length ruler with 5 markers** – an **Optimal Golomb ruler** with distance 6 units missing. In another solution 10 units are missing.

6 **17-unit length ruler with 6 markers** – an Optimal **Golomb ruler**. In this and other solutions the 14 and 15 units are missing. In a third solution the 10 and 15 units are missing.

7 **25-unit length ruler with 7 markers** – an **Optimal Golomb ruler**. No matter how the 7 markers are placed, you cannot measure 4 distances. In this placing of the markers the distances 11, 12, 16, and 20 cannot be measured. In another solution distances 10 16, 17, and 24 cannot be measured.

GOLOMB RULERS SOLUTIONS

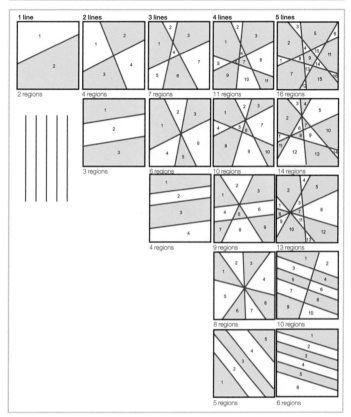

1 line / 1 / 2 / 2 regions

2 lines / 1 / 2 / 3 / 4 regions

3 lines / 7 regions

4 lines / 11 regions

5 lines / 16 regions

3 regions

4 regions / 6 regions / 10 regions / 14 regions

9 regions / 13 regions

8 regions / 10 regions

5 regions / 6 regions

As a general rule, to obtain the maximum number of separate regions try to place each new cut across all the previous lines. In that way every nth cut creates n new pieces. For example, if two cuts can make four regions, a third cut cutting the two previous lines will create three new regions, etc. This rule is seen in the first row, which illustrates the maximum number of regions.

Minimizing the number of regions is easy: make all the cutting lines parallel as shown in the last examples. Determining the maximum number of pieces in which it is possible to divide a circle (or a square) for a given number of cuts is called the *circle-cutting* or *pancake-cutting problem*. The minimum number is always n+1, where n is the number of cuts, and it is always possible to obtain any number of pieces between the minimum and maximum. Evaluating for 1, 2,... gives the sequence of maximal number of regions into which a plan can be cut by straight lines:

2, 4, 7, 11, 16, 22, 29, 37, ...

035

CUTTING THREE CAKES

a) The maximum number of pieces the three cakes can be cut by 3,4, and 5, a total of 12 straight line cuts is, 7,11, and 16 pieces respectively – a total of 34 pieces.

This solution can be considered the minimal "best" solution, but there can be other solutions, if more than two cuts (lines) are allowed to meet in a point.

For example, like cutting the cakes by 2, 4, and 6 cuts into 4 (max.), 8, and 22 (max.) pieces respectively, etc., in which some cuts are not minimal solutions

This problem is a simple example of a branch of mathematics called combinatorial

geometry, in which there is a fascinating interplay between shapes and numbers.

b) With the requirement of cutting the cakes into identical pieces we have to cut each cake radially from the center into 12 pieces, altogether 36 pieces (in which case there will be a piece of cake for you and me as well).

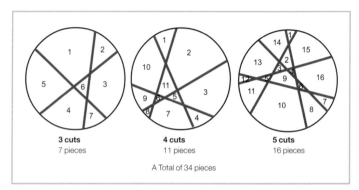

3 cuts
7 pieces

4 cuts
11 pieces

5 cuts
16 pieces

A Total of 34 pieces

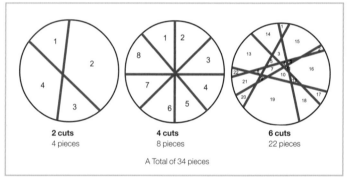

2 cuts
4 pieces

4 cuts
8 pieces

6 cuts
22 pieces

A Total of 34 pieces

CON-NECT 1

You will find this puzzle in its many variations in books testing IQ and visual perception. The puzzle is an exercise in topology and graph theory. You could topologically distort the puzzle by a continuous deformation, shown at right, to obtain the answer staring in your face.

CON-NECT 2

The graphic shows the solution.

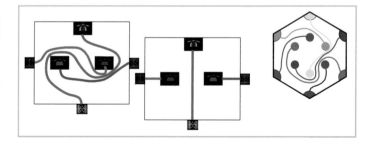

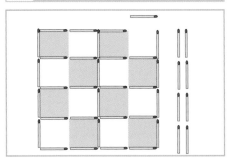

MATCHSTICK SQUARES ELIMINATION

Nine matchsticks must be eliminated. A simple proof of this minimum is by shading the pattern. Thus, eliminating eight matchsticks shared by both colors will eliminate all 16 cells. Another matchstick must be eliminated from the outline of the big square.

Thus, nine matchsticks must be eliminated as a minumum.

MATCH-MATCH 4	MATCH-MATCH FIVE	
1–2	1–9	7–11
3–7	2–17	10–20
4–10	3–14	12–19
5–6	4–15	13–16
8–9	5–21	18–23
	6–8	22–24

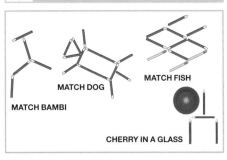

MATCH DOG

MATCH FISH

MATCH BAMBI

CHERRY IN A GLASS

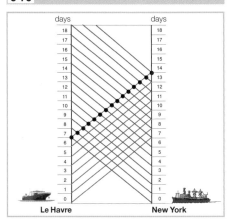

If your guess was seven, you were wrong, because there were ships already on the move before your ship began its voyage. The ships leaving Le Havre will meet 15 ships – 13 ships at sea and one in each harbor. The meetings occur daily, at noon and at midnight.

GRASSHOP

1. The next three lengths with solutions: **n = 9, n = 13, n = 16**.

2. For the first **n = 40**, there are **16** solutions as shown.

3. It is believed that for all n: **0 or 1 mod 4** are possible for **n = 20** or more, so the grasshopping number sequence can be extended accordingly.

042

The solutions up the first 40 lengths are shown in the graphic.

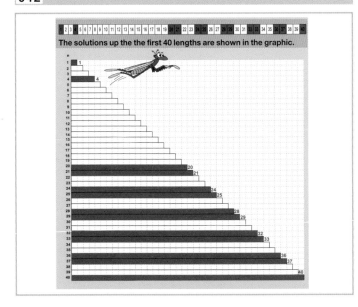

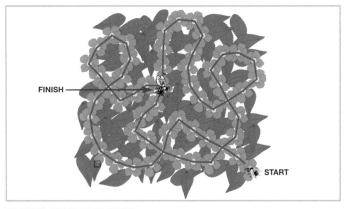

FINISH

START

FROM FLOWER TO FLOWER

The flowers can be considered as nodes (points) of a graph. If a flower has an even number of boundary crossings (overlaps with other flowers), Mr.Bee can enter and leave it, whereas a flower with an odd number of boundary crossings can be entered and left by Mr. Bee, but when he finally reenters he cannot leave again. Observing the flowers, the only flower with an odd number of crossings is the flower on which Mrs. Bee will be waiting.

By drawing a line through all the leaves that have only two crossings, and marking the multiple crossed flowers, you can easily complete a continuous line through all the flowers without ever retracing the line.

In general, according to Euler's theorem (see page 71/72), a graph like this can be traversed if only 0 or 2 of the flowers have an odd number of adjacent flowers. If it's "0," you can start anywhere because it is a closed loop. If it is "2" those two flowers are the start and finish points. That is what we have in this case – the start point has one adjacent flower and the finish point has three adjacent flowers. All the other flowers have even number of adjacent flowers.

044

EULER'S THEOREM

1- A graph has an Eulerian circuit if and only if it is connected and all of its vertices are even,

2- A graph has an Eulerian path if and only if it is connected and has either no odd vertices or exactly two odd vertices. If two of the vertices are odd, then any Eulerian path must begin at one of the odd vertices and end at the other.

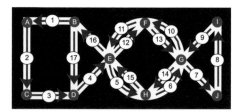

045

EULERIAN PATHS

We can conclude at the outset that the graph does not have an Eulerian circuit since it has two odd vertices (B and D). So the start and end points must be different, namely B and D. One of our choices, therefore, is to start an Eulerian path at point B. In creating the path we have to be careful not to make a move which would result in disconnecting the uncovered paths.

046

EULER CHARACTERISTIC FORMULA

It seemed easier to choose to count the number of intersection points and the number of regions:

Number of intersection points (V): **48**

Number of regions (F): **46**

Number of edges (E): **92**

Euler discovered the formula for any connected graph in the plane, also known as 'Euler Characteristic:

V - E + F = 2

which in our example: 48 - 92 + 46 = 2

48 + 46= 92 + 2

94 - 2 = E = **92**

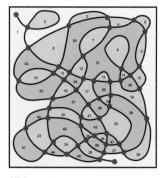

047

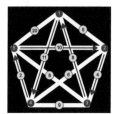

TRAVELING SALESMAN PROBLEM

The simplest idea about how to solve the problem is to find the weight of every Hamiltonian circuit and to select the one whose weight is the minimum. The total number of of Hamiltonian circuits starting at a particular vertex for a graph with 'n' vertices is given by (n - 1) x (n - 2) x .....3 x 2 x 1 otherwise written as (n – 1)!

Growth of (n-1)! table:

n	(n-1)!
3	1
4	6
5	24
8	5,040
12	39,916,800

From the table we can see the difficulty of solving such problems. For graphs with a great number of vertices no computer could cope with the problem. There is no known efficient algorithm that will solve the traveling salesman problem, there are algorithms enabling us to find circuits whose weight are fairly close to the minimum possible weight *(approximate algorithms)*.

048

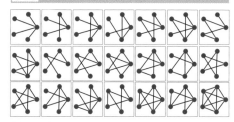

CONNECTED GRAPHS

The solution is shown in the graphic.

A path to all points

For those fascinated by number series, the number series for unlabeled connected graphs from n=1 to n=9 is: **1, 1, 2, 6, 21, 112, 853, 1117, 261080**

049

STAIRCASE PARADOX

All the staircase paths in all generations are of the same length: twice the side of the unit square, 2.

On the other hand, as the steps of the progression grow, they approach their limit, which is the length of the diagonal, which is, following the Pythagorean theorem

$$1^2 + 1^2 = \sqrt{2}$$

It looks like we have just proved a paradoxical relationship $2 = \sqrt{2}$, haven't we? In the 10th generation there will be $2^{10} = 1,024$ stairs, and in the 100th generation, the staircase will be indistinguishable from the diagonal, which is $\sqrt{2}$.

STAIRCASE WALKS

The missing steps.

050

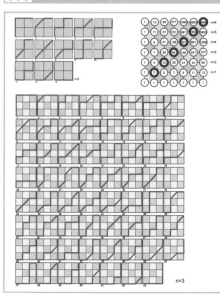

KING WALKS

For every grid intersection we can easily determine its "predecessors": the intersections from which the king can move directly to it. The number of different paths that lead to an intersection is the sum of the number of different paths that lead to each of its predecessors, as seen in the table above

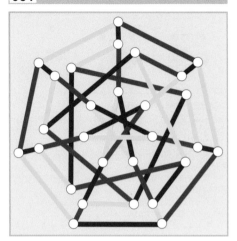

EDGE COLORING COXETER GRAPH
Three colors are sufficient.

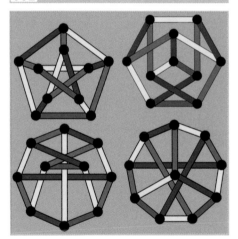

The four graphs are four equivalent topological variants of the same graph, the so-called Petersen graph (graph 1).

SAM LOYD'S MARS PUZZLE
Loyd received in fact 10,000 solutions with the correct answer: "There is no possible way."

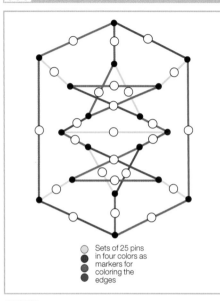

Sets of 25 pins in four colors as markers for coloring the edges

SNARK
Edge coloring Snark

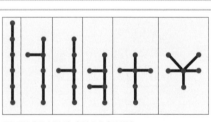

TREE GRAPHS ON 6 POINTS
There is just one more tree graph possible as shown. No matter how you try to connect 6 points to form a tree graph, topologically they will always belong to one of the graphs shown.

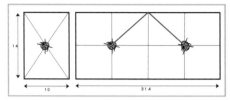

LADYBUG MINIMAL CROSSING
The outside ladybug must cross a distance of 21.04 cm to meet its friend on the inside.

By Pythagoras, distance

= square root of $(14^2 + (10 \text{ pi}/2)^2)$
= square root of $(196 + 246.74)$
= 21.04 cm

ANT'S JOURNEY ON TIN CAN
Both are right. In general when the two results are compared:

$$H + 2r = \sqrt{H^2 + \pi^2 r^2} \qquad (H + 2r)^2 = H^2 + \pi^2 r^2$$

The result is: $\dfrac{H}{r} = \dfrac{\pi^2}{...} - 1 = 1.467$

Thus the two lengths are equal when the ratio of the tin can's height to its radius is equal to 1.467. So both conclusions can be the right solutions, depending on the proportions of the cans:

1. When this ratio is smaller than 1.467, Mike's solution is right.

2. If higher, John is right, which can be seen in the nets of the two cans.

(*An ant on a tin can* by Igor Akulich, Quantum Sep/Oct 1997)

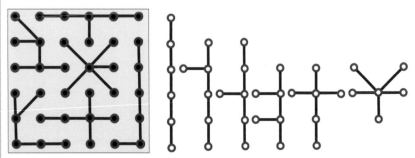

SIX POINT TREE GRAPHS PEGBOARD

058

TREE GRAPHS – THE LONGEST ROUTE

The longest path is shown above (yellow lengths). Very often beautifully simple and ingenious analog gadgets can solve complex mathematical problems. Jos Wennmacker of Nijmegen, The Netherlands, devised a simple gadget which can solve our problem and even more complex problems of this kind in no time. Wennmacker creates an analog model of the graph by knotting together pieces of string in exact scale (or connecting the pieces of string to small rings or eyelets). The result is obtained by two simple operations. Pick up the string structure at any node (point) and let it hang freely. Pick it up again at the lowest node and hang it again, and you have the longest path. As simple as that!

We are demonstrating the process to check our result obtained by hard work. The selected node for the first step is shown with a red circle around it.

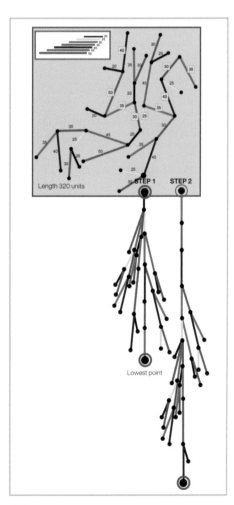

TOPOLOGICAL EQUIVALENCE TRANSFORMATION

RAMSEY GAME II

You can avoid having three in a group of four or five who either love or hate each other. This is proven by coloring each line of the graph in either of two colors, avoiding creating a triangle interconnecting any three points in one of the colors. But you can't avoid having three in a group of six who either love or hate each other. As you can see, no matter which color you use for the last uncolored line, you will be forced to create either a red or blue triangle of a solid color. This is one of the applications of Ramsey theory; there are many others.

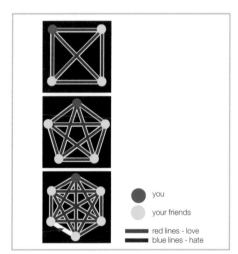

you
your friends
red lines - love
blue lines - hate

061

PARTY PROBLEMS

No matter how you chose to color the remaining lines, you can't avoid creating

WORLD TRIP

One possible New York to Paris route is: New York – London – Tel Aviv – Amsterdam – Tokyo – Cairo – Berlin – Paris, but there are others.

Can you find a more economical route?

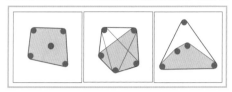

CONVEX QUADRILATERAL

It takes five points to guarantee a convex quadrilateral. This was elegantly proven by the Erdos-Szekeres theorem. If you surround the given points with a rubber band (like lassoing the points), there can be only three possibilities:

1. The band forms a convex quadrilateral (with the fifth point inside).

2. The band forms a pentagon; connecting two vertices will always result in a convex quadrilateral.

3. The band will form a triangle with two points inside. Draw a line through the two interior points – on one side of the line will be one vertex, and on the other will be two. Take the latter two vertices and the two interior points – these will make a convex quadrilateral.

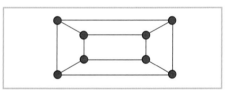

CONVEX PENTAGON

It has been proven that nine points will unavoidably create a convex pentagon in any configuration of randomly placed points. Eight points can be placed still avoiding a convex pentagon. Any additional point will unavoidably create a convex pentagon.

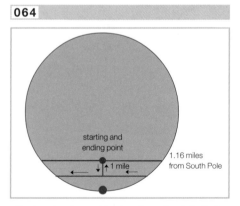

starting and ending point
↕ 1 mile
1.16 miles from South Pole

The beauty of recreational mathematics is that often new solutions are found to old classics, upgrading them, and giving them new creative twists like this one.

There is not just one point, but an infinite number of starting points. The explorer can start from any point on a circle drawn around the South Pole at a distance slightly more than 1 + 1/2 pi miles (or about 1.16 miles taking into account the Earth's curvature). After walking a mile south, his next walk will take him on a complete tour around the Pole, and the walk one mile north from there will take him back to the point where he started.

065

The secret is the color sequence on all but one piece of the serpent. As shown, if you start from the part of the serpent on the far top left and place the parts clockwise you can see that the color sequence on each consecutive piece starts with the next color on from the previous piece: yellow, orange, red, pink, light green, dark green, light blue, violet, and yellow again.

067

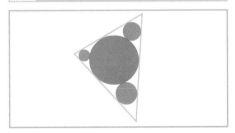

SEVEN CIRCLES THEOREM

The three circles that get larger and larger ultimately become the sides of a triangle. The orange circle becomes the inside circle of the resulting triangle. The rules about the meeting of the tangency remains.

A recognizable example is the curvature of the Earth's surface, which is so negligible that it appears flat. An infinite circle is therefore a straight line, believe it or not.

Something to think about: if a straight line is an infinite circle, then where is its center?

068

CONWAY'S GROUPING OF PI DECIMALS

Surprisingly and coincidentally, as it can be seen, this happens already in the seventh grouping of ten pi's decimals:

3.1415926535 8979323846 2643383279 5028841971 6939937510 5820974944 5923078164 ....

066

MYSTIC ROSES

You don't have to count the lines. You can calculate them easily. In a mystic rose for n number of point, n-1 lines emanate from ech point, so the total number of lines from all points is n (n-1). But since each line is shared by two points, the number of lines is half of that or .n (n-1) /2. Thus in the 19-point mystic rose there are 171 lines. Using Euler's theorem it is also easy to discover which mystic rose can be traced in one continuous line (or with one length of a string) without retracing any of the connections. Thus the mystic roses on 5, 19, and 21 points can all be traced.

In the mystic rose on 21 points, the jumping problem with step sizes 15 (missing 14 points) will close and cover 7 vertices. And with step sizes 13 (missing 12 points) all the vertices will be covered.

069

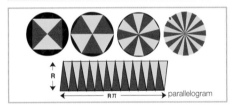

AREA OF A CIRCLE

The circle is cut into sectors that are arranged as in the drawing to form a parallelogram. The more sectors the circle is divided into, the clearer the sectors resemble triangles. The triangles becoming smaller and smaller, and the figure approaches the form of a rectangle. "In the limit" the polygons inscribed in the circle become the circle itself. This limit can never be reached but it can be approached as nearly as we wish. This principle is the main foundation of the modern mathematical calculus. The unrolling of the circle's sectors form an approximation of a parallelogram with: height = radius, and width = $^1/_2$ circumference.

070

BUFFON

This is a version of the famous Buffon's Needle experiment that you can easily perform yourself and which will allow you to calculate number pi with fair accuracy. Georges Louis Leclerc, a French

mathematician, showed that if a needle is dropped from a random height on a piece of paper covered with parallel lines, the length of the needle being equal to the distance between the lines, then the probability of the needle falling across a line is equal to 2/pi.

If the needle is shorter than the distance between lines than the probability that the needle will fall across a line is

2 c/pi x a

where a is distance between lines c is length of the needle.

Thus by throwing the needle at random a large number of times (n) and counting the number (m) of times the needle falls on a line, we can calculate an experimental value of pi as

pi = 2 c x n/a x m or pi = 2n/m if c = a

At first it seems almost magical that the answer involves pi.

This beautiful experiment was long forgotten until Pierre Simon Laplace (1749 – 1827) in 1812 published a major work in probability popularizing the needle experiment. In 1901, Lazzarini, an Italian mathematician, was patient enough to make 3,408 throws in the course of such an experiment, obtaining a value for pi of 3.1415929, a result which contains an error of only 0.0000003. Compare your results with the results of Lazzarini's experiment.

073

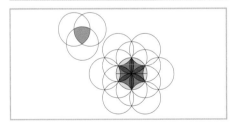

TRIPLE CIRCLES OVERLAP

Tad Dunne of Willowdale, Ontario, a reader of Martin Gardner, found a beautiful visual "look and see" solution, which involves no formulas and arithmetic, only a compass, as shown.

One quarter of a circle's area equals the sum of one-and-a-half deltas (green) plus three bananas (red and yellow). Therefore the overlapping areas of the three circles is smaller than a quarter circle (by an amount of half a delta).

071

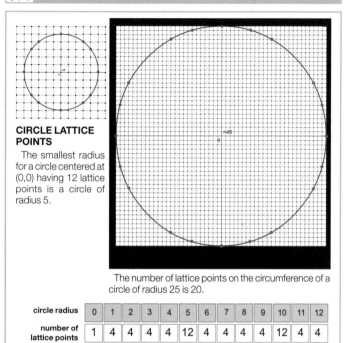

CIRCLE LATTICE POINTS

The smallest radius for a circle centered at (0,0) having 12 lattice points is a circle of radius 5.

The number of lattice points on the circumference of a circle of radius 25 is 20.

circle radius	0	1	2	3	4	5	6	7	8	9	10	11	12
number of lattice points	1	4	4	4	4	12	4	4	4	4	12	4	4

072

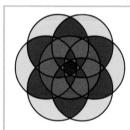

The answer for seven interescting circles is 44 regions, as shown. Euler's Formula for polyhedra is also valid for connected graphs: imagine that a polyhedron is distorted and flattened onto the plane. Each circle can intersect each other at two points. For each circle that makes 2(n-1) points. Counting all circles, and dividing by 2 (since each point is counted twice), we get n(n-1) points of intersection – or "vertices." Similarly, each circle is divided by the 2(n-1) points into 2(n-1) segments. This gives a total of 2n(n-1) edges.

Euler's Formula gives:
$$F = E - V + 2 = 2n(n-1) - n(n-1) + 2 = n^2 - (n - 2) \text{ regions}$$

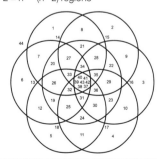

074

OVERLAPPING CIRCLES

The areas of the seven circles overlapping the big circle are equal to the area of the big circle. Therefore the blue and red areas are equal. The black overlapping areas take away the same amount from the overlapping circles. Both the red plus black, as well as blue plus black areas are equal to the area of the big circle. They are also equal to the green area, which is the biggest.

075

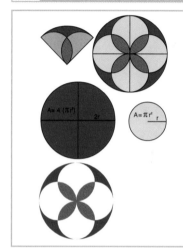

MUSHROOM QUADRANT

The big red circle has twice the radius of the little circle, therefore its area is four times as big. We can see that the four red regions are not included in the smaller circle, while the four overlapping green regions are used twice. Because of the complete symmetry of the pattern, you can use a leap of imagination to conclude that each of the red regions must be equal in area to each of the green regions

076

The sum of the arcs "appears" to be approaching the length of the diagonal AB, creating a paradox which may be considered a geometrical fallacy. In fact, it doesn't. Imagine the diameter of the large semicircle as 2 (as in our first example). Then the sum of the arc lengths of the semicircles equals pi. If the sum of the small semicircles would become the length of the diameter, their length would equal 2, which we know it isn't true.

No matter how small the semicircles become, their total length will always be equal to the length of the large semicircle, and only faulty reasoning may have led to the fallacy.

077

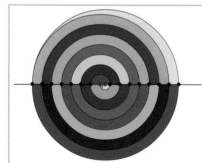

SEMICIRCLES SPIRAL

With the help of π we can find the length of the spiral and the areas of the semi-annuli, by calculating each portion separately.

Semicircle (yellow) (M, r) refers to the semicircle with center M, and radius length r.

Its arc length is $B = r \times \pi$.

Its area is $A = 1/2 \, \pi \times r^2$.

The length of the spiral is the sum of the Bs.

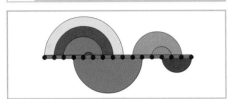

SEMICIRCLES CHAIN PUZZLE

One of the many solutions.

080

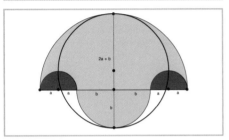

SALINON OF ARCHIMEDES

Subtract the area of the two equal semicircles from the large semicircle and then add the area of the middle semicircle to obtain the area of salinon.

081

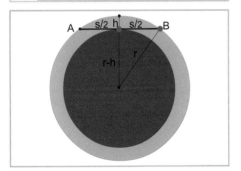

CIRCLE RINGS

By Pythagorean theorem:

Area of large circle = $\text{Pi } r^2$

Area of the small circle = $\text{Pi } (r-h)^2 = \text{Pi } r^2 - \text{Pi } rh + \text{Pi } h^2$

Area of the ring = $\text{Pi } (s/2)^2$

Thus the area of the ring depends only on the length of the chord and Pi. Note that the diameter of the circles was not given and does not need to be known.

If you imagine that the diameter of the small circle becomes smaller and smaller until its length is zero; the ring then becomes the larger circle whose diameter is then the chord ($2r=s$) and its area the area of this circle:

Area = $\text{Pi } r^2 = \text{Pi } (s/2)^2$

079

JOGGING PATHS ALONG SEMICIRCLES

The four joggers will arrive at the same time. The four paths are of equal length.

082

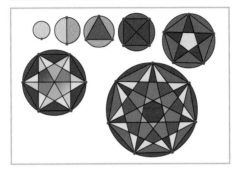

CIRCLE CUTTING CHORDS

Seven points circle

1. The general formula for the number of chords for "n" points:

$\{n \times (n-1)\}/2$

2. It is interesting to note that in spite of the seeming doubling sequence for the smaller circles, the answer for the six-point circle is not 32 as one would tend to guess. This is one of the beautiful examples in math of why guessing at an answer is not always the best way to solve a problem.

The seven-point circle has 21 chords, which divide it into 57 separate pieces.

083

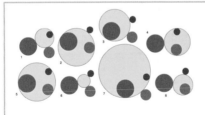

APOLLONIUS' THEOREM

Surprisingly enough, there are only eight different ways that three circles may touch a fourth on a plane. For our three given circles these are illustrated separately.

For the general case, take three circles and move them together so that they are mutually tangent, then, in the space between the three, draw a circle that touches all of them. You may also draw a circle around all three that is mutually tangent. In that way four circles can be mutually tangent (see the first and second diagrams). Four circles is the maximum number of circles that may be mutually tangent on a plane.

DESCARTES AND BEECROFT'S CIRCLE THEOREMS

There are two possible solutions as shown. Beecroft's Circle Theorem for the four mutually touching circles is shown at right.

084

SPHERE PACKING BOX

Theoretically, after many shakings of the box the best packing pattern (hexagonal packing) could be achieved, which would take about 14% less space in the box than before. But in practice, when the box is rotated, tapped, or shaken, the spheres assume an infinity of visually compelling configurations, reminiscent of cracks in crystals. The resulting configurations reflect processes in nature. It can be seen that there are always several regions of regular arrangements, set at angles to each other (grain boundaries), corresponding by analogy to atomic arrangements in crystals, metals, and other materials that occur as a crystal grows. Key properties of different materials can be determined according to the way in which atoms are arrayed and the way they are joined together. The difference among solids, liquids, and gaseous states are explained by the patterning of their atoms and the relative closeness of their molecules.

085

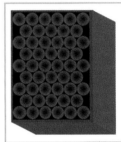

PACKING BOTTLES

You can repack the bottles in hexagonal packing in 9 rows, as shown, and you will be able to pack an additional two bottles for a total of 50 bottles in the crate.

PACKING SPHERES IN A CUBE **PAGE 180**

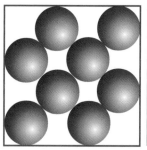

086

Layers 1, 3

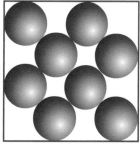

Layers 2,

PACKING SPHERES IN A CUBE

You can pack 32 spheres in four layers as shown.

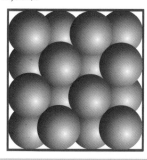

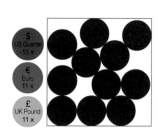

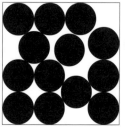

087

11 circles packed in a unit square   13 circles packed in a unit square

PACKING 11- AND 13 CIRCLES IN UNIT SQUARES

The illustration shows the solutions.

For circles of other sizes, you will need to calculate the size of corresponding unit squares.

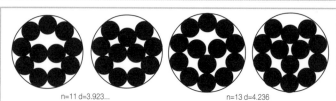

n=11 d=3.923...   n=13 d=4.236

PACKING CIRCLES IN CIRCLE

Puzzle 1 - 11 circles.

The best packing has two different forms as shown. This was proved by H. Melissen in 1994.

Puzzle 2 - 13 circles.

The best packing for 13 unit circles also comes in two different forms. It is interesting to note that one of these is totally rigid while in the other one there are three loose circles, as shown.

Both solutions were discovered independently by Kravitz in 1967 and later by Hugo Pfoertner and James Buddenhagen.

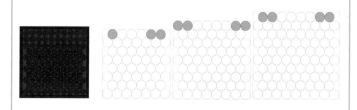

PACKING 100 BOTTLES IN A SQUARE CRATE

Yes! By combining the two packings, you can squeeze in another bottle, making a total of 106, as shown. Again, the best solution is not necessarily the most ordered and regular one. Needless to say, packing problems such as these are very important for manufacturing.

PACKING BOTTLES IN SQUARE CRATES PROBLEM

By rearranging the bottles in crates holding 49, 64, and 81 bottles into a hexagonal packing array, they can be repacked in their original square crates with the advantage of packing a larger number of bottles.

or, repack them into smaller rectangular crates and still packing an additional number of bottles, as the illustration demonstrates.

49 bottles packed in their original square crate, packed with additional 3 bottles.

64 bottles packed in a rectangular crate (of 99% smaller volume than the square crate), packed with additional 4 bottles.

81 bottles packed in a rectangular crate (of 98% smaller volume than the square crate), packed with additional 4 bottles.

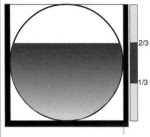

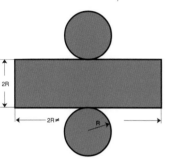

SPHERE SURFACE AREA – VOLUME

$A_{cylinder} = 2R \times 2R\pi + 2R2\pi = 6R2\,\pi$

$A_{sphere} = 4R2\pi$

$V_{cylinder} = R2\pi \times 2R = 2R3\,\pi$

$V_{sphere} = 4/3 \times R3\pi$ 🍎

> "Every cylinder whose base is the greatest circle in a sphere and, whose height is equal to the diameter of the sphere has a surface area, including the bases, 3/2 the surface of the sphere, and 3/2 of the volume of the sphere."
>
> *Archimedes*

WATER SPHERE

The sphere and the cylinder have the same surface area. The volume of the cylinder is exactly equal to the volume of the sphere plus the volume of the cone of the same dimensions.

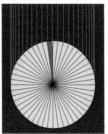

NOTES ON THE VOLUME OF A SPHERE

Volume of Cylinder – Volume of Sphere = Volume of Cone.

This is the fundamental theorem on which the measurement of spheres depends.

The ratios of the volumes of a cone, sphere, and cylinder, all of the same height and radius are in proportion 1 : 2 : 3.

Archimedes considered it one of his greatest achievements and it is said he wanted the discovery to be inscribed on his gravestone.

ROPE THE EARTH

The intuitive answer is that since one meter is inconsequential compared to the circumference of the Earth, the rope would hardly budge. But in this case intuition is wrong. A little analysis shows why. The circumference of the Earth is 2 x Pi times its radius, and the length of the rope is 2 x Pi both the radius of the Earth and the height that the rope is pulled off the surface. If the difference between those two lengths is one meter, then:

2 Pi(r + x) – 2 Pi r = 1 meter

2 Pi r + 2 Pi x – 2 Pi r = 2 Pi x = 1 meter

x = 1/Pi meters or about 0.33 meters, which is a surprisingly counterintuitive answer.

MEASURING THE EARTH WITH ERATOSTHENES

Eratosthenes knew that sunrays travel in parallel lines and so deduced that the difference in the angles was caused by the curvature of the Earth. Knowing the distance between Alexandria and Syene, which is about 490 miles (787 km), he multiplied this distance by 50 to determine the circumference of the circle that passes through these two towns and the North and South Poles: in other words, the circumference of the Earth.

360 / 7.5 = X / 787

where X= 39350 km, is the circumference of the Earth.

His estimate was remarkably accurate. Today, we know that the circumference at the Equator is 24,889 milies (40,056 km).

093

HOLE IN A SPHERE

Since calculus is outside the scope of this book, let's try to solve the problem by an intuitive explanation. If we imagine an infinitely small hole in a 6-inch sphere, it leaves nearly all the volume of the sphere intact:

4/3 Pi 3 ^{3} = 36 Pi cubic inches.

The bigger the sphere the larger the hole has to be for its length to be 6 inches. Calculus reveals that the volume of the remaining napkin-ring-shaped solid remains the same, no matter the hole's diameter or the size of the sphere. Quite amazingly the residual volumes of the spheres, the drilled spheres and drilled Earth are exatcly the same. Now that sounds quite counterintuitive. But even though the Earth is vastly larger than the spheres the drill had to take out proportionally more in order to make the thickness of the hole the same. The volume left does not depend separately on the initial size of the sphere or of the hole, but only on their *relation*, which is forced by requiring the hole to be exactly 6 inches long. Therefore the residue of the spheres no matter of what size initially must equal the volume of the initial sphere with a diameter of 6 inches, namely 36 Pi, a counterintuitive result.

It's not what your eyes will tell you, but in fact the circumference is larger than the height. You can calculate this to check by measuring the diameter and multiplying it by Pi (3.142…) to get the circumference. You'll find that even in a tall thin glas such as this, the height is the lesser sum. This is so counter-intuitive that it is often a convincing party trick – or a good way to win a round of drinks in a bar!

PICK'S THEOREM

You can work out the area through time-cosuming hard work without Pick's theorem, but the beauty of the theorem is its astonishing simplicity.

A= I + 1/2 B -1

B = the number of boundary points.

I = the number of inside points

REULEAUX TRIANGLE

The blue point will describe a near perfect square. The principle was exploited in the invention of a patented drill that drills square holes.

REULEAUX POLYGONS

When the three wheels are revolving, the platform with the cocktail glasses remains horizontal, without rising or tilting. Among all the curves of constant width the reuleaux triangle has the smallest area.

CURVES OF CONSTANT WIDTH

Curves that have the same width in every direction are called curves of constant width. Any curve of constant width can turn between two fixed parallel lines or within a square. Although some curves of constant width, such as the circle, are smooth, others have corners; and while some are highly symmetrical others are quite irregular. Indeed, any regular polygon with an odd number of sides can be rounded up to create a curve of constant width.

The width of a closed convex curve is defined as the distance between parallel lines bounding it. Curves of constant width have the same width regardless of their orientation between the parallel lines. There is an infinite number of them including the circle, which has the largest area, and the well-known Reuleaux triangle. The two irregular wheels have outlines which are curves of constant width. One is a Reuleaux triangle, which is created by drawing a circular arc from one corner passing through the other two. The width of such a curve in every direction is equal to the side of the equilateral triangle.

Any polygon with an odd number of sides can be rounded off like the Reuleaux triangle to create a curve of constant width, like other wheels based on a pentagon. Such curves are called Reuleux polygons.

096

PARABOLA

The best compromise is to throw the stone in a direction upwards at an angle of 45 degrees to the horizontal. Its path will be a parabola. The mathematical model for this answer takes into account several simplified assumptions. That the only force acting on the stone is the Earth's gravitational field, not taking into account air resistance, the rotation of the Earth, and a few other factors. If you want to take into account air resistance, you should make your throw a bit flatter.

Parabolas, like circles, always have the same shape, although the shape can be enlarged or diminished. The suspended weights will always form a parabola no matter what is the position of the rod.

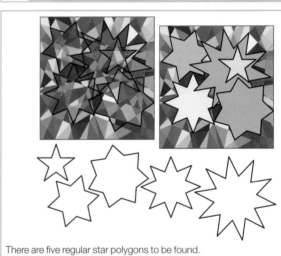

There are five regular star polygons to be found.

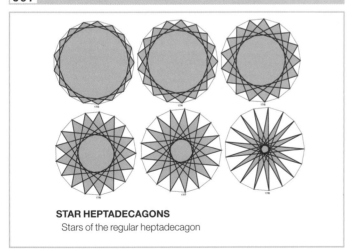

STAR HEPTADECAGONS

Stars of the regular heptadecagon

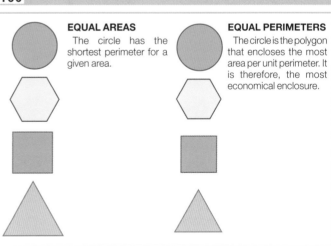

EQUAL AREAS

The circle has the shortest perimeter for a given area.

EQUAL PERIMETERS

The circle is the polygon that encloses the most area per unit perimeter. It is therefore, the most economical enclosure.

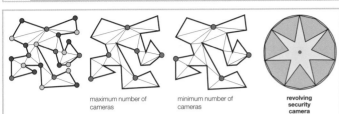

maximum number of cameras   minimum number of cameras   revolving security camera

CHVATAL ART GALLERY THEOREM

Initially, a theorem to solve the problem was suggested by Vasek Chvatal and Steve Fisk: for any gallery with "n" walls, n/3 cameras suffice. But this result is the worst case. Later an ingenious argument by Steve Fisk provided a truly beautiful proof. Triangulate the whole layout and color the vertices of each triangle in three different colors, the same three colors used for each triangle. The cameras should be placed at the points that have the color that appears the fewest times. This theorem provides the theoretical maximum number of the required cameras, but it does not guarantee the possible minimum. In our case triangulation gives six cameras as a maximum, but in practice this number can be reduced to four as shown.

ART GALLERY

If the shape of the gallery is a convex polygon, then one camera would be enough placed anywhere in the gallery. A simple solution would be a circular shape or a polygon of 14 sides. But another solution would be a star-shaped gallery, which would require a minimum floor area.

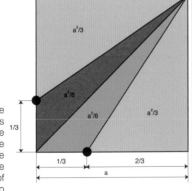

103

TRISECTING SQUARE AREA

The diagonal divides the square into two triangles, each of which is again divided into two triangles. The smaller triangle if half the area of the bigger. Since the two triangles have the same altitude, the base of the smaller triangle is half of the base of the larger. The trisecting lines also trisect the two sides of the square as shown.

TRISECTING TRIANGLE

The equilateral triangles can be dissected into five pieces which can be rearranged to form three shapes of equal area as shown

NINE - POINT CIRCLE

Brianchon and Poncelet published the theorem in 1821, though an otherwise unknown Englishman, Benjamin Bevan, proposed a problem in 1804 which is practically equivalent. The nine-point circle is half the size of the circumcircle of the triangle, and its center is half-way between the circumcenter and the orthocenter. Thales' theorem states that if the circumcenter is located on one side of the triangle, then the opposite angle is a right angle. If the circumcenter is inside the triangle, then the triangle is acute; if the circumcenter is outside the triangle, then the triangle is obtuse.

104

POLICE CHASE

The answers to our problems are related to the basic geometry of triangles.

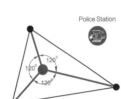

Police Station

Puzzle 1:
The Minimal Triangle Problem

In essence, we want to build three straight "roads" from each town to a point in the middle of the triangle. The puzzle asks us to minimize the total length of these roads. As it happens, this occurs when the roads meet at 120 degrees, as shown. The place where the roads meet, and thus where we would build the police station, is called the Fermat point.

Police Car 1

Puzzle 2:
Circumscribing a Circle about a Triangle

The point that is nearest to any of the three towns can be found by constructing a circle that will pass through the three vertices of the triangle. The center of this circle is the point we are looking for. To find it, we have to draw the three perpendicular bisectors on each side of the triangle, the point where they intersect is called the CIRCUMCENTER of the triangle. Since the three towns are on the same circle they are at the same distance from the circumcenter.

Police Car 2

Puzzle 3:
Inscribing a Circle in a Triangle or, The Angle Bisection Theorem

The point that is nearest to any of the three main roads, can be found by constructing a circle inside the triangle which will be tangent (touching) the three sides of the triangle. To find the center of this circle, called the INCENTER of the triangle, we have to bisect each angle and the point where the bisection lines meet is out point. Since the tangents are on the same circle they are at the same distance from the center point.

→	**1**	**2**	**3**	**4**	**7**			
43	**29**	**19**	**9**	**1**	**0**			

MANDALA

Puzzle 1. It is sufficient to remove five triangles out of the nine to eliminate all the red triangles. The quickest descending sequence of the remaining red triangles is by removing triangles 1, 2, 3, 4, and 7, as shown above

Puzzle 2. There are 120 triangles of all sizes altogether: 59 pointing up and 61 pointing down

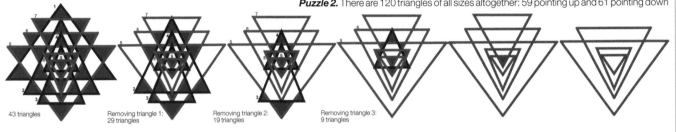

43 triangles

Removing triangle 1: 29 triangles

Removing triangle 2: 19 triangles

Removing triangle 3: 9 triangles

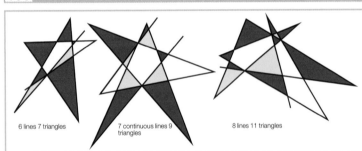

106

6 lines 7 triangles

7 continuous lines 9 triangles

8 lines 11 triangles

KOBON TRIANGLES

The requirement of continuous broken lines solutions for 6, 7, and 8 lines are shown. Can you do better?

Solutions for n = 3, 4, 5, and 9 lines are already continuous closed broken lines.

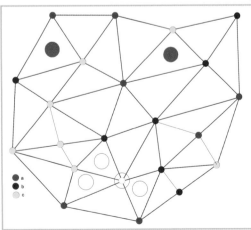

- a
- b
- c

COLORING TRIANGLES IN POLYGONS

At the outset two complete triangles were created but at the last dot a third complete triangle seems unavoidable, no matter how the colors are chosen. This will always happen.

This is the conclusion of Sperner's lemma for triangles:

If there is an odd number of complete edges on the boundary, then there is an odd number of complete triangles. If there is an even number of complete edges on the boundary, then there is an even number of complete triangles.

'a' and 'b' is a complete edge.

NOTES

Emanuel Sperner (1905–80) stated his lemma for triangles, but it can be generalized to all dimensions.

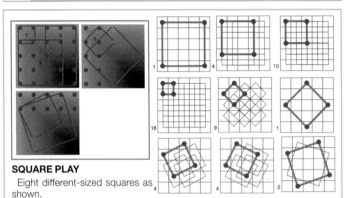

108

SQUARE PLAY

Eight different-sized squares as shown.

SQUARE PLAY

There can be eight different sizes of square, some of them in different orientations as shown, altogether 51 squares.

It is possible to have 15 children on the board so that no four of them are at the vertices of a square.

A classical paper-and-pencil game for two or three players can be played on this principle on squared paper. A square outline of any size is drawn. Each player places in turn a counter on a square. A player is eliminated if his or her counter completes a square with three counters already on the board. The winner is the last person left in the game.

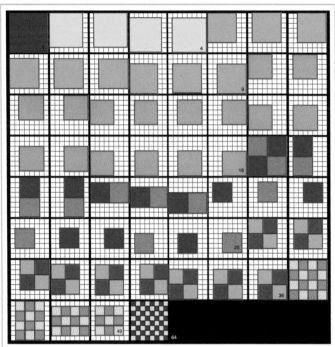

109

CHESSBOARD SQUARES

There are 204 squares, forming the sequence:
$$8^2 + 7^2 + 6^2 + 5^2 + 4^2 + 3^2 + 2^2 + 1^2 = 204$$

The total number of different squares on a square matrix with n units on a side is the sum of the squares of the first n integers.

CHESSCUBE

There are 8 x 8 x 8 individual cubes.
There are 7 x 7 x 7 cubes of 2 x 2 x 2.
There are 6 x 6 x 6 cubes of 3 x 3 x 3.
And so on until one large cube of 8 x 8 x 8.
Total $8^3 + 7^3 + 6^3 + 5^3 + 4^3 + 3^3 + 2^3 + 1^3 = 1{,}296$

There is an alternative formula that can be used to get to the same answer: Sum of cubes from 1 to n = [n/2 x (n + 1)] 2 = 1,296 when n = 8

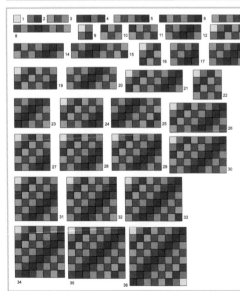

110

SQUARE LATTICE NUMBERS

Puzzle 1:

The number of rectangles (including squares) on square lattices from L(2) to L(8)

L(2) = 9
L(3) = 36
L(4) = 100
L(5) = 225
L(6) = 441
L(7) = 784
L(8) = 1296

which number is the sum of the cubes from 2 to 8. In general, for an n x n square lattice the lattice numbers are expressed by the general formula:

Puzzle 2:

In a L(8) square lattice (chessboard) there are 36 different sizes of squares and rectangles.

111

A SQUARE - BUT WHERE?

Orange.

112

PERMUTATIONS AND FACTORIALS PUZZLE

In how many different ways can you arrange in a row the ten numbers, in which some are identical as shown?

n=10 a=1 b=2 c=3 d=4

The general formula is

$P_{a,b,c,d} = n!/a!b!c!d! = 10!/ 1! 2! 3! 4! = 12600$

114

HOUSES, CATS, WHEAT, MICE

Ahmes's puzzle

16,807 unit measures of flour: 7 x 7 x 7 x 7 x 7

The solution is the sum of geometric progression of five terms, of which the first term is 7, and the multiplier is also 7:

houses 7
cats 49
mice 343
ears 2,401
grains 16,807

ST. IVES' RIDDLE

Only one. All the others were coming from St. Ives

115

FIFTY MAILBOXES PUZZLE

In the extreme case, where the mail is evenly distributed, there would be three letters in each mailbox, except one with four letters. This is a very simple example of the so-called *Pigeonhole principle* or Dirichlet's box principle, which is a principle of reasoning that can be applied to solve and a prove a great variety of different problems.

NUMBER OF HAIRS PUZZLE

The same principle can give us the answer to the hair problem as well, by going through a proof to show that there must be pairs of people who have exactly the same number of hairs. We can estimate the number of hairs on one person's body and come up with a safe upper limit for the number of hairs in one square centimetre. We can also estimate the number of square centimetres on the human body. If we multiple the two numbers we get an estimate of the number of hairs on a human body. We might multiply this number by 10 to get an upper limit. In this way we could get a result that no one human being has more than, say, 100 million hairs. This fact guarantees that there must be at least two people on Earth who have the same number of hairs.

113

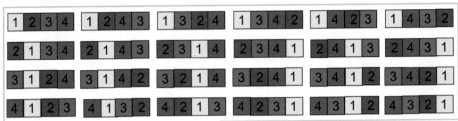

PERMUTATIONS, COMBINATIONS, FACTORIALS
CHARLIE'S SHELF

The number of permutations of eight different objects:

8 x 7 x 6 x 5 x 4 x 3 x 2 x 1 = 40,320

Charlie would need more than 110 years to succeed.

According to the Pigeonhole Principle, with 6.3 billion people on Earth, all having fewer than 100 million hairs, we *must* have pairs of people who have the exact same numbers of hairs. Imagine we have 100 million rooms and label them from 1 to 100 million and we line up all 6.3 billion people, telling each of them to step into the room whose number is the number of hairs on their body. What happens after 100 million people have gone into their appropriate rooms? Even in the worst scenario if all 100 million people went into different rooms, there are still a lot of people left.

116

SKYDIVING

Four skydivers can jump from the airplane in 24 different ways. Following the restriction that three of them always jump one after the other, the number of different ways they can jump is 2 x 6 = 12. The permutations of the jumps of the three superstitious skydivers alone are 3 x 2 x 1 = 6. The fourth skydiver can jump either before these permutations (6) or after (6) leaving 12 ways in all for them to jump.

117

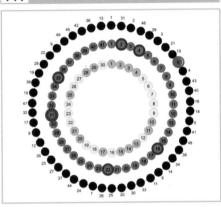

JOSEPHUS' PUZZLE

1. The original Josephus' Puzzle consists of a circle of 41 men (red circle). Josephus occupies position **31** to be the last in the count staying alive. The other ringed positions are those for his five friends to be saved too.

2. In a circle with 30 men (blue circle), with every ninth man eliminated, the group of 15 men to stay alive must occupy places: 1, 2, 3, 4, 10, 11, 13, 14, 15, 17, 20, 21, 25, 28, 29.

3. In a circle of 50 men, the men are eliminated around the circle as before, but now the jump between eliminations increases at each step (i.e. the first man is eliminated, then the second man after him (3), then the third (6), then the fourth, etc.). Which man will be the lucky survivor?

118

step K	door N									
	1	2	3	4	5	6	7	8	9	10
1										
2		•		•		•		•		•
3			•			•			•	
4				•				•		
5					•					
6						•				
7							•			
8								•		
9									•	
10										•

HOTEL DOORS

Doors 1, 4, and 9 will be open at the end. Door "N" is altered at step "K" if, and only if, "K" into divides "N." A door is closed or open according to the parity (even or odd numbered) of the number of times the door's state changes. You may have worked it out, or your guess was right. In our example, we see that the doors open at the end are exactly the perfect squares, 1, 4, 9, 16, 25, 36, 49, 64, 81, and 100.

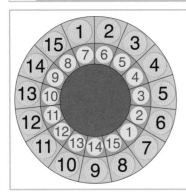

NUMBER CAROUSEL

When the set of numbers is odd, a simple pattern that prevents more than one pair of identical numbers from being next to each other, regardless of how the inner carousel is rotated, is to arrange them in a counterclockwise order on the inner carousel.

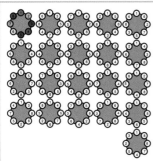

KNIGHTS OF THE ROUND TABLE

The general problem for "n" knights:

$(n - 1)(n - 2)/2$

n	1	2	3	4	5	6	7	8	9	10	
Permutations linear	1	2	6	24	120	720	5040	40320	362880	3638800	n!
Circular Puzzle 1	1	1	2	6	24	120	720	5040	40320	362880	(n-1)!
Circular Puzzle 2	1	1	1	3	12	60	360	2520	20160	181440	(n-1)/2!

CIRCULAR PERMUTATIONS

Puzzle 1 - The number of different **fixed circular permutations**, when the circles are not allowed to be taken out of the plane and flipped over.

Puzze 2 – **The number of** free circular permutations, **when flipping over is allowed**.

LOST SOCKS

The total number of different pairing combinations of ten pairs of socks (20 socks in all) is 190.

Because it takes two socks to make the first pair, there are 19 possible choices for the first pair plus 18 for the second pair plus 17 for the third pair, and so on.

Of the 190 possible pairs, in only ten cases will the two lost socks make a matching pair, because with 20 socks, there can be only ten matching pairs. So, if there are 190 possible combinations, 180 cases will result in pairs of socks that do not match and ten cases will result in matching pairs.

GLOVES IN THE DARK

To solve the problem you have to consider the worst scenario. This is the one in which you are unlucky enough to pick out all the left-handed or all the right-handed gloves, of each of which there are 15 gloves.

In such a case you need only one more, the 16th glove, in order to have the first pair. This is visualized in the graphic, below.

But in fact it's easy to do better than that if you have well-made gloves because, even though it is completely dark, you can still distinguish between left- and right-handed gloves by their shape. In this way you can separate the gloves into two groups, the left-handed and the right-handed ones. In this way you can choose 14 right or left- handed gloves and then choose one more, from the other group, so that the 15th chosen glove will make perfect pair with one of those already picked out.

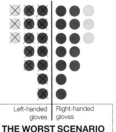

Left-handed gloves | Right-handed gloves

THE WORST SCENARIO

⊠ 15 gloves picked out, no pair

GIRLS AND BOYS IN A ROW

The illustration shows the 21 different patterns

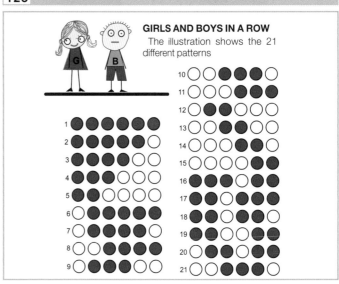

Therefore, it is 18 times more likely (180 divided by 10) that the worst-case scenario will occur, and there will only be eight remaining pairs of socks that match.

SOCKS IN THE DARK

To ensure to have a pair of socks of any color you must draw four socks in the dark.

To ensure to have pair of each color, in the worst scenario, you must draw all the socks of two colors (18 socks) and then two socks more: altogether that's 20 socks.

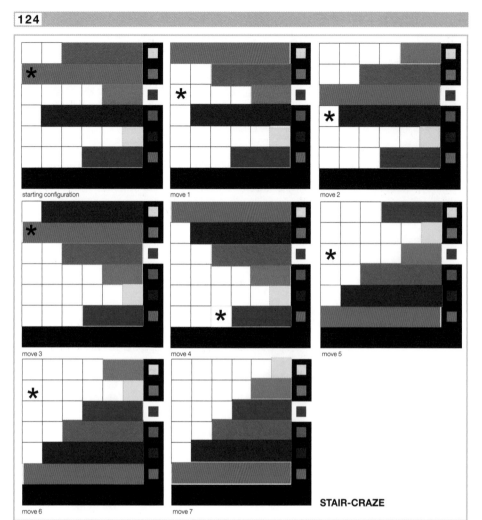

starting configuration

move 1

move 2

move 3

move 4

move 5

move 6

move 7

STAIR-CRAZE

1	2	3	4	5
6	7	8	2	9
4	10	9	11	6
12	8	1	10	5
3	12	11	7	●

POSI-NEGA MEMORY GAME